Top Federal Tax Issues for 2024 | CPE Course

Klaralee R. Charlton, J.D., LL.M.

Ariele R. Doolittle, Esq.

James R. Hamill, CPA, PhD

Susan Harper, CFE

Robert K. Minniti, CPA, CFE, CrFA, CVA, CFF, MAFF, CGMA, PI, DBA

Barbara Weltman, J.D.

Greg White, CPA

Contributors

Contributing Editors . . . . Kelen Camehl, CPA, MBA

Klaralee R. Charlton, J.D., LL.M.

Ariele R. Doolittle, Esq.

James R. Hamill, CPA, PhD

Susan Harper, CFE

Robert K. Minniti, CPA, CFE, CrFA, CVA, CFF, MAFF, CGMA, PI, DBA

Barbara Weltman, J.D.

Greg White, CPA

Production Coordinator . . . . Mariela de la Torre; Jennifer Schencker;

Gokiladevi Sashikumar; Leila Taylor

Production . . . . Sharon Sofinski; Anbarasu Anbumani

ISBN: 978-0-8080-5994-3

2700 Lake Cook Road
Riverwoods, IL 60015
800 344 3734
CCHCPELink.com

Printed in the United States of America

Introduction

Each year, a handful of tax issues typically require special attention by tax practitioners. The reasons vary, from tax legislation, a particularly complicated new provision in the Internal Revenue Code, to a planning technique opened up by a new regulation or ruling, or the availability of a significant tax benefit with a short window of opportunity. Sometimes a developing business need creates a new set of tax problems, or pressure exerted by Congress, or the Administration puts more heat on some taxpayers while giving others more slack. All these share in creating a unique mix that in turn creates special opportunities and pitfalls in the coming year and beyond. The past year has seen more than its share of these developing issues.

Top Federal Tax Issues for 2024 CPE Course identifies those recent events that have developed into the current "hot" issues of the day. These tax issues have been selected as particularly relevant to tax practice in 2024. They have been selected not only because of their impact on return preparation during the 2024 tax season but also because of the important role they play in developing effective tax strategies for 2024 and beyond.

This course is designed to help reassure the tax practitioner that he or she is not missing out on advising clients about a hot, new tax opportunity; or that a brewing controversy does not blindside their practice. In addition to issue identification, this course provides the basic information needed for the tax practitioner to implement a plan that addresses the particular opportunities and pitfalls presented by any one of those issues. Among the topics examined in the *Top Federal Tax Issues for 2024 CPE Course* are:

- Legislative History and Overview
- Required Beginning Date Changes
- Expanded Catch-Up Contributions
- Automatic enrollment and escalation rules
- Employer Matching and Code Sec. 529 Rollovers
- Expansion of Options for Part-Time Employees
- Changes for Beneficiaries
- Planning Ideas for Clients
- Business Use
- Personal Use
- Energy-Related Credits
- Other Vehicle-Related Matters
- Residency Rules Refresher
- Allocating Employee Compensation
- Resident Tax Credit Issues
- State Withholding Tax Considerations for Employers
- Telecommuting and Nexus
- Organization of the Form 1065 and Related Schedules
- Code Sec. 199A Reporting
- Guaranteed Payments

- Entity-Level Elections
- Schedule K
- Allocations of Profit and Loss
- Code Sec. 704(c) Reporting
- Distributions
- Partner Shares of Liabilities
- Disability Income
- Using Artificial Intelligence in Tax Practice
- Deductions
- Trusts and Estates
- Accounting Method Changes
- IRS Developments
- Information Reporting
- E-filing of Forms 1099 and W-2
- Social Security and Decision-Making
- Foreign Bank Account Reporting
- The 2022 Dirty Dozen Tax Scams
- New Scams in the 2023 Dirty Dozen
- Recognizing Illegal Tax Avoidance Schemes
- Tips from the IRS on Choosing a Tax Preparer
- Reporting Suspected Abusive Tax Promotions or Preparers
- Tips to Fight Fraud
- Overview of Cryptocurrency
- Bitcoin
- Legal Issues Associated with Virtual Currencies
- Initial Coin Offerings
- Virtual Currencies and Taxes
- The IRS Strategic Operating Plan
- Progress Toward SOP Objectives

Study Questions. Throughout the course you will find Study Questions to help you test your knowledge, and comments that are vital to understanding a particular strategy or idea. Answers to the Study Questions with feedback on both correct and incorrect responses are provided in a special section beginning at ¶ 10,100.

Final Exam. This course is divided into two Modules. Take your time and review all course Modules. When you feel confident that you thoroughly understand the material, turn to the Final Exam. Complete one, or both, Module Final Exams for continuing professional education credit.

Go to **cchcpelink.com/printcpe** to complete your Final Exam online for immediate results. My Dashboard provides convenient storage for your CPE course Certificates. Further information is provided in the CPE Final Exam instructions at ¶ 10,300. **Please note, manual grading is no longer available for Top Federal Tax Issues. All answer sheets must be submitted online for grading and processing.**

Note: The material contained in this publication was current at the time it went to print.

October 2023

PLEDGE TO QUALITY

Thank you for choosing this CCH® CPE Link product. We will continue to produce high quality products that challenge your intellect and give you the best option for your Continuing Education requirements. Should you have a concern about this or any other Wolters Kluwer product, please call our Customer Service Department at 1-800-344-3734.

COURSE OBJECTIVES

This course was prepared to provide the participant with an overview of specific tax issues that impact 2023 tax return preparation and tax planning in 2024. Each impacts a significant number of taxpayers in significant ways.

Upon course completion, you will be able to:

- Describe how the SECURE Act and SECURE 2.0 Act passed Congress and their primary provisions
- Explain the new increased catch-up contribution rules
- Identify the potential tax impacts related to IRA withdrawals by participants and beneficiaries under the legislation
- Recognize how to recommend tax planning to clients and beneficiaries affected by the SECURE Act and SECURE 2.0 Act
- Identify the changes affecting employer-sponsored plans, including automatic enrollment requirements and student loan repayment matching options
- Describe the limitations on deducting depreciation for business vehicles
- Identify the situations in which personal use of a vehicle is tax deductible
- Explain the tax incentives for purchasing certain types of vehicles
- Recognize which expenses are taken into account when deducting the costs of a business vehicle purchased in 2023
- Identify which elements must be substantiated when a taxpayer uses the standard mileage rate
- Recognize which method to use to figure an employee's personal use of a company vehicle
- Describe the corporate tax implications of having employees working in different states
- Recognize where (in which states) an employer may have corporate income tax nexus
- Identify the number of states that have a "convenience rule"
- Explain how to advise clients on sourcing of wages received while working remotely
- Identify how the primary domicile factors are considered for residency
- Explain what counts as a workday, and what does not, for wage allocation purposes
- Describe essential reporting issues and obligations in partnership taxation
- Identify planning opportunities with partnership tax returns

- Recognize how to apply best practices for preparing partnership returns
- Identify correct statements with respect to guaranteed payments
- Describe capital account reporting
- Describe characteristics of Schedule K-1s
- Identify important new tax cases
- Recognize how to apply important new IRS guidance
- Identify the impact of new legislation on clients
- Identify the Dirty Dozen tax scams
- Recognize how to educate clients to avoid falling prey to scammers
- Describe the consequences of participating in a tax scam
- Describe cryptocurrency
- Recognize how virtual currencies work
- Identify the tax implications of using cryptocurrency
- Describe the IRS Inflation Reduction Act's transformational opportunities for future tax administration
- Recognize what is true and not true about the $80 billion expenditure
- Identify resources to seamlessly help taxpayers and paid preparers

---

Additional copies of this course may be downloaded from **cchcpelink.com/printcpe**. Printed copies of the course are available for $15.00 by calling 1-800-344-3734 (ask for product 10024491-0011).

Contents

MODULE 1: BUSINESS—Chapter 1: Overview of the SECURE 2.0 Act

¶ 101 WELCOME

Congress seemingly cannot stop tinkering with the rules governing retirement plans in an effort to further encourage taxpayers to save for retirement and to incentivize employers to offer savings opportunities to employees. The Securing a Strong Retirement Act, dubbed the "SECURE 2.0 Act," passed Congress in 2022 as part of the year-end omnibus spending bill. This chapter focuses on the main points of the act affecting retirement plans for small businesses and taxpayers' future withdrawal requirements from their retirement plans. It provides a history of this legislation, a summary of its main provisions, and planning ideas for clients affected by the act.

¶ 102 LEARNING OBJECTIVES

Upon completion of this chapter, you will be able to:

- Describe how the SECURE Act and SECURE 2.0 Act passed Congress and their primary provisions
- Explain the new increased catch-up contribution rules
- Identify the potential tax impacts related to IRA withdrawals by participants and beneficiaries under the legislation
- Recognize how to recommend tax planning to clients and beneficiaries affected by the SECURE Act and SECURE 2.0 Act
- Identify the changes affecting employer-sponsored plans, including automatic enrollment requirements and student loan repayment matching options

¶ 103 LEGISLATIVE HISTORY AND OVERVIEW

The Setting Every Community Up for Retirement Enhancement Act of 2019 (known as the SECURE Act) was introduced in the House on March 29, 2019 (H.R. 1994) and passed the House on May 23, 2019. It was eventually incorporated into the Further Consolidated Appropriations Act of 2020, which passed the House and Senate in December 2019 and was signed into law on December 20, 2019 (P.L. 116-94).

The Securing a Strong Retirement Act of 2021 (known as the SECURE 2.0 Act) was introduced in the House on May 4, 2021 (H.R. 2954) and passed March 29, 2022. This bill became part of the Further Consolidated Appropriations Act of 2023, which became law on December 29, 2022 (P.L. 117-328). The direct links to each act are as follows:

- SECURE Act: Contained in Division O of HR 1865 (pp. 604–649), https://www.congress.gov/116/bills/hr1865/BILLS-116hr1865enr.pdf
- SECURE 2.0 Act: Contained in Division T of HR (pp. 817–939), https://www.congress.gov/117/bills/hr2617/BILLS-117hr2617enr.pdf

Changes under the original SECURE Act included the following:

- Delayed required beginning date
- Part-time worker participation opportunities
- Small business retirement plan credits
- Repeal of IRA contribution age limit
- IRA beneficiary withdrawal period changes

The SECURE 2.0 Act changes include:

- Delayed (again) required beginning date
- Increased part-time worker participation opportunities
- Expanded catch-up contributions
- Mandatory automatic enrollment and escalation terms
- Roth matching opportunities
- Student loan matching
- Lost and found retirement account database

Most of the SECURE Act provisions became effective for tax years starting after December 31, 2019, whereas most of the SECURE 2.0 Act provisions are effective for tax years starting after December 31, 2022.

¶ 104 REQUIRED BEGINNING DATE CHANGES

The qualified plan withdrawal rules permit individuals to make tax-free contributions to qualified retirement plans during their working years up to stated annual limits. For example, an individual can contribute on a pretax basis up to $6,500 to a traditional retirement account (IRA) or $22,500 to a 401(k) account in tax year 2023.

If funds are withdrawn from these accounts before the account owner reaches age 59½, a 10 percent penalty applies to the amount withdrawn in addition to the income being included as part of the owner's taxable income. There are some exceptions for hardship, education, a home purchase, and other circumstances. After an individual reaches age 59½, they can take unlimited voluntary withdrawals (without a penalty). Mandatory withdrawals (required minimum distributions, or RMDs) start after the employee's "required beginning date."

Delayed Required Beginning Date

The required beginning date is defined by Internal Revenue Code Sec. 401(a)(9)(C) as follows:

> "(C) Required beginning date.—For purposes of this paragraph—
>
> (i) In general.—The term "required beginning date" means April 1 of the calendar year following the later of—
>
> (I) the calendar year in which the employee attains age 70½, or
>
> (II) the calendar year in which the employee retires."

NOTE: Code Sec. 401(a)(9)(C)(i)(II) applies to a plan sponsored by the employee's current employer only, not to other retirement funds carried over from prior employers.

The SECURE Act delayed the required beginning date by replacing age 70½ with age 72, which was effective for tax years started after December 31, 2019. Subsequently, the SECURE 2.0 Act replaced age 72 with ages 73 and 75 based on the following timeline:

- Age 73 starting in 2023
- Age 75 starting in 2033

Previous versions of the SECURE 2.0 Act included an intervening increase to age 74 starting in 2030; however, the final legislation as confirmed by later commentary eliminated this interim increase.

The second increase is effective for taxpayers reaching age 73 after December 31, 2022. Since the effective date is based on when the taxpayer reaches the applicable required beginning date, there will be some taxpayers under ages 72 or 73 who need to take RMDs if they reached the applicable required beginning date prior to the effective date of the legislation. Those who already reached age 70½ were not grandfathered in. Based on year of birth, the following summarizes the birth dates associated with each required beginning date age:

- Those born before June 30, 1949, must start taking RMDs no later than April 2020 based on age 70½. (The CARES Act allowed participants to delay their first RMD until 2021.)
- For those born after June 30, 1949, but before January 1, 1951, RMDs start no later than April 2023 based on age 72.
- For those born in 1951–1957, RMDs start on April 1 of the year after they turn age 73.
- Those born in 1958 or later must start taking RMDs on April 1 of the year after they turn age 75.

The following charts illustrate how the SECURE Act affects taxable income and account growth.

Taxable Income and Account Growth Post–SECURE Act

RMD Begins at 70 1/2			
Life Expectancy	Age	Acct Value (5%) Growth	RMD
27.4	70	$500,000	$18,248
26.5	71	$505,839	$19,088
27.4	72	$511,089	$18,653
26.5	73	$517,058	$19,512
25.5	74	$522,423	$20,487
24.6	75	$527,033	$21,424
23.7	76	$530,889	$22,400
22.9	77	$533,913	$23,315
22	78	$536,128	$24,369
21.1	79	$537,347	$25,467
	Total Withdrawals		$212,964
Withdrawals + Account Value			$750,310

RMD Begins at 72			
Life Expectancy	Age	Acct Value (5%) Growth	RMD
27.4	70	$500,000	
26.5	71	$525,000	
27.4	72	$551,250	$20,119
26.5	73	$557,688	$21,045
25.5	74	$563,475	$22,097
24.6	75	$568,447	$23,108
23.7	76	$572,606	$24,161
22.9	77	$575,868	$25,147
22	78	$578,257	$26,284
21.1	79	$579,571	$27,468
	Total Withdrawals		$189,428
Withdrawals + Account Value			$768,999

RMD Begins at 73			
Life Expectancy	Age	Acct Value (5%) Growth	RMD
27.4	70	$500,000	
26.5	71	$525,000	
27.4	72	$551,250	
26.5	73	$578,813	$21,842
25.5	74	$584,819	$22,934
24.6	75	$589,979	$23,983
23.7	76	$594,296	$25,076
22.9	77	$597,681	$26,100
22	78	$600,161	$27,280
21.1	79	$601,525	$28,508
	Total Withdrawals		$175,723
Withdrawals + Account Value			$777,248

Missed RMD Withdrawal Penalty Reduction

Code Sec. 4974(a) imposes a penalty if an employee (or any beneficiary) withdraws less than the RMD. The penalty was historically 50 percent of the amount that should have been withdrawn; however, the SECURE 2.0 Act reduces the penalty to 25 percent. In addition, Code Sec. 4974(e) was added to allow a further penalty reduction to only 10 percent if the taxpayer withdraws the previously un-withdrawn amounts during a "correction window" and pays tax on those amounts. The correction window ends on the earlier of:

- The date a notice of deficiency is mailed relating to the Code Sec. 4974(a) penalty,
- The date the taxpayer addresses the Code Sec. 4974(a) penalty, or
- The last day of the second year after the penalty is imposed.

If the taxpayer does not act within the correction window, the 10 percent reduced penalty is no longer available. This addition is seemingly designed to incentivize taxpayers to address unwithdrawn RMDs instead of ignoring or waiting out the statute of limitations.

Currently, the IRS permits taxpayers to request a waiver of the penalty for reasonable cause. To do so, the taxpayer attaches a statement to Form 5329, *Additional Taxes on Qualified Plans (including IRAs) and Other Tax Favored Accounts*, explaining the circumstances surrounding the missed withdrawal and explaining how they are correcting it. Currently, it is unclear if the SECURE 2.0 Act reduced penalty provision will eliminate the IRS's voluntary penalty waiver process.

¶ 105 EXPANDED CATCH-UP CONTRIBUTIONS

The SECURE 2.0 Act introduces several new catch-up contribution opportunities. The catch-up contribution amount is now indexed for inflation, there is an additional catch-up for employees who are ages 60–63, there is an increased catch-up for SIMPLE plans, and Roth characterization is required for catch-ups to employer plans.

Pre-SECURE 2.0 Act IRA and 401(k) Plan Contribution Limits

For tax year 2022, the contribution limits were as follows:

- IRA and Roth IRA limits
  - — Under age 50 = $6,000
  - — Age 50 or over = $7,000 (includes the $1,000 catch-up)
- 401(k) plan limits
  - — Under age 50 = $20,500
  - — Age 50 or over = $27,000 ($6,500 catch-up)
- SIMPLE limits
  - — Under age 50 = $14,000
  - — Age 50 or over = $17,000 ($3,000 catch-up)

Expanded SECURE 2.0 Act IRA and 401(k) Plan Contribution Limits for 2023

- IRA and Roth limits
  - — Under age 50 = $6,500
  - — Over age 50 = $7,500 ($1,000 catch-up **will now be adjusted for inflation (AFI)**)
- 401(k) plan limits
  - — Under age 50 = $22,500
  - — Over age 50 = $30,000 ($7,500 catch-up)
  - — **Ages 60–63 = $32,500 (starting in 2025, the catch-up is increased to the greater of $10,000 AFI or 150 percent of the regular catch-up)**
- SIMPLE limits
  - — Under age 50 = $15,500
  - — Over age 50 = $19,000 ($3,500 catch-up; **in 2024, this will increase 10 percent)**
  - — **Ages 60–63 = $32,500 (starting in 2025, the catch-up increases to the greater of $5,000 AFI or 150 percent of the regular catch-up)**

Note that these amounts are subject to taxable compensation limits. The portions in bold above are the SECURE 2.0 Act changes. Any other revisions are related to normal inflation adjustments.

Catch-Up Contributions Characterized as Roth

The Act provides that catch-up contributions under Code Secs. 401(k), Code Sec. 403(b), or Code Sec. 457(b) plans are subject to mandatory Roth tax treatment, except those made by participants whose wages for the preceding calendar year do not exceed $145,000, as annually indexed for inflation. This rule does not apply to simplified employee pensions under Code Sec. 408(k), or to SIMPLE IRAs under Code Sec. 408(p).

Effective January 1, 2024, catch-up contributions to employer-sponsored plans (i.e., 401(k), 403(b), and 457(b) plans) must be made to a Roth account if the taxpayer earns more than $145,000 AFI.

EXAMPLE: The 401(k) plan limits are as follows:

- Under age 50 = $22,500 (all pre-tax)
- Over age 50
    - — $22,500 (pre-tax)
    - — $7,500 (post-tax Roth)
- Ages 60–63
    - — $22,500 (pre-tax)
    - — $10,000 (post-tax ROTH)

Amounts are subject to taxable compensation limits.

Excess IRA Contribution Penalty

Employees who contribute too much to their IRA must withdraw the excess contribution before the due date of their tax return. As mentioned earlier, withdrawals made prior to age 59½ are subject to a 10 percent early withdrawal penalty. The SECURE 2.0 Act exempts the earnings on the overcontribution from the 10 percent early withdrawal penalty.

When an overcontribution occurs, the taxpayer must file Form 5329 to report it. The SECURE 2.0 Act imposes a six-year statute of limitation for taxpayers who had an overcontribution to their account and failed to file Form 5329.

Early Withdrawal Penalty Exceptions Expanded

Code Sec. 72(t) allows taxpayers to withdraw retirement funds before age 59½ without paying the 10 percent penalty for a multitude of reasons (medical expenses, college, first-time homebuyer, disability, etc.). The SECURE 2.0 Act adds to this list of exceptions by allowing taxpayers to make a one-time withdrawal of up to $1,000 per year for an unforeseeable or immediate financial need related to personal or family emergency expenses. The taxpayer can repay the withdrawal within three years. If it is not repaid, the taxpayer cannot make further withdrawals based on the emergency exception during the three-year period. This provision is effective starting January 1, 2024.

Retirement "Savings" Accounts

Also effective January 1, 2024, retirement plans can offer linked emergency savings accounts to non–highly compensated employees. An employee can contribute 3 percent of their salary up to a total account balance of $2,500 on a post-tax (Roth) basis. The participant can withdraw up to $1,000 once per year for an emergency without triggering the 10 percent early withdrawal penalty.

The withdrawal can be repaid within three years of taking it, but if it is not repaid, the taxpayer cannot take further withdrawals from this savings account during the three-year term. This provision is intended to address lower income earners' worries that saving for retirement leaves them without an emergency fund.

EXAMPLE: 2024: Employee contributes $2,000 to an emergency savings account.

2025: Employee's car breaks down on the Fourth of July, and the employee withdraws $700 from the savings account.

2026: Employee recontributes $200 to the savings account.

2027: Employee recontributes $100 to the savings account

2028: Employee encounters a health event in January but cannot access the savings account because repayment has not occurred during the three-year repayment term.

2029: Employee can again access the remaining savings account.

"Saver's Match" Replacing "Saver's Credit"

The "saver's credit" currently provides a nonrefundable tax credit for lower-income taxpayers who take advantage of retirement savings opportunities. Starting in 2027, taxpayers earning between $41,000 and $71,000 for married filing jointly and $20,500 and $35,500 for single taxpayers will be eligible for a federal retirement savings "match" of up to 50 percent of the employee's own contributions (up to $2,000 per year). This new match will replace the saver's credit. Details on how taxpayers will receive this match or where it will be deposited have yet to be released.

New Options for Lower-Income Plan Participants

In summary, SECURE 2.0 implements three new options to incentivize lower-income taxpayers to participate in retirement saving opportunities including the new early withdrawal exception for emergency expenses up to $1,000; the retirement savings account, which is similarly accessible for emergency expenses up to $1,000; and the saver's match providing a federal match for lower-income savers. Time will tell whether these incentives actually encourage savings among the target group or whether the complexity and seeming red tape surrounding these opportunities will detract from taxpayers' participation.

STUDY QUESTIONS

1. Most SECURE 2.0 Act provisions are applicable for tax years starting on which of the following dates?

a. January 1, 2019

b. January 1, 2020

c. January 1, 2023

d. January 1, 2024

2. As a result of the SECURE 2.0 Act, the combined 401(k) plan deferral and catch-up contribution limit for those aged 60–63 for 2025 is which of the following?

a. $7,500

b. $22,500

c. $30,000

d. $32,500

3. The new saver's match, which will replace the saver's credit, will be effective starting in which of the following years?

a. 2026
b. 2027
c. 2030
d. 2033

¶ 106 AUTOMATIC ENROLLMENT AND ESCALATION RULES

The SECURE 2.0 Act added Code Sec. 414A, which requires new defined contribution plans to include provisions that will automatically enroll employees once they are eligible. The initial automatic savings rate must be at least 3 percent but no more than 10 percent. That rate must automatically increase by 1 percent annually up to at least 10 percent but no more than 15 percent. Employees may elect out of saving or reduce their saving rates at any time. This provision is effective for new plans beginning after December 31, 2024. The goal is to increase employee participation by requiring employees to opt-out of retirement savings instead of opting-in.

EXAMPLE: An employer plan automatically enrolls employees in a defined contribution plan at 4 percent after they reach one year of service. Employee A does not realize that she has been enrolled in the plan. After five years, Employee A is saving at a 9 percent rate (due to the automatic 1 percent increase annually). Employee A contacts her employer to reduce her contribution rate to 2 percent.

The potential savings from automatic enrollment is illustrated in the following chart:

Savings Opportunities for Automatic Enrollee				
	Employee's Wage	Savings Rate	Annual Retirement Savings	Savings with 5% Growth
Year 1	$50,000	3%	$1,500	$1,500
Year 2	$51,500	4%	$2,060	$3,635
Year 3	$53,045	5%	$2,652	$6,469
Year 4	$54,636	6%	$3,278	$10,071
Year 5	$56,275	7%	$3,939	$14,513
Year 6	$57,964	8%	$4,637	$19,876
Year 7	$59,703	9%	$5,373	$26,243
Year 8	$61,494	10%	$6,149	$33,705
Year 9	$63,339	11%	$6,967	$42,356
Year 10	$65,239	12%	$7,829	$52,304
Year 11	$67,196	13%	$8,735	$63,654
Year 12	$69,212	14%	$9,690	$76,527
Year 13	$71,288	15%	$10,693	$91,046
Year 14	$73,427	15%	$11,014	$106,613
Year 15	$75,629	15%	$11,344	$123,288

¶ 107 EMPLOYER MATCHING AND CODE SEC. 529 ROLLOVERS

SECURE 2.0 Act introduces some new ways for employers to match their employees' own retirement contributions and also recognizes the impact student loan debt could play on employees' ability to start saving for retirement. Employers will now be able to match employees' contributions on a Roth basis and provide matching contributions for employees paying down student debt. New options for rolling over unused educational savings funds to retirement accounts was also incorporated in the legislation.

Employer Roth Matching

Matching contributions by employers or nonelective contributions by employers currently are only made on a pre-tax basis. The SECURE 2.0 Act allows plans to permit employees to choose whether all or part of the employer's contribution will be added to a Roth account. The employer's plan must include this as an option. This provision is effective for any employer contributions made after December 29, 2022; however, the plan must incorporate this option, which may not be adopted by all employers.

> **EXAMPLE:** Employee B earns $100,000 per year and contributes 10 percent of his earnings to a pre-tax 401(k) plan and 10 percent of his earnings to a post-tax Roth 401(k) plan. His employer offers a match of an employee's contributions up to 6 percent of the employee's salary, so Employee B is eligible for a $6,000 contribution from his employer. If the employer's plan allows, Employee B may choose to have all of the contribution added to either the 401(k) plan or the Roth 401(k) plan, or part to each account.

Student Loan Matching

IRS Private Letter Ruling 201833012 permitted employers to provide a retirement plan matching contribution based on an employee's student loan payments (instead of actual retirement contributions). The SECURE 2.0 Act makes this ruling a permanent statutory fixture. Note that all other tests for the retirement plan must still be met, including antidiscrimination calculations.

> **EXAMPLE:** An employee earns $50,000 annually and pays $500 per month ($6,000 annually/12 percent of salary) toward student loans. The employee cannot afford to save for retirement on top of the student loan payments.
>
> The employer who has adopted this plan provision and who normally matches the employee's contributions up to 4 percent of the employee's salary, can now deposit $2,000 in the employee's retirement account even if the employee contributes nothing.
>
> The employee's payments toward their student loans count as retirement contributions for purposes of the employer's matching calculations.

529 Plan Rollovers

The SECURE 2.0 Act amends Code Secs. 408A and 529 to permit unused 529 savings to be rolled into Roth IRA accounts. This is beneficial for students who did not fully deplete their educational savings accounts and would have been subject to nonqualifying use penalties plus tax on any earnings withdrawn from the account. This provision is effective for tax years starting after December 31, 2023. Note the following considerations:

- Transfers must be done on a trustee-to-trustee rollover.
- The beneficiary of the 529 plan and the owner of the Roth IRA must be the same person.
- The 529 plan must be open for 15 years prior to the rollover.
- Total rollovers cannot exceed $35,000 during the beneficiary's lifetime.
- Annual Roth IRA contribution limits apply (without considering the taxpayer's income), which means the rollovers must occur over multiple years.

EXAMPLE: Maria's parents and grandparents contribute $200,000 to a 529 savings account for her educational expenses. Maria receives scholarships and has $30,000 remaining in her 529 account upon graduation. In 2024, Maria can roll over $6,500 AFI to a Roth IRA account. The next year, Maria can roll over another $6,500 AFI, and so on until the account is empty. Maria now has a solid start to retirement savings during years when her income levels may have been too low to contribute.

NOTE: Do not forget about the other opportunities to use 529 plan monies.

- The original SECURE Act created an option for students to use 529 plan balances to pay off up to $10,000 in student loans.
- The account owner (often a parent or grandparent) can change the beneficiary to a sibling, cousin, grandparent, aunt, uncle, or the account owner themselves to pay additional educational expenses.
- The account owner can also use up to $10,000 for elementary, middle, or secondary school. (Some states have restrictions, so check first.)

¶ 108 EXPANSION OF OPTIONS FOR PART-TIME EMPLOYEES

Along the lines of changes to employer-sponsored plans is a new rule that now requires employers to permit long-term, part-time employees to participate in a retirement plan if it is offered. Before the SECURE Act, an employer could limit plan participation to employees who are at least 21 years old and either (1) work 1,000 hours in 12 months or (2) have 12 months of service.

Under the SECURE Act, an employer using the "1,000 hours in 12 months" requirement must now also offer a "500 hours in three consecutive years" eligibility option. This rule is effective for plan years beginning after December 31, 2020. The three-year counting does not begin until January 2021.

EXAMPLE: UNDER THE ORIGINAL SECURE ACT: John has worked 600 hours per year for his employer since 2015. He is 45 years old. John's employer is now required to permit John to participate in the company's retirement plan if he works until January 1, 2024 (three consecutive years after the original effective date of January 1, 2021).

The SECURE 2.0 Act shortens the time period for part-time employee eligibility to 500 hours in two consecutive years, effective for plan years beginning after December 31, 2024. The two-year counting still begins on January 1, 2021, and the two-year period applies for both participation and vesting requirements. Top-heavy plans will be eligible for an exemption if they do not provide safe-harbor matching contributions to long-term, part-time employees. Since the two-year rule is only effective for plan years starting after December 31, 2024, part-time employees should still look to the original SECURE Act's three-year rule if they desire to participate sooner than 2025.

EXAMPLE: UNDER THE SECURE 2.0 ACT: John has worked 600 hours per year for his employer since November 1, 2022. He is 45 years old. John's employer will be required to permit John to participate in the company's retirement plan for the plan year that starts *after* December 31, 2024, if he works until November 1, 2024 (two consecutive years after the original effective date of January 1, 2021).

Employers of part-time employees should consider the following:

- If the employer used the 1,000-hour test, its plan must be amended to permit long-term, part-time employees to participate.
- Participation will start on January 1, 2024, under the original SECURE Act if the employee was employed back on January 1, 2021.
- Only employees who started more recently will benefit from the SECURE 2.0 Act since it applies only to plan years after December 31, 2024.

All employers will have until the end of the first plan year beginning on or after January 1, 2025 (instead of 2022) to amend their plan documents to comply with all of the new required provisions passed under the SECURE Act, SECURE 2.0 Act, CARES Act, and Taxpayer Certainty and Disaster Tax Relief Act of 2019. Employers can operate as though those future amendments are already made without violating the anti-cutback requirement applicable to all plans.

Current laws require a multitude of notices regarding the plan and plan activities to be sent to all employees (even if employees opted out of participation in the plan). The SECURE 2.0 Act reduces the scope of notices required to be sent to employees who opt out. Nonparticipants must now receive (1) an annual participation reminder and (2) any documents requested by the employee.

¶ 109 CHANGES FOR BENEFICIARIES

Lost and Found Retirement Account Database

By the end of 2024 (two years after passage of the SECURE 2.0 Act), the Department of Labor must create a "Retirement Savings Lost and Found" database. The goal is to prevent orphan retirement savings accounts from going unclaimed. This follows the trend begun by many states to create unclaimed fund search websites. A similar site is currently maintained by the National Association of Insurance Commissioners for life insurance policies and annuities.

Expanding on Surviving Spouse's Withdrawal Options

The SECURE 2.0 Act requires the IRS to amend Treas. Reg. § 1.401(a)(9)-5, Q&A 5(a), to allow the surviving spouse of an employee to use the uniform tables based on the employee's date of death to calculate required distributions as originally intended. Now, spouses inheriting both IRAs and employer-sponsored accounts can choose from all the available distribution options applicable to surviving spouses.

Post–SECURE Act IRA Beneficiary Withdrawal Options

After the passage of the original SECURE Act, there are now four categories of retirement plan distribution options: those for spouses, eligible designated beneficiaries, designated beneficiaries, and no designated beneficiary. The four categories are detailed in the following chart:

Post-SECURE Act Distribution Options	
Spouses	Menu of options—rollover, stretch IRA, etc.
Eligible designated beneficiary (disabled, ill, and minors)	Stretch IRA
Designated beneficiaries	10-year plan with or without RMDs depending on the age of the account owner
No beneficiary	5-year plan or decedent's life expectancy depending on whether the decedent died before or after their required beginning date

The payout options for surviving spouses remain unchanged compared to withdrawal options prior to the passage of the SECURE Act and SECURE 2.0 Act. Eligible designated beneficiaries receive the same withdrawal options practitioners historically applied to any named individual beneficiary. As described in the following section, the SECURE 2.0 Act, the proposed regulations, and notices from the IRS have recently clarified how designated beneficiaries and non-designated beneficiaries should calculate their withdrawal windows.

RMDs and the 10-Year Payout

The proposed regulations released after the passage of the SECURE Act clarify a widely misunderstood concept relating to whether beneficiaries subject to the 10-year withdrawal window must also withdraw RMDs if the account owner died after their required beginning date. As described in the regulations, if an account owner died before their required beginning date (under age 72 prior to the SECURE 2.0 Act or age 73 after the SECURE 2.0 Act), the beneficiary must simply empty the account by end of the 10th year after the death. However, if the account owner died *after* the required beginning date, the beneficiary must withdraw RMDs for the next 10 years *and* empty the account by end of the 10th year after the death.

The IRS acknowledges that the SECURE Act was not clear on the rule to take RMDs during the 10-year withdrawal period. IRS Notice 2022-53 suggests that in spite of pushback from practitioners concerned about the unwieldly nature of the regulations, the IRS intends to permanently adopt this bifurcated plan. In light of the original misunderstanding of the SECURE Act legislation, Notice 2022-53 offers relief to beneficiaries subject to the 10-year withdrawal window who failed to take RMDs during 2021 and 2022. If a taxpayer did not take an RMD for 2021 or 2022, the IRS will not assert any excise tax due under Code Sec. 4974 (2020 was an RMD holiday for all account owners under the CARES Act). If a taxpayer already paid an excise tax for a missed RMD, the taxpayer may request a refund of that excise tax.

EXAMPLE: Mom, age 70, and Dad, age 75, each have a $500,000 IRA. Sadly, both pass away in a car accident. Their child is named as the sole beneficiary of both accounts. Since Mom had not yet reached her required beginning date, the child must withdraw her account by the end of the 10th year after her death. Since Dad had already reached his required beginning date, the child must withdraw annual RMDs from Dad's account and also withdraw the remainder of the account by the end of the 10th year after his death.

RMDs and the 5-Year Payout

If an account owner dies before the required beginning date (under age 72 prior to the SECURE 2.0 Act or age 73 after the SECURE 2.0 Act) and the account is payable to the owner's estate, a charity, or a nonqualifying trust, the beneficiary must empty the account by the end of the fifth year after the death. No RMDs are required during this five-year withdrawal period. But if the account owner died *after* the required beginning date, the estate/charity/nonqualifying trust can withdraw the account over the remaining life expectancy of the account owner reduced by one each year after death. This period is sometimes referred to as the *ghost life expectancy*.

The following table illustrates a sample withdrawal period for an account owner dying after their required beginning date at age 75. Curiously, as illustrated in this table, a non-designated beneficiary such as an estate can actually withdraw funds over a longer period of time if the owner dies after their required beginning date and has a life expectancy greater than 10 years under the Single Life Table.

		Age	Account Value (5%) Growth	RMD
	27.4	70	$100,000	
	26.5	71	$105,000	
	25.6	72	$110,250	
	24.7	73	$115,763	$4,687
	23.8	74	$116,630	$4,900
Death	22.9	75	$117,316	$5,123
Switch to Single Life Table	14.1	76	$117,802	$8,355
	13.1	77	$114,920	$8,773
	12.1	78	$111,455	$9,211
	11.1	79	$107,356	$9,672
	10.1	80	$102,568	$10,155
	9.1	81	$97,034	$10,663
	8.1	82	$90,689	$11,196
	7.1	83	$83,468	$11,756
	6.1	84	$75,297	$12,344

NOTE: Once the RMDs are "turned on," they cannot be turned off. That means if an account owner turned on RMDs (by reaching their required beginning date), the RMDs cannot be turned off after his death.

However, if the surviving spouse transfers the deceased spouse's account to their own account, RMDs can be turned off.

Although RMDs can't be turned off, the plan beneficiary can always increase the flow of distributions or fully deplete the account during the 10- or 5-year term.

¶ 110 PLANNING IDEAS FOR CLIENTS

The changes imposed by the SECURE Act and SECURE 2.0 Act are, in part, linked to the fact that life expectancy in the United States increased from age 73.7 in 1980 to age 79.1 in 2023. Delaying the required beginning date increases the size of RMDs from retirement savings plans and increases the likelihood of an employee dying with a larger retirement account.

Unfavorable beneficiary withdrawal provisions will tax more dollars at higher rates because (1) withdrawals are compressed into a shorter withdrawal period and (2) beneficiaries may still be working, subjecting withdrawals to higher tax brackets.

Delayed Required Beginning Date

As mentioned earlier in this chapter, the SECURE 2.0 Act replaces "age 72" in Code Sec. 401(a)(9)(C) with "ages 73 and 75" (based on a timeline). The following two charts compare withdrawals for an inherited IRA both before and after passage of the Act:

	Pre-Secure Act Inherited IRA						Post-Secure Act 2.0 Inherited IRA			
	Required Withdrawal Factor	Age	Acct Value (5%) Growth	RMD Pre-Secure Act			Required Withdrawal Factor	Age	Acct Value (5%) Growth	RMD Post-Secure Act
Parent	N/A	68	$100,000	$0		Parent	N/A	68	$100,000	$0
	N/A	69	$105,000	$0			N/A	69	$105,000	$0
	29.1	70	$110,250	$0			N/A	70	$110,250	$0
	28.2	71	$115,763	$4,105			N/A	71	$115,763	$0
	27.4	72	$117,446	$4,286			N/A	72	$121,551	$0
	26.5	73	$119,032	$4,492			26.5	73	$127,628	$4,816
	25.5	74	$120,491	$4,725			25.5	74	$129,193	$5,066
	24.6	75	$121,791	$4,951			24.6	75	$130,587	$5,308
Child	41	45	$122,929	$2,998		Child	41	45	$131,808	$13,181
	40	46	$126,078	$3,152			40	46	$125,217	$13,913
	39	47	$129,230	$3,314			39	47	$117,565	$14,696
	38	48	$132,377	$3,484			38	48	$108,748	$15,535
	37	49	$135,513	$3,663			37	49	$98,650	$16,442
	36	50	$138,626	$3,851			36	50	$87,141	$17,428
	35	51	$141,706	$4,049			35	51	$74,069	$18,517
	34	52	$144,743	$4,257			34	52	$59,256	$19,752
	33	53	$147,723	$4,476			33	53	$42,466	$21,233
	32	54	$150,633	$4,707			32	54	$23,357	$23,357
	Total Withdrawals			$60,509			Total Withdrawals			$189,245

Planning for Potentially Shortened RMD Period

Ever since the SECURE Act was introduced in March 2019, planners have been trying to come up with ideas to help clients avoid the unfortunate 10-year withdrawal period. Some of the most common tax-saving proposals are detailed in the sections that follow.

Withdrawing funds during one's lifetime. Withdrawing funds over the owner's lifetime may very well be the best option for a client who is in a lower income tax bracket. Of course, analysis should be done to ensure this is the best option. Some clients are in lower tax brackets than their children. There are also many clients who incur significant medical expenses later in life, especially after they move into assisted living. Withdrawing taxable funds in years with excess medical deductions should be considered over using investments that will receive a basis adjustment at the client's death.

Making qualified charitable distributions (QCDs). Clients who are already charitably inclined should consider using these funds and make qualified charitable distributions instead of writing checks or cashing in nonqualified funds. After age 70½, taxpayers can make charitable contributions of up to $100,000 per year directly from an IRA (not a 401(k) plan). The age 70½ for purposes of QCD withdrawals was not impacted by either the SECURE Act or SECURE 2.0 Act. These QCDs are not includable in income. Under the SECURE 2.0 Act, the $100,000 limit is now indexed for inflation. The inflation index will start for tax years beginning after 2023.

New Code Sec. 408(d)(8)(F) allows up to $50,000 to be directed to a split-interest entity in the form of a QCD. The $50,000 limit is similarly indexed for inflation. Qualifying split-interest entities include charitable remainder annuity trusts, charitable remainder unitrusts, and charitable gift annuities. In comparison to most sums transferred to these types of entities, the $50,000 limit is relatively inconsequential and will likely cost more in administrative expenses than would be worth the tax savings.

Naming a charitable remainder trust as beneficiary. Charitable remainder trusts can be useful, though, if the charitable remainder trust (CRT) is named as the beneficiary of a client's retirement account. The client can achieve tax deferral similar to that with a stretch IRA and can maintain control over the monies, so the beneficiaries don't receive everything at once. The following steps can be taken to accomplish this:

- Have testamentary CRT language included in the participant's estate plan.
- Name a CRT as beneficiary of the plan.
- The CRT claims the account at the participant's death.
- The CRT can withdraw the account now but pays no tax as a charitable entity.
- Distributions are made over the participant's lifetime or a period of years to named beneficiaries who pay tax as the funds are received.

Naming multiple nonspouse beneficiaries. Another relatively simple consideration is dividing the account among multiple beneficiaries. By doing this, the taxpayer is spreading out the 10-year withdrawal payments among multiple taxpayers instead of conglomerating all the income onto one beneficiary's tax return.

> **EXAMPLE 1:** The taxpayer's son is the beneficiary of the taxpayer's $500,000 IRA. At a minimum, the son's income is increased by $50,000 per year if the IRA is withdrawn proportionately over the 10-year withdrawal period.

> **EXAMPLE 2:** The taxpayer's three grandchildren are the beneficiaries of the taxpayer's $500,000 IRA. Each grandchild's income is increased only by $16,666 per year if the IRA is withdrawn proportionately over the 10-year withdrawal period. The grandchildren may also be in lower tax brackets.

Converting an IRA to a Roth IRA. Lastly, clients might consider converting their traditional IRAs to Roth IRAs. Of course, this may not be ideal for every client depending on their current income tax bracket, but with tax rates at historical lows right now, it may be an idea that some clients want to consider. This requires income tax analysis similar to medical expenses, tax rates, losses, etc.

> **PLANNING POINTER:** When recommending tax planning to clients and beneficiaries affected by the SECURE Act and SECURE 2.0 Act, remember that one size does not fit all. The following are among the many factors that must be taken into account:
>
> - Relative ages of the taxpayer and beneficiary
> - Relative income tax brackets
> - Estate tax liability
> - Beneficiary immaturity or disability
> - Creditor issues (lawsuits/divorce)
> - Charitable intentions

STUDY QUESTIONS

4. With respect to 529 plan rollovers, the maximum amount of 529 plan assets permitted to be rolled over to a Roth IRA during a beneficiary's lifetime is which of the following amounts?

a. $22,500
b. $32,500
c. $35,000
d. $40,000

5. Employers have until the end of the first plan year beginning on or after January 1, ______ to amend their plan documents to comply with the SECURE Act, the SECURE 2.0 Act, the CARES Act, and the Taxpayer Certainty and Disaster Tax Relief Act.

a. 2021
b. 2022
c. 2023
d. 2025

6. After age 70½, taxpayers are permitted to make charitable contributions of up to ______ per year directly from an IRA without recognizing taxable income for such distributions.

a. $100,000
b. $125,000
c. $200,000
d. $250,000

MODULE 1: BUSINESS—Chapter 2: Tax Rules for Vehicles

¶ 201 WELCOME

This chapter covers the tax rules for vehicles—cars, light trucks, and vans used by individuals and businesses. It discusses write-offs for using vehicles, and new green energy incentives for buying clean vehicles. It also addresses vehicle-related tax rules, such as those associated with donating vehicles to charity.

¶ 202 LEARNING OBJECTIVES

Upon completion of this chapter, you will be able to:

- Describe the limitations on deducting depreciation for business vehicles
- Identify the situations in which personal use of a vehicle is tax deductible
- Explain the tax incentives for purchasing certain types of vehicles
- Recognize which expenses are taken into account when deducting the costs of a business vehicle purchased in 2023
- Identify which elements must be substantiated when a taxpayer uses the standard mileage rate
- Recognize which method to use to figure an employee's personal use of a company vehicle

---

¶ 203 INTRODUCTION

Vehicle usage in the United States—by both individuals and businesses—is widespread, and the costs are significant. In 2022, nearly 15 million new cars and light trucks were purchased,[1] and more than 290.8 million cars were registered in the United States.[2] As of November 2022, the average cost of a new car was $45,872.[3] Approximately one-fifth of all vehicle transactions were leases.[4]

Different tax rules apply, depending on whether the vehicle is owned or leased, whether it's used for business or personal driving, and whether it's a clean vehicle, a plug-in electric vehicle, or fuel cell vehicle versus one powered by fossil fuel.

Because of the complexity of some of the rules, this chapter only provides an overview, with references to additional resources on particular matters.

---

[1] MarkLines, "USA—Automotive Sales Volume," https://www.marklines.com/en/statistics/flash_sales/automotive-sales-in-usa-by-month#:~:text=Light%20vehicle%20seasonally%20ad-justed%20annualized,million%20units%20a%20year%20ago.

[2] Hedges & Company, "US Vehicle Registration Status," https://hedgescompany.com/automotive-market-research-statistics/auto-mailing-lists-and-marketing/.

[3] Business Wire, "U.S. Automotive Forecast for November 2022," https://www.businesswire.com/news/home/20221123005156/en/J.D.-Power-and-LMC-Automotive-U.S.-Automotive-Forecast-for-November-2022.

[4] Statista, "Percentage of New Vehicles on Lease in the United States from 3rd Quarter of 2017 to 3rd Quarter of 2022," https://www.statista.com/statistics/453122/share-of-new-vehicles-on-lease-usa/#:~:text=Nearly%20one%20fifth%20of%20new,the%20rest%20being%20sold%20outright.

¶ 204 BUSINESS USE

The use of cars, vans, pickup trucks, and panel trucks is common for business. Taxpayers who use a vehicle for business are generally permitted to write off the costs. In fact, the deduction for car and truck expenses for sole proprietors is one of the top two deduction categories each year. The deduction includes acquisition and most operating costs. However, various limitations apply and there are different ways to handle annual write-offs.

There are two ways to figure the deduction for business use of a vehicle: the *actual expense method* and the *standard mileage rate*. Usually, a taxpayer may choose which method to use. However, the standard mileage rate may *not* be used if the taxpayer:

- Operates five or more vehicles at the same time,
- Claimed depreciation using any method other than straight-line,
- Claimed a Code Sec. 179 deduction,
- Claimed a bonus depreciation allowance, or
- Deducted actual expenses after 1997 for a vehicle the taxpayer leases.

Note that if you claim the standard mileage rate in the first year of vehicle ownership, you may choose to deduct actual expenses or use the standard mileage rate in later years. In the case of a *lease*, once you claim the actual expense method, you cannot choose to use the standard mileage rate in a future year.

If the standard mileage rate is chosen by reporting it on a timely filed return, this choice cannot be changed for the year it was used.

> **EXAMPLE:** Taxpayer A bought a business car in December 2022 and filed her 2022 income tax return on April 18, 2023, using the standard mileage rate method to determine the deduction for the vehicle. She cannot amend this return to change to the actual expense method.

Using the actual expense method, the expenses factored into the standard mileage rate include:

- Depreciation or lease payments (depending on whether the vehicle is owned or leased)
- Gas and oil
- Insurance
- Registration fees and licenses
- Repairs and maintenance
- Tires

This list is not exclusive. Other costs, such as car washes—another maintenance expense—are deductible. Parking and tolls are separately deductible. Interest on a car loan is handled separately; it is not part of actual expenses deducted for car and truck expenses.

Depreciation of a Vehicle

While most of the expenses are self-explanatory, we should discuss depreciation and lease payments. Vehicles are five-year property, but a six-year recovery period applies due to the half-year convention under the Modified Accelerated Cost Recovery System (MACRS). The normal depreciation rates applied to the unadjusted basis (usually cost) of the vehicle are:

- 20 percent for the first year (half of the 40 percent double-declining balance factor for year 1)
- 32 percent for the second year

- 19.20 percent for the third year
- 11.52 percent for the fourth and fifth years
- 5.76 percent in the sixth year

There are various limitations that may alter or limit the deduction amount resulting from these percentages. Before discussing these limitations and their impact on the annual depreciation allowance, we should discuss the basis to use to compute the depreciation.

If the taxpayer buys a vehicle, the basis for depreciation is the vehicle's cost. This includes sales tax on its purchase. It cannot separately deduct the sales taxes on the vehicle in the year of purchase. It does not matter whether the taxpayer pays cash or finances the purchase in whole or in part. The borrowed funds are part of the cost basis.

> **EXAMPLE:** A business buys a $40,000 pickup truck for its business, putting $5,000 down and financing the balance. The cost basis is $40,000, even though the business only paid $5,000 cash.

Using a Personal Vehicle for Business

If a taxpayer begins to use a personal vehicle for business purposes, the basis for depreciation is the lesser of the vehicle's fair market value (FMV) on the date of conversion to business use or its adjusted basis on that date. Because a vehicle typically declines in value annually, the taxpayer will likely be using FMV for depreciation purposes because it would be lower than the adjusted basis.

Whether the taxpayer buys the vehicle for business use or converts it from personal use and uses it for both business and personal driving, the taxpayer must allocate basis to business and personal use.

> **EXAMPLE:** A taxpayer buys a vehicle for $40,000 and uses it 75 percent for business. The taxpayer figures depreciation on $30,000, the portion of basis allocable for business use.

Trade-Ins

If the taxpayer acquires the vehicle through a trade-in of another one, the taxpayer must report gain or loss on the transaction (the trade-in). Usually, gain results because of having depreciated the vehicle. In the past, trade-ins didn't necessarily trigger tax because they were treated as like-kind exchanges, but this tax treatment is now restricted to realty, so vehicle transactions are taxable. The good news is that the full cost of the new vehicle (including the trade-in allowance) is the tax basis for depreciation.

Listed Property

The depreciation percentages mentioned earlier in this chapter only apply if business use of the vehicle is more than 50 percent of the miles driven for the year. These percentages reflect the MACRS factors for 5-year property. A vehicle is listed property (Code Sec. 280F). This means that if business use is below 50 percent, only straight-line depreciation may be claimed.

Depreciation deductions for listed property must be reported in Part V of Form 4562, *Depreciation and Amortization*.

If business use is more than 50 percent but declines below this threshold in a later year, the taxpayer must change to the straight-line depreciation method. This is so even in the year of disposition, other than in the case of the owner's death. The MACRS deduction—the amount in excess of straight-line depreciation—must be recaptured.

The dollar limits apply to so-called luxury vehicles weighing under 6,000 pounds (the unloaded gross vehicle weight) (Code Sec. 280F). The IRS can adjust the dollar limits annually, and the limits to use are those applicable for the year in which the vehicle is placed in service. The dollar limits for depreciating luxury vehicles bought and placed in service in 2023 are as follows:

2023 Dollar Limits for Depreciating Luxury Vehicles	
Tax Year	**Placed in Service in 2023 (Rev. Proc. 2023-14)**
First year	$20,200*
Second year	$19,500
Third year	$11,700
Each succeeding year	$6,960

* If the vehicle does not use the additional first-year depreciation deduction under Code Sec. 168(k), the limit is $12,200.

In the past, there were different limits for passenger cars versus trucks and vans. Now, light trucks and vans are treated the same as passenger cars.

Looking Ahead and Back

Bonus depreciation begins phasing out in 2023, reducing the applicable amount by 20 percent each year until it expires at the end of 2026. For vehicles placed in service prior to 2023, different dollar limits may apply. These dollar limits are listed in IRS Publication 463, *Travel, Gift, and Car Expenses*. The percentage is different if the fourth quarter convention applies.

Safe Harbor Rule

If a vehicle is placed in service in 2022 and the taxpayer used 100 percent bonus depreciation, then the taxpayer must figure depreciation going forward using a safe harbor rule (Rev. Proc. 2019-13). To apply the safe harbor method, the taxpayer must use the applicable depreciation table in Appendix A of IRS Publication 946, *How to Depreciate Property*. The safe harbor method does not apply to a vehicle placed in service after 2022 because bonus depreciation is no longer 100 percent.

The safe harbor method also does not apply if the taxpayer elected out of the 100-percent additional first-year depreciation deduction or elected under Code Sec. 179 to expense all or a portion of the cost of the vehicle. To use the safe harbor method, no special form or election is needed; the taxpayer simply applies it to the depreciation allowance on the first taxable year following the year in which the vehicle was placed in service.

Allocating the Dollar Limit

If a taxpayer buys an expensive vehicle but doesn't use it entirely for business, the taxpayer must allocate the dollar limit.

> **EXAMPLE:** A vehicle bought and placed in service in 2023 cost $100,000 and is used 75 percent for business. The full dollar limit would ordinarily be $20,200, taking into account the additional first-year depreciation deduction (bonus depreciation). In this situation, the deduction cap is $15,150, or 75 percent of $20,200.

Heavy SUVs

Passenger vehicles are not subject to the dollar limit when rated at more than 6,000 pounds unloaded gross vehicle weight (Code Sec. 280F(d)(5)). For trucks and vans, the threshold is more than 6,000 pounds gross vehicle weight. There are dozens of such "heavy" sports utility vehicles (SUVs), ranging from the Audi Q7 to the Toyota Sequoia.

For heavy SUVs, the usual dollar limits and the full first-year expensing limit—$1,160,000 in 2023—do not apply. Instead, there is a special first-year expensing deduction of up to $25,000, adjusted for inflation, so the amount is $28,900 in 2023. There is an additional write-off:

- In 2023, with 80 percent bonus depreciation applicable, the full purchase price is not immediately deductible.
- The only requirement for using bonus depreciation for a heavy SUV is that the vehicle must be used more than 50 percent for business.

Vehicles Exempt from Dollar Limits and Substantiation Requirements

Certain vehicles are exempt from the dollar limits, including:

- Vehicles with an interior cargo bed length of less than 6 feet
- Passenger vans seating fewer than ten people behind the driver's seat
- Cargo vans
- Non–personal use vehicles (Reg. § 1.274-5T(k)), which include:
  - — Ambulances
  - — Delivery trucks with seating only for the driver (or with a fold-out jump seat)
  - — Farm vehicles (e.g., tractors)
  - — Flatbed trucks
  - — Hearses
  - — Specialized vehicles (e.g., tow trucks, moving vans, dump trucks)

To repeat, they are exempt from both substantiation requirements and the dollar limits that would otherwise apply. The IRS makes it very clear that merely putting a business sign on a vehicle does not transform it into a non–personal use vehicle.

Leased Vehicles—Actual Expense Method

If a leased vehicle is used 100 percent for business, then 100 percent of the lease payments are deductible, subject to an adjustment (discussed below). If the vehicle is used partly for personal driving, the taxpayer must allocate the lease payments; only the business portion is deductible.

If the vehicle is considered a luxury vehicle, then an *inclusion amount* reduces the deductible lease payment. More specifically, the inclusion amount is taken from an IRS table for this purpose. The taxpayer should use the table for the year in which the lease begins. For 2023, this means a vehicle first leased on or after January 1, 2022, and having a FMV at the start of the lease of over $60,000.

First Year	Second Year	Third Year	Fourth Year	Fifth Year and Later
$0	$0	$1	$3	$5

EXAMPLE: Assume a vehicle is leased in January 2023 with a fair market value of $75,000. The inclusion amount for the first year of the lease is $91. If the total vehicle lease payments for 2023 are $7,200, the deductible amount is $7,109 ($7,200 – $91).

The inclusion amounts for vehicles leased before 2023 are in IRS Publication 463.

Standard Mileage Rate for Business Driving

The IRS can adjust the standard mileage rate annually, and twice it has made two adjustments for a year when gas prices skyrocketed. The standard mileage rate cannot be used for business driving if:

- The taxpayer uses five or more cars at the same time, such as fleet operations;
- The taxpayer previously claimed accelerated depreciation, including first-year expensing and bonus depreciation for the vehicle; or
- The taxpayer is a rural mail carrier who is reimbursed for driving.

The standard mileage rate can be used regardless of business status, meaning it can be used by employees who are still eligible to deduct their work-related expenses, self-employed persons, and business entities.

Keep in mind that most employees can't deduct their mileage costs because of the suspension of miscellaneous itemized deductions subject to the 2 percent-of-AGI (adjusted gross income) floor. However, some employees deduct their business expenses in other ways and can still take their mileage deduction. These include:

- Reservists in the Armed Forces who deduct their travel costs as an adjustment to gross income
- State or local government officials paid on a fee basis who deduct their business expenses as an adjustment to gross income
- Performing artists who are eligible to deduct their business expenses as an adjustment to gross income

The standard mileage rate can also be used to reimburse employees on a tax-free basis using an accountable plan, which will be discussed later in this chapter. Also, note that the standard mileage rate can be used whether the vehicle is owned or leased.

For 2023, the standard mileage rate for business driving is 65.5¢ per mile (Notice 2023-03). In 2022, there were two standard mileage rates: 58.5¢ per mile for the first half of the year, and 62.5¢ per mile for the second half of the year. Rates for these and other years are shown in the following chart:

Year	Business Cents per Mile
2023	65.5¢
January – June 2022 July – December 2022	58.5¢ 62.5¢
2021	56¢
2020	57.5¢
2019	58¢
2018	54.5¢

The standard mileage rate deduction is figured by multiplying the number of business miles driven during the year by the rate.

EXAMPLE: If the taxpayer drives 13,468 miles for business in 2023, the deduction for car usage figured with the standard mileage rate is $8,822 (13,468 × 65.5¢).

Sole proprietors claim their vehicle use deduction in Part IV of Schedule C (Form 1040 or 1040-ES), assuming they are not required to file Form 4562 for depreciation purposes.

Deemed Depreciation

When the taxpayer sells or trades in a vehicle for which the standard mileage rate was used, it must adjust the basis of the vehicle by a deemed depreciation rate for each year of service. Like the standard mileage rate, this is a rate that is also set annually by the IRS. The adjustment is necessary because depreciation is factored into the standard mileage rate.

The deemed depreciation rate for 2023 is 28¢ per mile. It was 26¢ per mile in 2022. Apply the deemed depreciation rate for each year based on the applicable rate and the number of miles driven. The following chart lists the deemed depreciation rates since 2015. The deemed depreciation rate hasn't varied too much over the years.

Year	Deemed Depreciation Rate
2023	28¢
2021–2022	26¢
2020	27¢
2019	26¢
2017–2018	25¢
2015–2016	24¢

EXAMPLE: A taxpayer bought a car in 2020 and used it 10,000 miles each year, using the standard mileage rate. The car is sold at the end of 2023. The basis of the car is reduced by $10,700.

Year	Rate	Mileage	Deemed Depreciation
2020	$0.27	10,000	$2,700
2021	$0.26	10,000	2,600
2022	$0.26	10,000	2,600
2023	$0.28	10,000	2,800
Total			$10,700

Rural Letter Carriers

There are special rules for rural letter carriers and their reimbursements. For rural letter carriers, qualified reimbursements from the government are tax-free. However, these carriers may have higher vehicle costs than the amount reimbursed. Unfortunately for them, the additional costs cannot be deducted from 2018 through 2025 because of the suspension of miscellaneous itemized deductions for individuals.

In prior years, rural letter carriers deducted their driving costs and figured this unreimbursed employee business expense on Form 2106, *Employee Business Expenses*, using the actual expense method (the standard mileage rate method was not permitted) and then claimed them as a miscellaneous itemized deduction on Schedule A of Form 1040.

Substantiation

Claiming a deduction for business vehicles is predicated on substantiation. The tax law is very specific about this requirement. Failure to have adequate substantiation has led to much litigation, and the taxpayer often loses deductions to which he or she would otherwise be entitled. Substantiation means keeping a contemporaneous record noting the following:

- Dates of driving
- Business destination
- Purpose of each drive
- Total mileage for the year for allocation between business and personal use
- Cost of each separate expense

PLANNING POINTER: Using the standard mileage rate method relieves the taxpayer of recordkeeping for costs, but not for substantiation of other elements.

Recordkeeping can be simplified with smartphone apps, some of which use GPS and note the date and destination of each trip. However, it's still up to the user to note the purpose of the trip and any other necessary details, including costs when using the actual expense method.

Schedule C filers must note in Part IV whether they have evidence to support their deduction and whether this evidence is written. The IRS has not stated in any formal or informal way whether apps are treated as written, but they do enable users to make printouts.

Accountable Plans

Reimbursing employees for business driving in their personal vehicles can be done through an accountable plan or a non-accountable plan. An accountable plan is a win-win for both employees and employers. The employer effectively deducts all the reimbursements as write-offs for business driving. Thus, the reimbursements avoid income and employment taxes.

Accountable plan payments are more important than ever for employees since they cannot deduct their unreimbursed employee business expenses as miscellaneous itemized deductions until after 2025. An accountable plan is an arrangement established by the employer. It must contain all of the following elements:

- **There must be a business connection for the expenses.** This is easy to show when employees use their personal vehicle for company business.
- **The employee must adequately account to the employer for the expenses incurred within a reasonable time.** An accountable plan with a 60-day deadline following either (1) advance payments to employees or (2) incurring the expense is treated as reasonable, but the employer can set a shorter period. Substantiation means supplying all the required information outlined earlier. If the employer reimburses the employee at no more than the standard mileage rate, no substantiation of the actual expenses is needed.

  EXAMPLE: If the employer reimburses the employee for business driving in 2023 at 65.5¢ per mile, the employee does not need receipts for gas fill-ups. The employee must still substantiate the business purpose of the travel as outlined earlier.

The employee must account for and return to the employer any excess advances (monies not used for a business purpose) within a reasonable period of time. For this purpose, returning excess advances to the employer within 120 days of the advance of funds to the employee is treated as reasonable.

EXAMPLE: If an employer advances an employee $400 for driving during a quarter of the year, but the employee's mileage entitles her to only $375, she must return the $25 to the employer within this time period.

PLANNING POINTER: Although there is no requirement in the tax law that the accountable travel reimbursement plan be written or formalized, it is highly advisable for the employer to put the terms of the plan in writing and communicate them to employees.

Closely held corporations may want to adopt an accountable plan in their annual board meeting and note the adoption in the corporate minutes.

If the plan is not in writing, there must be some proof that a plan exists.

In one case, a couple who owned an S corporation could not show any proof, such as collecting documentation, to substantiate the purported expenses and the amount actually reimbursed (*Kyle D. Simpson*, TC Memo 2023-4). As a result, they were taxed on the reimbursements.

Nonaccountable Plans

If an employer has an accountable plan but an employee fails to meet all of the requirements, then expenses are treated as having been paid under a nonaccountable plan. Under a nonaccountable plan, reimbursements are treated as taxable compensation, which means they are:

- Taxable as compensation to the employee,
- Subject to income tax withholding and FICA and FUTA taxes, and
- Reportable on an employee's Form W-2.

The employee cannot deduct the cost of business driving on his or her personal income tax return due to the suspension of miscellaneous itemized deductions.

Fixed and Variable Rate Rule

Another rule relative to car usage is the fixed and variable rate rule, or FAVR. FAVR is used to figure reimbursements to employees who drive their own vehicles on company business. It's an alternative to the standard mileage rate for purposes of accountable plans and obviating the need to substantiate costs to the employer. The amount reflects fixed and variable costs (e.g., lease payments, which are fixed, and gas expense, which is variable). The burden is on the employer to make the necessary calculations for the FAVR.

The rule can only be used if the vehicle's cost does not exceed a set amount. For 2023, the cost limit is $60,800 (Notice 2023-03).

A complete explanation of FAVR can be found in Rev. Proc. 2010-51.

STUDY QUESTIONS

1. Which of the following statements regarding the deduction for business use of a vehicle is correct?

a. Usually, a taxpayer is permitted to choose which method they use to calculate the deduction.

b. There are three possible methods of calculating the deduction.

c. The standard mileage rate method may be used if a taxpayer operates five or more vehicles at the same time.

d. Parking and tolls are expenses factored into the standard mileage rate.

2. Regina, a real estate agent, buys an expensive luxury vehicle with an unloaded gross vehicle weight that is less than 6,000 pounds. The car cost $120,000, and she uses it for business 60 percent of the time. The car is placed in service in 2023. Assuming that Regina uses bonus depreciation in year 1, what is the amount of her deduction for 2023?

a. $7,320

b. $12,120

c. $20,200

d. $72,000

3. The standard mileage rate for 2023 is which of the following?

a. 54.5 cents per mile

b. 57.5 cents per mile

c. 62.5 cents per mile

d. 65.5 cents per mile

¶ 205 PERSONAL USE

A person may use his or her vehicle for various activities other than business. This nonbusiness use may nonetheless give rise to a deduction.

Commuting

Generally, commuting to and from work is a nondeductible personal expense (Code Sec. 262). This is true regardless of the distance of the commute or other special factors. The only exception is any additional cost incurred for bringing work-related tools along (***Fausner***, S.Ct., 73-2 USTC ¶ 9515).

Once at work, driving to a second work location is not commuting; it is business driving. Even so, it can't be deducted by an employee but may be reimbursed through an accountable plan.

Driving for Medical Purposes

Personal driving for medical purposes is deductible. This includes driving to the following:

- Doctors and dentists
- Hospitals and clinics
- Pharmacies
- Therapists
- Any other deductible medical treatment (e.g., acupuncturists)

The cost of driving for medical purposes is based on either (1) the total of actual expenses incurred or (2) applying the IRS-set standard rate for this purpose. For 2023, the standard rate is 22¢ per mile, plus parking and tolls. The rate for 2022 was 18¢ per mile for the first half of the year and 22¢ for the second half of the year.

Even if a taxpayer itemizes, the AGI limit on itemizing medical expenses may bar a deduction for medical driving. Total medical expenses must exceed 7.5 percent of AGI.

PLANNING POINTER: Substantiation is required for medical driving, just as it is for business driving.

Driving for Moving Purposes

In the past, driving for a work-related move was part of an above-the-line deduction for moving expenses. For 2018 through 2025, this deduction is limited to members of the military who relocate to a permanent station of duty pursuant to orders (Code Sec. 217). A taxpayer who qualifies for a moving expense deduction may include driving in this write-off, which is figured on Form 3903, *Moving Expenses* (line 2), and is an above-the-line deduction (no itemizing is required).

Driving for this purpose includes taking yourself, members of your household, and personal effects to your new home. It does not include driving associated with house-hunting trips or returning to a previous location to close on a former residence.

The cost of driving for moving purposes is also based on either (1) the total of actual expenses or (2) the IRS-set standard rate. For 2023, the standard rate is 22¢ per mile. The rate for 2022 was 18¢ per mile for the first half of the year and 22¢ for the second half of the year. Parking and tolls should be added to the deduction.

PLANNING POINTER: As in the case of business and medical driving, substantiation is required.

Driving for Charity

Driving related to charity can also be deductible. This type of driving entails using a personal vehicle on behalf of a charitable organization.

EXAMPLE: If a taxpayer volunteers for Meals on Wheels and uses his vehicle to deliver meals to homebound individuals, the taxpayer may deduct the driving.

The taxpayer may deduct the actual expenses or rely on a mileage rate fixed by the tax law: 14¢ per mile. (The same rate has been in effect since 1997.) The taxpayer can add parking and tolls to the deduction. Charitable driving must be substantiated and is then claimed as an itemized deduction.

Personal Use of Company Vehicle

The personal use of a company vehicle is generally treated as taxable compensation. This requires the employer to figure the value of personal use. There are several ways to do this.

Under the actual FMV rule, FMV is determined by looking at the cost of leasing a comparable vehicle at a comparable price at a comparable time. Essentially, this is the cost of a vehicle in an arm's-length transaction. There are two safe harbors under this method:

- Use the manufacturer's sticker price, plus 4 percent.
- Use the manufacturer's suggested retail price, minus 8 percent.

Then the portion of annual use for personal driving is reported as taxable compensation on the employee's Form W-2.

Another method for valuing personal use of a company vehicle is the car's annual lease value (ALV). The amount of the ALV used to determine personal use depends on the fair market value of the vehicle on the date it is first used for personal purposes.

EXAMPLE: A company car's FMV on the date the employee began to use it for personal purposes is $25,000. The ALV is $6,850. The ALV is multiplied by the percentage of personal miles to total miles driven by the employee for the year. Thus, if the employee drives 5,000 miles for personal driving and 15,000 miles on company business, the amount of reportable income resulting from personal use of the company car is $1,713 ($6,850 × 25%).

ALVs are listed in IRS Publication 15-B, *Employer's Tax Guide to Fringe Benefits*. The ALV does not include fuel costs, regardless of whether the employer provides fuel, reimburses its cost, or charges the employee for it. Employers must add a fuel charge of 5.5¢ per mile to the value of personal use figured under ALV, for personal driving (Reg. § 1.61-21(d)(3)(ii)(D)).

EXAMPLE: If an employee drives a company car 3,000 miles in the year for personal use, the additional taxable amount reported is $165.

Another valuation rule is the fleet-average valuation rule. This rule applies to employers with a fleet of at least 20 vehicles (Reg. § 1.61-21(d)). This valuation method is a variation on the ALV. The employer averages the FMV of its vehicles. The FMV must be recalculated every two years.

The maximum value of employer-provided vehicles first made available to employees for personal use for an entire year cannot exceed a set amount. For 2023, that amount is $60,800 (Notice 2023-03); for 2022, it was $56,100 (Notice 2022-03).

Another method for valuing personal use is the cents-per-mile rule. This rule is based on the standard mileage rate. More specifically, the employer values personal use based on the number of miles the company vehicle was driven for personal purposes.

EXAMPLE: Continuing with the facts in the previous example, $5,000 personal miles in 2023 would be valued at $3,275 ($5,000 × 65.5¢).

This method can be used only if the vehicle is also used in the employer's business; it can't be used if the vehicle is only used for personal purposes. The value of the vehicle when first made available to the employee must not exceed a set limit (see the "Fleet-Average Valuation Rule" section).

Another rule that can be used is the commuting rule. Under this rule, the value of personal use is $1.50 per day each way, or $3.00 per day for a round-trip commute. This method of valuation can only be used if personal use is restricted to commuting or *de minimis* use and a written policy reflects this. The commuting rule cannot be used for a "control employee." For 2023, this includes any of the following:

- A board or shareholder-appointed, confirmed, or elected officer whose pay is $130,000 or more
- A director
- An employee whose pay is $265,000 or more
- An employee who owns a 1 percent or more equity, capital, or profits interest in the business

Instead of using the definition of a ***control employee*** for purposes of the commuting rule, the taxpayer can choose to use the definition of a ***highly compensated employee***. A highly compensated employee is someone who meets either of the following tests for 2023:

- The employee was a 5 percent owner at any time during the current or preceding year, or
- The employee received more than $135,000 in pay in the preceding year.

The second test can be ignored if the taxpayer/employee wasn't also in the top 20 percent of employees when ranked for pay in the preceding year.

¶ 206 ENERGY-RELATED CREDITS

Over the years, various tax incentives existed for buying vehicles. For example, during the Great Recession in 2008 and 2009, the sales tax on the purchase of vehicles up to a set price and within a set period was deductible, regardless of whether the taxpayer itemized deductions. In the past, there were tax credits for buying hybrid vehicles. Now, tax incentives relate to so-called clean vehicles. These are plug-in electric vehicles (EVs) or fuel cell vehicles (FCVs).

The Inflation Reduction Act of 2022 made numerous changes to incentivize the purchase of electric vehicles (EVs) by consumers and businesses. The IRS provides answers to frequently asked questions about the clean vehicles credit at https://www.irs.gov/newsroom/frequently-asked-questions-about-the-new-previously-owned-and-qualified-commercial-clean-vehicles-credit.

Clean Vehicle Credit for Consumers Beginning in 2023

After 2022, there are different EV credits: two that apply for consumers and one that can be used by businesses for certain vehicles and movable equipment. Let's start with the one for consumers who buy a *new* EV.

The clean vehicle credit applies to the purchase of a plug-in EV or a fuel cell electric vehicle. This credit is up to $7,500 and is set to run through 2032. The 200,000-vehicle limit no longer applies. However, there are new eligibility requirements.

Like the pre-2023 credit, the amount is limited to $7,500, but the way in which it's figured is different. There's a crucial minerals portion of the credit up to $3,750 and a battery component portion up to $3,750. The critical minerals and battery components must be extracted or processed in the United States, by a U.S. free-trade agreement partner, or recycled in North America. The Department of Energy has a list of the percentages (https://bit.ly/3CQWVvg) to meet these requirements; they increase each year.

The clean vehicle credit is nonrefundable, with no carryforward. To claim the credit, the taxpayer's modified adjusted gross income (MAGI) may not exceed:

- $300,000 for married filing jointly,
- $225,000 for head of household, or
- $150,000 for other filers.

A taxpayer can use MAGI from the year in which he or she takes delivery of the vehicle or from the year before, whichever is less. If the taxpayer's MAGI exceeds the threshold amount in one year, it can still be claimed if it is below the threshold in the other year.

Additional clean vehicle credit rules include the following:

- The EV must be new.
- The seller must report information to the buyer—and to the IRS—at the time of sale. This information includes the buyer's name and taxpayer identification number (SSN).
- The vehicle's manufacturer suggested retail price (MSRP) cannot be greater than:
  - — $80,000 for vans, SUVs, and pickup trucks
  - — $55,000 for other vehicles

  NOTE: The MSRP includes options, accessories, and trim, but doesn't include destination fees.

Credit for previously owned EV. Starting in 2023, there is a separate credit for previously owned clean vehicles (Code Sec. 25E). This credit applies to the same type of vehicle covered by the clean vehicle credit, meaning vehicles that weigh no more than 14,000 pounds. The credit is 30 percent of the sale price, up to a maximum credit of $4,000. Like the new EV credit, this credit is nonrefundable and can only be claimed once every three years. It can't be claimed if the taxpayer claimed another used clean vehicle credit in the three years before the purchase date. The credit also may not be claimed by a person who is a dependent on another taxpayer's return.

There is an income limit for the previously owned EV credit. The taxpayer's MAGI may not exceed:

- $150,000 for married filing jointly and qualifying surviving spouse,
- $112,500 for head of household, or
- $75,000 for other filers.

As with the credit for a new EV, a taxpayer can use MAGI from the year in which he or she takes delivery of the vehicle or the year before, whichever is less. If the taxpayer's MAGI exceeds the threshold amount in one year, the credit can still be claimed if it is below the threshold in the other year.

To qualify for the previously owned EV credit, the vehicle must:

- Have a sale price of $25,000 or less
- Have a model year at least two years earlier than the calendar year when it is purchased (e.g., a vehicle purchased in 2023 would have to be a model year of 2021 or older)

- Not have already been transferred after August 16, 2022, to a qualified buyer
- Have a gross vehicle weight rating of less than 14,000 pounds
- Be an eligible FCV or plug-in EV with a battery capacity of at least 7 kilowatt hours
- Be for use primarily in the United States

Also, the vehicle must be purchased from a dealer who reports the following required information at the time of the sale to the purchaser and to the IRS:

- Dealer's name and taxpayer ID number
- Buyer's name and taxpayer ID number
- Sale date and sale price
- Maximum credit allowable under Code Sec. 25E
- Vehicle identification number (VIN), unless the vehicle is not assigned one
- Battery capacity

The previously owned clean vehicle credit is claimed on Form 8936.

> **PLANNING POINTER:** Starting in 2024, the clean vehicle credit and the previously owned clean vehicle credit can effectively be "sold" to the dealer to reduce the purchase price of the vehicle. Opting to sell the credit to the dealer means the taxpayer does not have to wait to file a return in order to reap the tax savings from the credit.

Commercial clean vehicle credit. Starting in 2023, there is a credit for commercial clean vehicles that may be claimed by businesses as well as tax-exempt organizations (Code Sec. 45W). This credit applies to vehicles similar to the ones covered by the clean vehicle credit for consumers as well as to heavier motor vehicles and mobile machinery (vehicles not designed to perform a function of transporting a load over a public highway).

The credit is the lesser of 15 percent of the vehicle's basis, or 30 percent if the vehicle isn't powered by gas or diesel, or the incremental cost of the vehicle. The maximum credit amount depends on the weight of the vehicle:

- Up to $7,500 for vehicles weighing under 14,000 pounds
- Up to $40,000 for vehicles weighing 14,000 pounds or more

Incremental cost is the excess of the purchase price of such vehicle over the price of a comparable vehicle. A comparable vehicle with respect to any qualified commercial clean vehicle is any vehicle that is powered solely by a gasoline or diesel internal combustion engine and is comparable in size and use to such qualified commercial clean vehicle.

The IRS stated that it reviewed the incremental cost for all street vehicles in calendar year 2023 (Notice 2023-9). The analysis shows that the incremental cost of all street vehicles, other than compact car plug-in electric hybrids, with a gross vehicle weight of less than 14,000 pounds is greater than $7,500 in calendar year 2023. The incremental cost won't limit the available credit amount for these street vehicles placed in service in calendar year 2023.

For compact car plug-in electric hybrids for which the incremental cost was calculated to be less than $7,500, the IRS will accept the incremental cost published by the Department of Energy.

> **PLANNING POINTER:** There is no limit on the number of credits a business may claim. A business that replaces a fleet of cars or buys multiple trucks can

claim a credit for each vehicle that qualifies. The depreciable basis of the vehicle or machine must be reduced by the amount of the credit claimed.

The commercial vehicle or machinery must also either be:

- A plug-in EV that draws significant propulsion from an electric motor with a battery capacity of at least:
  - — 7 kilowatt hours if the gross vehicle weight rating (GVWR) is under 14,000 pounds
  - — 15 kilowatt hours if the GVWR is 14,000 pounds or more; or
- A FCV that satisfies requirements listed in Code Sec. 30B

The business will have to include the VIN number on the tax return to claim the credit. At present, there is no draft form for this purpose.

Alternative fuel refueling property credit (Code Sec. 30C). Another green energy measure related to vehicles is the tax credit for installing a charging station. This credit applies for installing a charging station and runs through 2032. Different rules apply to individuals who install charging stations at their residences versus businesses that install charging stations on their premises. However, in both situations, the credit beginning in 2023 can only be claimed if property is located in low-income census tracts or non-urban areas.

Individuals who install an EV charging station in their residence may claim a tax credit of the lesser of 30 percent of the property's cost or $1,000. Various credits must be used to reduce the regular tax before this credit for a charging station may be claimed. The unused portion of the credit may not be carried forward; it is simply lost.

Although an individual may not owe alternative minimum tax (AMT), the taxpayer must still figure the tentative minimum tax (TMT) to figure the credit. The taxpayer should attach Form 6251, *Alternative Minimum Tax—Individuals* to Form 8911, *Alternative Fuel Vehicle Refueling Property Credit*.

For charging stations for businesses, the credit limit is as follows:

- For 2022: the lesser of 30 percent of the property's cost or $30,000
- For 2023 and beyond: the lesser of 6 percent of the property's cost or $100,000

Beginning in 2023, prevailing wage and apprenticeship requirements must be satisfied in order to claim the credit for property placed in service after December 31, 2022. The IRS provides some guidance on these requirements (IR-2022-208), which reflect proposed regulations that took effect on January 30, 2023 (87 FR 73580). The IRS noted that it would issue additional guidance, so watch for any developments, which would impact 2023 returns to be filed in 2024.

The credit is figured on Form 8911. Partnerships and S corporations must file this form to claim the credit. All other taxpayers are not required to complete or file this form if their only source for this credit is a partnership or S corporation. Instead, they report this credit directly on Form 3800, *General Business Credit*.

State-level green energy tax incentives. Taxpayers should check their state tax rules, as there may be incentives for buying EVs and/or installing charging stations in their state. State-level tax incentives can be found at https://www.dsireusa.org/ (enter a zip code or click on the state on the map).

¶ 207 OTHER VEHICLE-RELATED MATTERS

This section addresses some other matters that may arise because they relate to vehicles.

State and Local Taxes

Today, if taxpayers purchase a vehicle solely for personal use, they may still obtain a tax break. The state and local sales taxes on the vehicle—new or pre-owned—are deductible by individuals if they itemize deductions and forego the deduction for state and local income taxes. The total write-off is subject to the $10,000 cap on state and local taxes (SALT cap).

The taxpayer should figure the sales tax deduction from an IRS table and then to this amount, add the sales taxes on the vehicle purchase.

NOTE: Businesses add the sales tax to basis.

Registration Fees by Individuals

In addition to sales taxes on vehicle purchases, registration fees are deductible by taxpayers, but only those who itemize. To deduct state and local car registration fees as a state personal property tax (subject to the SALT cap), the fee must be:

- An ad valorem tax, which means it is based on a percentage of the car's value (e.g., 1% of value);
- Imposed on an annual basis, whether it is collected more or less frequently; and
- Imposed on personal property.

A tax based on weight, model, year, or horsepower is not a deductible ad valorem tax. If a tax is based on both value and some other factor or factors, then the portion of the registration fee based on value is deductible.

Interest on Car Loans

Interest on a loan to buy a vehicle for personal driving is not deductible. However, interest on a loan by a self-employed person to buy a vehicle used for business driving is a deductible business expense. However, this "business interest" is subject to the interest expense limitation. Small businesses—those that meet the gross receipts test—are automatically exempt from this interest limitation, so all of their interest payments are deductible. Farming businesses and real property businesses that elect out of the limitation may deduct all of the interest on a vehicle loan.

PLANNING POINTER: The loan to purchase a vehicle is carried as a liability on the balance sheet for a business.

Donating Vehicles to Charity

If an individual donates a car or truck to an IRS-recognized charity, it may be tax deductible if the taxpayer itemizes deductions and does not claim the standard deduction amount. Generally, the amount of the deduction is limited to 30 percent of the taxpayer's AGI. It is claimed as a charitable contribution on Schedule A of Form 1040 or 1040-SR.

Special substantiation rules apply to donations of vehicles valued at over $500. The organization must issue Form 1098-C, *Contributions of Motor Vehicles, Boats, and Airplanes,* within 30 days of the date of the contribution or the date the organization sells the vehicle without using it in any significant way. If the organization sells the vehicle without using it in a significant way in its charitable activities or making any improvements to the vehicle, the donor's deduction is limited to the amount of the sales proceeds.

If the value of the vehicle is $250 or more but not over $500 and the organization sells it, the donor can deduct the actual value and isn't limited to the sales proceeds. If the vehicle's value is over $500 but the organization sells it for $500 or less, the maximum deduction the donor can claim is $500.

EXAMPLE: A taxpayer donates a clunker worth $750 to a charity, and the charity sells it for $450. The donor can deduct $500.

It's up to the donor to substantiate the value of the donation (using such resources as Kelley Blue Book values at www.kbb.com). The donor should also retain a written acknowledgment of the gift.

Car Accidents and Thefts

Car accidents and thefts are all too common occurrences. For 2018 through 2025, no deduction for loss related to a personal-use vehicle can be claimed as a personal casualty or theft loss; this write-off has been suspended.

Federal Disasters

If a vehicle is damaged or destroyed in a federally declared disaster, the loss may be deductible.

Involuntary Conversions

If insurance or other reimbursements exceed the adjusted basis of the vehicle, then there is a tax gain (an involuntary conversion). The taxpayer may be able to defer reporting the gain by buying replacement property (Code Sec. 1033); this is property that is similar or related in service or use.

To postpone reporting all the gain, the taxpayer must buy replacement property costing at least as much as the amount realized for the old vehicle. If the cost of the replacement property is less than the amount realized, the taxpayer must report the gain up to the unspent part of the amount realized.

The replacement must be timely (buying another vehicle to replace the old one usually within two years of the end of the year of the casualty). For involuntary conversions resulting from federally declared disasters, there's an additional one year to replace the vehicle. Disaster areas are listed at https://www.irs.gov/newsroom/tax-relief-in-disaster-situations.

The basis of the new or repaired vehicle ("replacement property") is reduced by the amount of gain not recognized.

Disaster Losses for Vehicles

If a taxpayer suffers a loss on a business vehicle, it's fully deductible. If the vehicle is used for personal driving, it may be deductible as a disaster loss on Schedule A of Form 1040 or 1040-SR. To claim the deduction:

- **The taxpayer must prove that the loss arose from an event declared to be a federal disaster.** Having an insurance report or newspaper articles on the disaster is helpful. Pictures of the vehicle are also helpful.
- **The taxpayer must establish the amount of the loss.** If the vehicle is damaged, the taxpayer should measure the loss by comparing the value before and after the event, and then reduce this amount by any insurance or other reimbursement. The taxpayer can use the cost of repairs as a measure of loss, provided it is not excessive and merely restores the vehicle to its pre-casualty event condition.
- **The taxpayer must reduce the loss by $100.** The $100 reduction applies to each casualty or theft loss event in the same year. The $100 reduction applies only to personal vehicles; it does not apply to business vehicles.
- **The taxpayer must reduce the loss by 10 percent of AGI**. Only the amount of total losses for the year in excess of 10 percent of AGI is deductible.

EXAMPLE: In 2023, the taxpayer's vehicle was totally destroyed in a flood declared to be a federal disaster. The vehicle's value before the incident was $18,100, or $18,000 after the $100 reduction. Insurance paid the taxpayer $6,000, so its loss is $12,000. The taxpayer's AGI is $48,000. The deductible loss is $7,200 ($12,000 – [10% of $48,000]).

A disaster loss can be deducted on the tax return prior to the year of the disaster. This can generate a tax refund if the prior year return has already been filed. To obtain the refund, the taxpayer must file an amended return.

If the disaster occurs before the prior year return has been filed, the taxpayer should simply report the loss on that return to reduce their tax bill. There is a time limit for electing to report the loss on a prior-year return. The due date for making the election is six months after the due date for filing the tax return for the disaster year (determined without regard to any filing extension). The deadline for revoking an election is on or before the date that is 90 days after the due date for making the election.

STUDY QUESTIONS

4. Which of the following statements regarding driving for medical purposes is correct?

- **a.** Driving to pharmacies is not considered driving for medical purposes.
- **b.** The cost of driving for medical purposes is based only on the total of actual expenses incurred.
- **c.** If a taxpayer itemizes deductions, total medical expenses must exceed 2 percent of adjusted gross income to be deductible.
- **d.** For 2023, the amount that can be deductible is the standard rate (22 cents per mile), plus parking and tolls.

5. The maximum amount of the 2023 credit for the purchase of a new qualified electric vehicle is which of the following?

- **a.** $2,500
- **b.** $5,000
- **c.** $7,500
- **d.** $10,000

6. The amount of the state and local tax cap for individuals who itemize deductions is which of the following?

- **a.** $7,500
- **b.** $10,000
- **c.** $12,500
- **d.** $15,000

MODULE 1: BUSINESS—Chapter 3: Tax Implications in a Remote Work Environment: State Tax Nexus and Income Tax Issues

¶ 301 WELCOME

The COVID-19 pandemic prompted a drastic shift to remote work, and many people are still working remotely. Employers have been allowing employees to work remotely in different states. Allowing employees to work remotely from states in which they do not normally work can create a host of issues for employers, but the two big tax issues relate to nexus and income tax.

First, will the presence of an employee working from home create taxable nexus for the employer in that state? Second, for income tax purposes, which state is owed income tax when an employee is working remotely from an out-of-state location? Is it possible that states could have contradictory rules, creating a double tax situation for many employees? (Spoiler alert: yes).

This chapter explains how states have responded to the new remote work environment and identifies potential issues for both individuals working remotely and their employers.

¶ 302 LEARNING OBJECTIVES

Upon completion of this chapter, you will be able to:

- Describe the corporate tax implications of having employees working in different states
- Recognize where (in which states) an employer may have corporate income tax nexus
- Identify the number of states that have a "convenience rule"
- Explain how to advise clients on sourcing of wages received while working remotely
- Identify how the primary domicile factors are considered for residency
- Explain what counts as a workday, and what does not, for wage allocation purposes

---

¶ 303 RESIDENCY RULES REFRESHER

Let's begin with a quick refresher on residency rules since, of course, the state tax consequences of remote employees depend on the employee's resident status. In general, states use three types of residency tests:

- **Domicile.** *Domicile* is generally defined as the location or area that a person intends to be their permanent home. This is the place they intend to return to whenever they might be absent. This test is often referred to as the "home is where the heart is" test. It's more of a subjective inquiry that looks at different factors to determine where the person intends their home to be.
- **Statutory residency.** The most widely used test for statutory residency defines the term *resident* to include an individual who is not domiciled in the state, but

who maintains a permanent place of abode there *and* is in the state for more than 183 days in a given taxable year. This test is sometimes called the "183-day rule." Implicit in this test is that a person can be a resident of more than one state. There are other variations of statutory residency. For example, a variation used in Ohio takes into account "contact periods," where a person is treated as a statutory resident only if they have more than 212 contact periods in Ohio during the year.

- **Rebuttable presumption of residency.** Other states, like California, use a rebuttable test. Under California's test, a person who spends more than 9 months in California during any tax year is presumed to be a resident, but that presumption is rebuttable. The following examples discuss residency in particular states.

EXAMPLE: RESIDENCY IN NEW YORK STATE: Residency is generally established by looking at:

- Domicile: Determined using five primary factors—home, time, business, family, and the "near and dear" factor, which is essentially the location of one's prized possessions.
- Statutory residency: A person not domiciled in New York in a particular year, but who spends more than 183 days (including part days) and maintains a "permanent place of abode" in New York.

In New York, income tax is based on resident status:

- New York State (NYS) residents are subject to tax on their worldwide income.
- NYS nonresidents are subject to tax on NYS-source income only.
- New York City (NYC) tax applies to residents only, so a nonresident working in NYC will be subject to NYS tax but not to the NYC personal income tax.
- The tax for the city of Yonkers applies to residents and nonresidents alike.

EXAMPLE: RESIDENCY IN CALIFORNIA: Residency is generally established by determining:

- Whether the taxpayer is present in California for other than a temporary or transitory purpose
- Whether the taxpayer is domiciled in California, but outside California for a temporary or transitory purpose

California also has a rebuttable presumption of residency if the taxpayer spends at least nine months of the year in California. Income tax is based on resident status:

- California residents are subject to tax on their worldwide income.
- California nonresidents are subject to tax on California-source income only.

There are no local individual income taxes.

¶ 304 ALLOCATING EMPLOYEE COMPENSATION

If an employee is a resident of the state where they work, then generally 100 percent of their compensation income is subject to that state's income tax, and the employer must withhold tax on 100 percent of their compensation. If an employee is a nonresident, state tax generally is still due to the extent of the taxpayer's workdays in the state. The formula for determining the workday percentage is:

[In-State Workdays] ÷ [Total Workdays] = [Workday Percentage]

The employer generally must withhold state tax based on that workday percentage, and the employee reports allocable income based on that workday percentage.

Allocating "Regular" Wages/Salary

Allocation is required when a nonresident's in-state workdays/compensation exceeds the state's applicable threshold (if any). The standard allocation formula is as follows:

$$\frac{In - State\ Workdays}{Total\ Workdays} \times Total\ Wages$$

A *workday* typically includes days worked in the employee's office, travel days, days worked from home, and days worked on weekends. It typically excludes holidays, vacation days, sick days, and weekends. The following chart shows how workdays may be counted:

Counting Workdays		
Total Days in Year		365
Nonworking Days		
Saturdays/Sundays	104	
Holidays	10	
Vacation Days	14	
Sick Days	5	
Other nonworking days	2	
Total Nonworking Days		135
Total Days Worked in Year		230
Total Days Worked Out-of-State		55
Total Days Worked In-State		175

EXAMPLE: You were employed in Colorado and were a resident of that state. Your employer required you to spend 15 days during 2022 at the company's main office in Wisconsin. Your annual salary was $40,000, which was compensation for 260 days. The amount of wages allocable to Wisconsin is $2,307.69, computed as follows:

$15/260 \times \$40,000 = \$2,307.69$

Source: Wisconsin Pub. 122 (3/2023).

State Withholding Guidance During COVID-19

During the COVID-19 pandemic, there were three general approaches to state guidance regarding withholding for teleworkers:

- The state issued no guidance, so normal withholding rules presumably applied;
- The state issued guidance that specifically confirmed that the pre-pandemic rules remained in full force and effect; and
- The state adopted temporary laws, regulations, or other guidance that changed the normal pre-pandemic withholding rules.

As far as the temporary pandemic rules are concerned, the guidance generally fell into one of two categories.

- States that sought to maintain the status quo for their outbound residents, or
- States that allowed inbound residents who worked out of state pre-pandemic to continue sourcing their wages to their out-of-state pre-pandemic location.

The "start" and "end" dates varied by state and were tied to:

- The federal government's state-of-emergency,
- The state's state-of-emergency (e.g., Pennsylvania),
- The employer's mandatory work-from-home order (e.g., New Jersey), or
- A specific date (i.e., starting on March 13, 2020, and ending on July 1, 2021) (e.g., Connecticut, Massachusetts, South Carolina)

The states' responses to telecommuting during the pandemic are summarized in the following chart:

State Responses to Telecommuting and COVID-19

State	Sourced to Employer's Home State	Sourced to Employee's Home State
Alabama	X	
Arkansas	X (until 12/1/20)	X (as of 1/1/21)
California		X
Colorado		X
Connecticut		X (2020 only)
Delaware		X
Georgia	X	
Illinois*		X
Iowa		X
Kansas	X (both until 12/31/20)	X (only as of 1/1/21)
Kentucky		X
Maine	X (until 6/30/21)	
Maryland		X
Massachusetts	X (until 9/13/21)	
Minnesota		X
Mississippi	X	
Missouri	X (for some employers if elected until 7/19/21)	X
Montana		X
Nebraska	X (until 7/30/21)	
New Jersey**	X	X
New York	X	
North Carolina		X
Ohio (municipal income tax)	X (until 12/31/21)	
Oregon		X
Pennsylvania		X (until 6/20/21)
Rhode Island	X	
South Carolina	X (until 9/30/21)	
Vermont		X
Wisconsin		X

* Withholding required if employee is telecommuting from IL for more than 30 days.
** Rules of employer's home state dictate which state gets the tax.

Note that nearly all of this guidance was limited to the pandemic period and is no longer in effect.

The "Convenience of the Employer" Rule

This is a rule that applies to a small number of states, and it reflects an issue that has come to the forefront in recent years. A small number of states apply this rule. With respect to those states, in general, an employee's days worked from home are deemed to be days worked at their assigned work location to the extent that the employee is working remotely for their own convenience, broadly defined, rather than for the employer's necessity. Applications of this rule include:

- Nonresident income allocation,
- Employer withholding, and
- Resident credit purposes.

Six states—New York, Connecticut, Pennsylvania, Delaware, Nebraska, and New Jersey—currently have a "convenience rule." Connecticut and New Jersey's rules only applies if the other state is a convenience state. Several states (Georgia, Massachusetts, Maine, Mississippi, Nebraska, New York, Pennsylvania, Rhode Island, and South Carolina) issued guidance or temporary legislation during the pandemic requiring that days worked at home to continue to be treated as if worked at the employee's regular place of work.

Convenience Rule States	
Connecticut Conn. Gen. Stat. § 12-711(b)(2)(C)	"For purposes of determining the compensation derived from or connected with sources within this state, a nonresident . . . shall include income from days worked outside this state for such person's convenience if such person's state of domicile uses a similar test."
Delaware 2020 Schedule W 30 Del. C. § 1124(b).	For nonresidents, non-Delaware workdays "must be based on necessity of work outside . . . Delaware in performance of duties for the employer, as opposed to solely for the convenience of the employee. Working from [a home office] does not satisfy the requirements of 'necessity' of duties for your employer and is considered for the convenience of the employee unless working from home is a requirement of employment with your employer."
Nebraska 316 Neb. Admin. Code 22-003.01C(1)	"If the nonresident's service is performed without Nebraska for his or her convenience, but the service is directly related to a business, trade, or profession carried on within Nebraska and except for the nonresident's convenience, the service could have been performed within Nebraska, the compensation for such services shall be Nebraska source income."
New Jersey N.J. Stat. § 54A:5-8(e) P.L. 2023, c. 125 (effective 1/1/2023)	Similar to Connecticut's rule: "If an employee's state of residence uses a 'convenience of the employer' test when determining the source of income of a nonresident, income or wages earned by a nonresident are allocated to the employer's location, unless the nonresident works from an out-of-state location due to the necessity of the employer, rather than the convenience of the employee."

Convenience Rule States	
New York 20 NYCRR 132.18(a) TSB-M-06(5)I	"Any allowance claimed for days worked outside New York State must be based upon the performance of services which of necessity, as distinguished from convenience, obligate the employee to out-of-state duties in the service of his employer"
Pennsylvania 61 Pa. Code § 109.8	If a nonresident employee (including corporate officers but generally excluding salesmen) performs services both within and without PA, their PA-sourced income includes the ratio of PA workdays over total workdays. For this ratio, Non-PA workdays include days worked out-of-state performing services "which, of necessity, obligate the [employee] to perform out-of-State duties in the service of his employer."

New York's "Convenience of the Employer" Rule

In 2020, New York began sending desk audit notices to taxpayers who previously allocated most or all of their W-2 income to New York, and who began filing nonresident income tax returns allocating a lower percentage of their wages to New York. Some of the 2020 notices stated:

> We have determined that you were unable to access your office located in New York due to a temporary office closure resulting from COVID-19. If an employee's assigned or primary work location was New York prior to COVID-19 temporary office closure, and the employer continues to maintain the New York office for the employee, the employer's assigned and primary work location is still New York. The fact that the New York office is not used during the COVID-19 office closure does not affect the conclusion.

EXAMPLE: The July 2020 New York State FAQ on COVID Telecommuting included the following:

My primary office is inside New York State, but I am telecommuting from outside of the state due to the COVID-19 pandemic. Do I owe New York taxes on the income I earn while telecommuting?

If you are a nonresident whose primary office is in New York State, your days telecommuting during the pandemic are considered days worked in the state unless your employer has established a bona fide employer office at your telecommuting location.

There are a number of factors that determine whether your employer has established a bona fide employer office at your telecommuting location. In general, unless your employer specifically acted to establish a bona fide employer office at your telecommuting location, you will continue to owe New York State income tax on income earned while telecommuting.

https://www.tax.ny.gov/pit/file/nonresident-faqs.htm#telecommuting

The Convenience Rule After COVID-19

Telecommuting is likely here to stay and may become even more prevalent. Therefore, convenience rule issues will take center stage. But what happens if an employer no longer has a physical office? Employers need to be careful about nexus and convenience rule issues if they continue to allow employees to work from home.

Options to avoid New York's convenience rule include the following:

- **Option 1:** Assign the employee to a non–New York office.
- **Option 2:** Establish a bona fide home office under the TSB-M-06(5)I factors (see the chart that follows).
- **Option 3:** No New York workdays.

<table>
<tr><th colspan="2">The TSB-M-06(5)I Factors</th></tr>
<tr><td colspan="2">Step 1: Primary Factor: Employee's duties require the use of special facilities that cannot be made available at the employer's place of business, but those facilities are available at or near the employee's home.
If the home office does NOT satisfy the primary factor, proceed to Step 2.</td></tr>
<tr><td colspan="2">Step 2: The Secondary and "Other" Factors: The home office may still qualify as a "bona fide employer office" if it meets four out of the six Secondary Factors plus three out of the ten "Other" Factors.</td></tr>
<tr><td>Secondary Factors (4 out of 6 required)
1. Home office is a requirement or condition of employment.
2. Employer has a bona fide business purpose for the employee's home office location.
3. Employee performs some core duties at the home office.
4. Employee meets with clients, patients, or customers at the home office.
5. Employer does not provide the employee with office space or regular work accommodations.
6. Employer reimburses expenses for the home office.</td><td>"Other" Factors (3 out of 10 required)
1. Employer maintains a separate telephone line and listing for the home office.
2. Employee's home office address and phone number are on the employer's business letterhead and/or cards.
3. Employee uses a specific area of the home exclusively for the employer's business.
4. Employee keeps inventory of products or samples in the home office.
5. Employer's business records are stored at the home office.
6. Employer signage at the home office.
7. Home office is advertised as employer's place of business.
8. Home office covered by a business-related insurance policy.
9. Employee properly claims a deduction for home office expenses for federal income tax purposes.
10. Employee is not an officer of the company.</td></tr>
</table>

Reassignment to a Non-New York Office

There is no written guidance as to what constitutes an individual's primary office. On audit, New York has looked at facts such as:

- Which office does the individual visit more than any other?
- Where is the employee's administrative support?
- Where does the employee's supervisor, managers, or "team" sit?
- Does the employee still have designated office space in New York?
- What do the employer's HR records designate as the primary office?

There must be evidence other than geographical proximity to reassign an employee to another office.

EXAMPLE: NEW YORK TO FLORIDA MOVE: Facts

Matt lives and works in New York City, but he has decided to give up his NYC lease and move to Florida for good. Matt's employer is based in NYC and doesn't have a Florida office, but is okay with Matt doing remote work indefinitely, with occasional visits to the NYC office.

So, Matt telecommutes from his home office in Florida.

Issues

This is an easy domicile case, and there are NYC tax savings. But Matt's wages will still be subject to NYS tax based on the "convenience rule." Matt's employer is still required to withhold 100 percent NY tax.

EXAMPLE: DOUBLE TAX ON REMOTE WORK?: Facts

James (a NY resident) historically worked in his employer's NYC office. Since March 2020, he has been working remotely from his ski home in Colorado. James expects to return to NY by the end of 2022.

Issues

James is a NY resident, so NY withholding must continue. Colorado's rules require James to source his wage income to Colorado based on his physical work location in Colorado.

New York, on the other hand, calls those Colorado physical presence workdays "New York workdays" under its convenience rule.

James's employer may also have Colorado withholding obligations.

Multiyear Allocations

Multiyear allocations are triggered when a taxpayer receives compensation attributed to services performed in a different tax year. Common sources of deferred compensation include deferred bonuses, equity awards (restricted stock units/stock options), and termination/severance pay.

Deferred bonuses. Deferred bonuses are bonuses received by a nonresident for services performed in a previous taxable year. For example, a bonus received on April 1, 2023, for performance in 2022 is allocated based on the 2022 (not 2023) allocation percentage. This can be particularly important when a bonus is received in the year of one's change in residence.

Equity awards. Several key dates are associated with equity awards:

- **Grant date:** When the employee is granted an option to purchase stock from the employer at a fixed price within a set period.
- **Vest date:** When the employee satisfies all employment-related conditions, making the options exercisable.
- **Exercise date:** When the employee actually buys the stock.
- **Sale date:** When the employee sells the stock.

Restricted stock. Restricted stock units (RSUs) are generally taxable for federal purposes as ordinary income in the year of vesting. The taxable amount equals the difference between the amount paid (if any) and the fair market value at the time of vesting (unless a Code Sec. 83(b) election is made).

The amount taxable as ordinary income for federal tax purposes can represent taxable compensation to a nonresident for state income tax purposes. It is generally allocable to the extent that the compensation is taxable for federal income tax purposes and where it is earned.

Example: New York RSU allocation. Employee A works in Employer's Florida office and is a New York nonresident every year. In 2022, Employer informs Employee A that he'll receive an RSU award valued at $1,000,000, which was granted on April 1, 2022, and would vest over the next five years on the following schedule:

- 10 percent on the first anniversary of the grant date (April 1, 2023)—$100K
- 10 percent on the second anniversary of the grant date (April 1, 2024)—$100K
- 20 percent on the third anniversary of the grant date (April 1, 2025)—$200K

- 30 percent on the fourth anniversary of the grant date (April 1, 2026)—$300K
- 30 percent on the fifth anniversary of the grant date (April 1, 2027)—$300K

From 2022 through 2027, Employee A has 240 workdays for Employer each year and he works in New York on 10 percent of those days (24 days/year), except that he works an extra six days in New York in March 2024 (30 days total for 2024).

In 2023, Employee A will receive W-2 compensation based on his 10 percent vesting ($100K) in wages, plus any appreciation that has occurred between the grant and vest dates, which will be allocated to New York based on the number of workdays between the date of the grant (April 1, 2022) and the date of vest (April 1, 2023). Thus, in 2023, $10,000 (or 10 percent of the $100K, plus appreciation) will be sourced to and taxable by New York.

The 2024 allocation will be computed as follows:

	New York		Total
Workdays 4/1/2022 – 3/31/2023	24		240
Workdays 4/1/2023 – 3/31/2024	30		240
Total Workdays Grant-to-Vest Period	**54**		**480**
	NY Allocation % (54 ÷ 480) = 11.25%		
	Total vested in 2024 (assume no appreciation) = $100K (10% of $1M)		
	Amount sourced to/taxable by NY = $11,250 (11.25% of $100K that vested in 2024)		

The 2025 allocation will be computed as follows:

	New York	Total
Workdays 4/1/2022 – 3/31/2023	24	240
Workdays 4/1/2023 – 3/31/2024	30	240
Workdays 4/1/2024 – 3/31/2025	24	240
Total Workdays Grant-to-Vest Period	**78**	**720**
NY Allocation % (78 ÷ 720) = 10.83%		
Total vested in 2025 (assume no appreciation) = $200K (20% of $1M)		
Amount sourced to/taxable by NY = $21,660 (10.83% of $200K that vested in 2025)		

Stock options. Statutory/qualified options (e.g., incentive stock options or ISOs) are generally taxed only once (when sold), and the character of the gain is capital in nature. Nonstatutory/nonqualified stock options are taxed twice: at the exercise date (ordinary income on the W-2) and when sold (capital gain).

Allocation methodologies for stock options vary. Most (but not all) states tax a nonresident on option income when and where it was earned versus when it was received. It doesn't matter if the individual was a resident of the state when it was earned.

- Workdays from grant-to-vest—e.g., New York, Georgia, Idaho
- Workdays from grant-to-exercise—e.g., Arizona, California, Connecticut, New Jersey, Pennsylvania
- Exceptions:
  - — Five-year—Illinois
  - — Location of grant rule—North Carolina

The difference between the option price and the fair market value on the exercise date represents compensation for services to a nonresident. The compensation is generally taxable for state tax purposes when it is recognized for federal income tax purposes. For qualified/ISOs, this is the date of sale; for nonqualified stock options (NQSOs), it is the date of exercise.

For qualified/ISOs, the compensation element is limited to the appreciation in stock between the grant and exercise dates. Any further appreciation between the exercise and sale dates is investment/intangible income and is not included in New York taxable income for a nonresident.

Termination/severance pay. This is generally allocated based on prior in-state services, but with varying periods. In New York, termination/severance pay is allocated based on the year of termination and three prior years. Note that New York uses a "comp-to-comp" method for this period.

> **EXAMPLE:** If Julia separates from employment in 2021 and receives a severance, she measures total New York compensation and total everywhere compensation in 2018, 2019, 2020, and 2021 and computes the allocation percentage using a total New York compensation over total everywhere compensation fraction over that period.

In Minnesota, termination/severance pay is allocated based on the percentage of time worked in the state in total.

> **EXAMPLE:** Andy worked for nine years in Minnesota and one year in Florida. He is a Florida resident when receiving his severance payment. He must allocate 90 percent of his severance pay to Minnesota.

Allocating Director's Fees

Director's fees are generally allocated based on the location of board meetings. New York requires nonresidents to allocate board compensation like a W-2, salaried employee (days in/out during the current year). However, generally only the days when there are board meetings are counted, and not the time spent preparing for the board meetings.

There is some inconsistency in audit treatment here, but it seems that most auditors do not count out-of-state attendance by telecommuting as a New York day. California has also issued Chief Counsel Ruling 2019-03, which expresses a similar view. Director's fees are non-wage income, so there are no convenience rule issues. By contrast, Pennsylvania has issued guidance stating that director's fees should be allocated "based upon working days within and outside the Commonwealth." *See* PA Department of Revenue, Answer ID 3570 (updated 6/29/2018).

> **EXAMPLE:** Kayla is on the board of a multinational company and received director's fees totaling $100,000 in 2021. The board held eight meetings in 2021: four in New Jersey, three in New York, and one in California.
>
> Kayla's director's fees are allocated as follows: $50,000 (50%) to New Jersey; $37,500 (37.5%) to New York; and $12,500 (12.5%) to California.

Proposed Federal Legislation to Address Remote Work Tax Issues

In 2021, two bills addressing remote work tax issues were introduced in Congress: the Remote and Mobile Workforce Relief Act of 2021 and the Multi-State Worker Tax Fairness Act of 2021. Both had goals of establishing some sort of nationwide uniformity so that tracking the changing rules and thresholds for remote work tax issues will not be a compliance nightmare.

The Remote and Mobile Worker Relief Act addresses "State and Local Tax Certainty During the 'Covered Period,'" including topics such as nexus hold harmless and remote work location versus primary work location. It broadly applies to a number of state and local taxes. The Multi-State Worker Tax Fairness Act calls for federal preemption of the convenience of the employer test.

STUDY QUESTIONS

1. Each of the following is one of the five primary domicile factors, ***except?***

a. Business

b. Forwarding address

c. Near and dear items

d. Time

2. In response to telecommuting during the pandemic, which of the following states is sourced to the employer's home state?

a. California

b. Mississippi

c. Oregon

d. Minnesota

3. In response to telecommuting during the pandemic, which of the following states does an employee have to work in for their income to be sourced to their home state and not necessarily their employers?

a. Wisconsin

b. New York

c. Rhode Island

d. Mississippi

¶ 305 RESIDENT TAX CREDIT ISSUES

When sourcing income, for residents, taxable income includes everything. For nonresidents, income from in-state sources is taxable. Income from in-state sources includes:

- Wages for services performed in-state
- Income/loss from real property
- Income/loss from in-state business

Note that not all income has a source. For example, "unearned income" or income from investments/intangibles is generally not taxable for nonresidents. Note that double taxation is possible for dual residents.

Resident Tax Credits

States generally allow their residents a credit for taxes paid to other states. The credit cannot exceed the tax due in the home state. There are two general approaches:

- The most common approach is to allow a credit for the tax paid to the other state on income sourced to that state, typically based on the home state's allocation rules (i.e., if we would tax a nonresident on the income, we will give the resident credit on taxes paid to the other state on that income). New York and Rhode Island use this approach.
- The less common approach is to allow a credit for tax paid to the other state on income not sourced to the home state (intangible income). New Jersey is an example of a state that uses this method.

Resident Tax Credit Statutes

In some states, the credit is limited to tax paid on income sourced to the taxing state. According to New York's statute:

> A resident shall be allowed a credit against the tax otherwise due . . . for any income tax imposed on such individual for the taxable year by another state of the United States, a political subdivision of such state, the District of Columbia or a province of Canada, *upon income both derived therefrom* and subject to tax under this article." [N.Y. Tax Law § 620(a) (emphasis added)].

Connecticut's statute reads as follows:

> Any resident . . . of this state shall be allowed a credit against the tax otherwise due under this chapter in the amount of any income tax imposed on such resident . . . for the taxable year by another state of the United States or a political subdivision thereof or the District of **Columbia *on income derived from sources therein*** and which is also subject to tax under this chapter." [Conn. Gen. Stat. § 12-704(a)(1) (emphasis added)].

California's statute is similar:

> The credit shall be allowed only for taxes paid to the other state . . . *on income derived from sources within that state* which is taxable under its laws irrespective of the residence or domicile of the recipient." [Cal. Rev. and Tax Code § 18001(a)(1) (emphasis added)].

In New Jersey, the resident credit is only limited to the extent that (1) the income is not from New Jersey sources and (2) the income is actually taxed by the other jurisdiction. The result is that New Jersey allows a resident credit for tax paid to another jurisdiction on intangible income. Michigan, Montana, and Oregon offer similarly structured resident credits.

Resident Tax Credit Challenges: The Convenience Rule

This would be a non-issue if all states used the same methods to source income. Most states limit the resident credit to taxes paid on income derived from the taxing state. Whether income is derived from sources in the state is determined under the rules of the state offering the credit.

If New York, for example, would tax nonresidents on that income, then New York would provide a New York resident a credit for taxes paid on that income to another state. There can be overlap and conflict in these situations. There are varying definitions of "in-state workday" in convenience and non-convenience states.

Resident Credit Examples: Working and Living in Different States

EXAMPLE 1: Employee A lives in New Jersey and receives wages from her New York employer. Employee A also received $1 million in dividends.

New York taxes all of Employee A's wage income.

New Jersey taxes all of Employee A's income (wages and dividends) but gives her a credit for the tax paid to New York on her wage income.

EXAMPLE 2: Employee B is domiciled in New York and telecommutes from California during the COVID-19 pandemic.

California taxes all of Employee B's wage income.

New York taxes all of Employee B's wage income but doesn't allow a credit for the tax paid to California since the employee's days commuting from California are deemed New York workdays under New York's convenience rule.

Resident Credit Examples: Dual-Resident (Resident of Two States)

EXAMPLE 1: Executive C is domiciled in New Jersey and is a statutory resident of New York City where she works and has an apartment. Executive C received $1 million in dividends.

New York taxes all of Executive C's income (wages and dividends). New York State and New York City personal income tax is imposed.

New Jersey taxes all of Executive C's income (wages and dividends) but gives her a credit for the tax paid to New York on all non–New Jersey income (which covers wages and dividends).

EXAMPLE 2: Executive D is domiciled in Connecticut and is a statutory resident of New York City, where she works and has an apartment. Executive D received $1 million in dividends.

New York taxes all of Executive D's income (wages and dividends). New York State and New York City personal income tax is imposed.

Connecticut taxes all of Executive D's income (wages and dividends) but gives her a credit for the tax paid to New York on New York–sourced income (which covers wages only). No credit is allowed for tax paid to New York on her dividend income.

Reciprocal Tax Agreements

If an employee works in State A but lives in State B, a reciprocal tax agreement between States A and B may provide that the employer need only withhold for, and the employee need only file in, State B.

However, reciprocal tax agreements typically exist only between neighboring states, and not all neighboring states have them. Such agreements are applicable to local taxing jurisdictions. They do not apply to income earned in a third state that is not party to the agreement.

States with reciprocal agreements allow a resident to work in another state without being subject to wage withholding or personal income taxes in the worksite state. The following chart provides a state-by-state list of reciprocity states:

State	Reciprocity States
Arizona	California, Indiana, Oregon, and Virginia
Illinois	Iowa, Kentucky, Michigan, and Wisconsin
Indiana	Kentucky, Michigan, Ohio, Pennsylvania, and Wisconsin
Iowa	Illinois
Kentucky	Illinois, Indiana, Michigan, Ohio, Virginia, West Virginia, and Wisconsin
Maryland	Pennsylvania, Virginia, Washington, D.C., and West Virginia
Michigan	Illinois, Indiana, Kentucky, Minnesota, Ohio, and Wisconsin
Minnesota	Michigan and North Dakota
Montana	North Dakota
New Jersey	Pennsylvania
North Dakota	Minnesota and Montana
Ohio	Indiana, Kentucky, Michigan, Pennsylvania, and West Virginia
Pennsylvania	Indiana, Maryland, New Jersey, Ohio, Virginia, and West Virginia

State	Reciprocity States
Virginia	Kentucky, Maryland, Pennsylvania, Washington, D.C., and West Virginia
Washington, D.C.	Maryland and Virginia
West Virginia	Kentucky, Maryland, Ohio, Pennsylvania, and Virginia
Wisconsin	Illinois, Indiana, Kentucky, and Michigan

¶ 306 STATE WITHHOLDING TAX CONSIDERATIONS FOR EMPLOYERS

States generally require employers to withhold personal income taxes on behalf of their employees. However, employer withholding requirements differ widely among the states. Many states have no thresholds (e.g., require withholding on the first dollar earned or the first day worked in the state). These states include Colorado, Indiana, Massachusetts, Maryland, Michigan, North Carolina, Ohio, Pennsylvania, and Virginia.

Among states that impose personal income taxes, more than half require employers to withhold tax from a nonresident employee's wages beginning with the first day the nonresident employee travels to the state for business purposes. Other personal income tax states provide for a threshold before requiring tax withholding for nonresident employees.

Employer Withholding Audits

States are becoming increasingly aggressive in enforcing withholding requirements, which are viewed as a new revenue source. There are multiple difficulties associated with withholding for a mobile workforce, including:

- Insufficient payroll system capabilities
- Burdens placed on employees to document travel
- No uniformity across states and cities

¶ 307 TELECOMMUTING AND NEXUS

Issues to consider when examining the tax impact of telecommuting include nexus, withholding changes, the "convenience of the employer" rule, and before stay-at-home orders and after.

Nexus means that there must be a link, some "minimum connection between a state and the person, property or transaction," for a state to impose tax. Does the presence of a telecommuter create nexus for a company? In most states and in "normal" circumstances, the answer is yes. This could mean nexus for employment, income, sales, and other taxes.

Nexus Considerations

Physical presence, or more specifically the presence of employees, in a state generally provides the state with jurisdiction to impose corporate income and franchise taxes. There have been cases holding that the presence of a single, telecommuting employee creates nexus (*see, e.g., Telebright Corp. v. New Jersey Division of Taxation,* 25 N.J. Tax 333 (Tax 2010), *aff'd* 424 N.J. Super. 384 (2012)).

Many states have adopted an economic nexus factor presence standard asserting nexus on a taxpayer if its sales, property, or payroll in the state exceed a certain threshold. The question is whether temporarily remote employees cause corporate taxpayers (employers) to exceed any of these thresholds.

Taxpayers with P.L. 86-272 positions should also consider whether the activities of temporarily remote employees exceed the scope of P.L. 86-272. During the pandemic, a handful of states released guidance providing that the presence of remote employees due to COVID-19 would not alone cause a taxpayer to establish nexus in the state. In certain cases, nexus relief was only available during the official state of emergency period.

Nexus Thresholds for Business Taxes

Approaches to nexus standards for business activity taxes include economic presence and factor presence. The Multistate Tax Commission (MTC) factor presence standard thresholds are:

- $50,000 of property;
- $50,000 of payroll;
- $500,000 of sales; or
- 25 percent of total property, total payroll, or total sales

State economic presence thresholds are detailed in the following chart:

State	Economic Presence
Connecticut	$500,000 in annual gross receipts
Maine	(1) $250,000 of property; (2) $250,000 of payroll; (3) $500,000 of sales; or (4) 25% of taxpayer's property, payroll, or sales (starting with tax years beginning on/after January 1, 2022)
Massachusetts	$500,000 (Presumption of corporate excise tax nexus if annual sales in MA exceed)
Michigan	$350,000 in annual gross receipts and "actively solicits" sales in Michigan
New York	$1,138,000 in annual receipts (threshold was $1 million until January 1, 2022)
Ohio (CAT)	$500,000 in annual taxable gross receipts; also uses MTC factors
Oregon	$750,000 in annual commercial activity
Hawaii	$100,000 in gross income in current/prior year or at least 200 transactions
Pennsylvania (CNIT)	$500,000 threshold (rebuttable presumption for pass-through entities held by a corporate entity)
Texas (franchise tax)	$500,000 in annual gross receipts
Washington (B&O)	More than $53,000 of in-state property or payroll; more than $267,000 of in-state receipts; or at least 25% of total property/payroll/sales

NOTE: Twenty-eight states and Washington, D.C., have adopted market-based sourcing to date.

State	Factor Presence
Alabama	MTC factors (adjusted for inflation; currently $54,000 property, $54,000 payroll, $538,000 sales, or 25% of total P/P/S)
California	MTC Factors (adjusted for inflation; currently $61,040 property, $61,040 payroll, $610,395 sales, or 25% of total property/payroll/sales)
Colorado	MTC factors
Ohio (CAT)	MTC factor
Tennessee	MTC factors

STUDY QUESTIONS

4. Which of the following states is one of the six states to have a "convenience rule"?

a. Pennsylvania
b. Florida
c. Hawaii
d. Missouri

5. Which of the following is excluded within the scope of "income from in-state sources"?

a. Income/loss from real property
b. Income from mutual funds
c. Wages for services performed in-state
d. Income/loss from in-state business

6. An employee works in State X but lives in State Y. If there is an agreement between States X and Y that provides that the employer need only withhold for, and the employee need only file in State Y, then this is an example of a ______ agreement.

a. Mutual
b. Reciprocal
c. Common
d. Jurisdictional

MODULE 1: BUSINESS—Chapter 4: Partnership Tax Filing Issues

¶ 401 WELCOME

Practitioners often encounter partnership tax filing issues regardless of their area of specialty. Increased information reporting and the complex nature of partnership tax transactions make compliance with the filing requirements particularly challenging. This chapter provides a practical review of the issues that most commonly arise in preparing partnership tax returns. It also addresses how to tackle partnership tax return complexities during the extended filing season.

¶ 402 LEARNING OBJECTIVES

Upon completion of this chapter, you will be able to:

- Describe essential reporting issues and obligations in partnership taxation
- Identify planning opportunities with partnership tax returns
- Recognize how to apply best practices for preparing partnership returns
- Identify correct statements with respect to guaranteed payments
- Describe capital account reporting
- Describe characteristics of Schedule K-1s

¶ 403 INTRODUCTION

In 2022, 4.3 million partnership returns were filed in the United States, and the IRS conducted 7,800 audits of partnerships. That is an incredibly low rate, so it's no surprise that the IRS plans to significantly increase the audit rate of partnerships. One of the ways the IRS will accomplish this is by using expert systems and artificial intelligence (AI).

Some of the questions on the partnership return are fairly new, so when practitioners answer those questions, they must consider how the IRS will use that information in an audit. Chances are that, in the future, the IRS will be using AI to identify those partnerships that are most likely to be audited based on the way preparers respond to these questions.

> **NOTE:** A preparer would be well advised to consider how the responses to the new information items (most first appeared in 2020) on Form 1065 and its related schedules will be used in audits.

Other topics addressed in this chapter include allocation of profit and loss, partner shares of debt, entity-level elections, centralized audits, capital accounting, unrecognized Code Sec. 704(c) reporting, distributions, and guaranteed payments.

¶ 404 ORGANIZATION OF THE FORM 1065 AND RELATED SCHEDULES

Form 1065, *U.S. Return of Partnership Income,* and its related schedules contain many questions. Some of these questions are simple, but others are designed to highlight areas of controversy. The following chart identifies certain types of partnership transactions and matches them to the questions asked on the partnership tax return.

Examples of Form 1065 Questions		
1	1065, page 1, Item K	Code Secs. 465, 469 groupings done by partnership
2	1065, page 2, Q6	Cancellation of debt (COD) event(s)
3	1065, page 2, Q10	Sec. 754 election
4	1065, page 3, Q11	Swap-and-drop
5	1065, page 3, Q12	Drop-and-swap
6	1065, page 3, Q25	Qualified opportunity fund (QOF) status
7	1065, K-1, item I2	Partner is a retirement plan
8	1065, K-1, Item J	Shares of capital, profit, and loss (P&L)
9	1065, K-1, Item K	Shares of debt (three types)
10	1065, K-1, Item L	Tax basis capital reconciliation
11	1065, K-1, Item M	Contributed Sec. 704(c): Yes/No
12	1065, K-1, Item N	Unrecognized Sec. 704(c)
13	1065, K-1, Boxes 22 and 23	Check if more than one passive activity loss (PAL) or at-risk activity statement attached

When preparing an individual return, if a taxpayer has not experienced a particular event, that does not have to be indicated. But in preparing a partnership return, the practitioner generally has to indicate whether certain events happened to the taxpayer during the year. A partnership has ordinary and separately stated items because a partnership is a pass-through entity; partnership income flows through and retains its character. Partners need separate reporting for anything that might impact their tax reporting.

Page 1 of Form 1065 reports those items that are treated the same for all partners, such as:

- Ordinary business income or loss
- Code Sec. 162 classification of a business
- Deduction for partner guaranteed payments

Recent tax law changes have greatly increased the required information to be reported on Form 1065. This information includes:

- Code Sec. 199A reporting (aggregation; unadjusted basis of assets [UBIA]; W-2 wages)
- Code Sec. 1400Z-2 opportunity zone deferrals
- Activity reporting
- Code Secs. 469, 465, and 1411 reporting, including grouping decisions
- Specific Schedule K-1 questions

All of this information must be separately detailed. In fact, the first substantive question on Form 1065 is exactly the first question on Form 1120-S (*U.S. Income Tax Return for an S Corporation*), that is, check this box if the taxpayer aggregated activities for purposes of Code Sec. 465 or grouped activities for Code Sec. 469. The Schedule K-1 asks a similar question for each partner.

¶ 405 CODE SEC. 199A REPORTING

Taxpayers can aggregate businesses, but they do not have to. Reg. § 1.199A-6 provides fairly detailed rules as to when taxpayers can aggregate businesses and what types of businesses they are allowed to aggregate. However, the decision to aggregate is entirely up to the taxpayer.

The decisions that are made at the partnership level are then binding on the partners because anything that is aggregated cannot be disaggregated. The partnership also has to make the following decisions:

- How many businesses does the partnership have?
- Of these businesses, which are specified service trades or businesses (SSTBs)?
- What is the qualified business income (QBI) three-step process for each business?
- What are the W-2 wages for each business?
- What is the UBIA for each business?
- What is the amount, if any, of real estate investment trust (REIT) dividends?

NOTE: REIT dividends are subject to the 20 percent deduction, but they are also unique in that they are not subject to the high-income taxpayer rule.

¶ 406 GUARANTEED PAYMENTS

Guaranteed payments are determined without regard to income; that is, they are not entrepreneurial risk–type payments. However, it is not always clear what constitutes a guaranteed payment.

The payments are treated as if made to a non-partner. They are deductible to the partnership and separately reported (ordinary) income to the partner. Guaranteed payments may be for capital or services, which can affect self-employment tax treatment (and the 0.9 percent Code Sec. 1411 surtax).

It is not always clear how to classify a guaranteed payment, so there is actually quite a bit of flexibility in determining the classification.

Preference versus Guarantee

Preferences may mimic guaranteed payments, and although some people use the terms *preference* and *guarantee* interchangeably, there are distinctions. A preference return is a priority that is intended to be matched with an allocation of income (per the disguised sale regulations). The intent may not be realized, and the preference could carry over. "Target" allocations, discussed later in this chapter, make it easy to see the link between the preference (distribution) and the allocation of income.

A guaranteed payment is not determined by reference to income. Guaranteed payments create their own income and deduction. The recipient of the guarantee has separately stated income, and the partnership has a deduction for the guaranteed payment.

If a partner is asked, "Do you want a guaranteed payment?" the answer is presumably yes for economic purposes. However, can the "guarantee" be replaced with a priority distribution matched with "target" income allocations? This will allow for an increased Code Sec. 199A deduction. Note that if the partnership is generating business income, guaranteed payments are not eligible for the qualified business income deduction (QBID). Priority distributions do not impact the QBID.

¶ 407 ENTITY-LEVEL ELECTIONS

Page 2 of Form 1065 asks what type of entity the partnership is. Generally, this is based on the classification ("check-the-box") regulations. Reg. § 301.770-3 states that if an unincorporated business entity, such as a general partnership, limited partnership, limited liability company (LLC), limited liability partnership (LLP), or unincorporated business entity, has two or more owners, by default, it is a partnership. If it has one owner, by default, it is a disregarded entity. The regulations also state that if the taxpayer does not agree with the default rules, it can elect to treat the entity as something else. The taxpayer can choose the "Other" classification to classify the entity as a joint venture, for example.

There is a great deal of flexibility in reporting in community property states. Rev. Proc. 2002-69 provides that a married couple who own all of the interests can elect to treat that entity as a disregarded entity or a partnership if the husband and wife are the only owners and hold interests as community property.

In all states, if a husband and wife own a joint venture and both spouses materially participate in the trade or business, they have the same flexibility in choosing disregarded entity or partnership status (Code Sec. 761(f)).

> **EXAMPLES:** Assume Husband A and Wife B establish an LLC. If they are in a community property state, they can elect that the LLC be treated as a partnership or a disregarded entity by administrative fiat (Rev. Proc. 2002-69). If they are in a separate property state, their LLC likely will be treated as a partnership.
>
> Assume Husband C and Wife D run a joint venture (not an LLC). Their joint venture is treated the same whether they are in a community property or separate property state. If they have a trade or business, and both materially participate in it, they have the choice of partnership or disregarded entity status by statute.

Consider a partnership LLC with one equity partner and several carried interests. Is it a partnership or a disregarded entity? Assume one partner has contributed capital and the others have profits interests only. If it is a partnership, a partnership tax return must be filed to avoid penalties.

But is this actually a partnership? Although most people will treat the entity as a partnership, the answer is unclear. Under old IRS guidelines (prior to 1997), this entity would not be considered a partnership because only one person has a capital interest. However, the IRS has taken other positions more recently.

Determining whether an entity is a partnership can sometimes be a challenge (e.g., especially with a joint venture or co-tenancy; see Rev. Proc. 2002-22). It is unclear what minimum interest triggers partner status, and if the taxpayer incorrectly believes it is not a partnership, it could face penalties for failure to file a partnership return. There could also be missed elections and reporting issues, such as the following:

- Opportunity zone deferral
- Code Sec. 1031 deferral
- Charitable deduction appraisals

Typically, an entity does not want partnership status; it is easier not to have to file Form 1065. The entity can also avoid foot faults on entity-level elections. In some cases, it can be helpful to have a separate entity, such as for deliberate controlled-entity sales.

More recently, the state and local tax (SALT) workaround may be available only for a partnership (or other pass-through entity) tax filing. Some states allow Schedule C to qualify, but most require a separate entity filing a return. This could create a need for a partnership filing.

Schedule B Questions

Schedule B of Form 1065 asks a set of questions, some that are merely informative and others that are potential audit traps. The first question is whether the taxpayer has made a Code Sec. 754 election in the past or is first making the election now. It may be helpful for practitioners to ask this question of a new client.

The next question is whether something happened this year that would cause an adjustment triggered by the Code Sec. 754 election, such as a distribution, a sale, or a change of an interest. The next question asks if the partnership has distributed undivided interests in its property. This is to identify a "drop and swap" transaction. The IRS may question whether the partners held the property in a manner that allows a Code Sec. 1031 exchange. Then it asks if the partnership has distributed property acquired in an exchange. This is meant to target "swap and drops." A swap and drop occurs when a taxpayer makes a like-kind exchange at the partnership level and then distributes one or more of the properties that it receives. This question is likely included in the partnership return because the IRS could then argue that the partnership did not hold that property for investment or trade or business purposes but rather held it for the purpose of distributing it to the partners.

More commonly seen is the "drop and swap" noted above. If the partnership wants to sell some real estate it owns, and one or more of the partners want to cash out while the others want to do a Sec. 1031 exchange, the partnership first distributes the property as tenant-in-common interest to the partners, and then has them individually make Sec. 1031 exchanges or not, as they see fit. Often the partnership has already negotiated the terms of the sale. This may throw the sale of distributed property back to the partnership.

Partnership Code Sec. 754 Elections

The Code Sec. 754 election is an entity-level election that affects two transactions:

- The sale or exchange of an interest (Code Sec. 743). This affects the basis of the purchasing partner only, but the partnership must track the adjustment (if notified).
- Distributions of money or property from the partnership (Code Sec. 734). An adjustment may be made to the basis of partnership properties.

NOTE: The Sec. 754 election is important because once made, it is binding on all future years.

Code Sec. 743 adjustments are designed to equate the "inside" and "outside" basis. The outside basis refers to the partner's basis in the interest. This is cost if purchased; it may also be the fair market value for an inherited interest, carryover basis for a gifted interest, or substituted basis for an interest acquired in an exchange. The inside basis is a percentage share of the partnership's basis attributable to the partner's interest. The partnership uses it to report entity transactions to the partner.

The Code Sec. 743 adjustment arises outside the partnership and creates no capital account adjustments because it is triggered by one partner buying an interest from another partner. That does not involve the partnership; it happens outside the partnership. Therefore, it is absolutely clear that Sec. 743 adjustments do not affect tax or book capital.

The Sec. 743 adjustment is allocated among assets using a hypothetical sale of assets. This allocation may need to follow Code Sec. 1060 principles where the partnership is operating a trade or business or where goodwill could reasonably attach to the assets. However, the taxpayer is not required to file Form 8594, *Asset Acquisition Statement Under Section 1060*, even if Code Sec. 1060 applies. It must follow the principles of Form 8594 but does not have to actually file it.

Code Sec. 734 adjustments are triggered by a distribution to a partner. This occurs "inside" the partnership and impacts capital accounts. These adjustments do affect the book and tax capital because they affect the partnership's balance sheet, and the basis of assets of the partnership.

There are four scenarios when an adjustment occurs. A partner usually takes a carryover basis in distributed property. It may be less if the basis of the interest is insufficient to allocate the full carryover, or it may be more if the distribution liquidates the partner's interest. There are positive and negative adjustments, both of which are triggered by what happens to the partner.

- Positive adjustments
  - Gain is recognized by the distributee.
  - The distributee's basis in the property is less than the carryover.
- Negative adjustments
  - Loss is recognized by the distributee.
  - The distributee's basis in the property is more than the carryover.

Both negative adjustments occur only when a partner's interest is liquidated; the partnership must continue after the one partner's interest is liquidated to book an adjustment, so negative adjustments are less common than positive adjustments.

Generally, Code Sec. 734 and 743 adjustments are not made unless a Code Sec. 754 election is in effect. If an adjustment was not made already, it would not be made for a negative adjustment. However, a mandatory adjustment occurs if the adjustment is negative and exceeds $250,000. This applies to both Code Sec. 734 and 743 adjustments.

STUDY QUESTIONS

1. Which of the following statements is correct regarding guaranteed payments?

a. It is always clear how to classify them.
b. They are determined without regard to income.
c. They are not deductible to a partnership.
d. They are treated as if made to a partner.

2. Which of the following appropriately describes the type of election a Code Sec. 754 election represents?

a. Account-level election
b. Partner-level election
c. Entity-level election
d. Transaction-level election

3. A mandatory adjustment occurs when the adjustment is both negative and exceeds what amount?

a. $50,000
b. $100,000
c. $150,000
d. $250,000

¶ 408 SCHEDULE K

Schedule K of Form 1065 summarizes the ordinary and separately stated items shown on the individual partners' Schedule K-1s. However, decisions must also be made, related to the following:

- Code Sec. 179 expense elections
- Aggregation for Sec. 199A

- Aggregation for Sec. 465 at-risk purposes
- Grouping of activities for purposes of
  — Passive activities and at-risk
  — But the passive activity grouping may affect Code Sec. 1411 net investment income tax (NIIT)

Reporting Passive Loss Activities

Although a partnership is not subject to the PAL rules, it must determine such "activities" because what the partnership aggregates cannot be disaggregated by the partner. The partnership must attach a statement to the return showing the income or loss for each PAL activity or classification.

The partnership grouping may affect the partners in two ways: (1) passive loss application, and (2) the Sec. 1411 Medicare surtax application. Although what the partnership binds together cannot be separated, a partner may add additional activities to the partnership's grouping.

It is generally best to disaggregate to allow the partners the greatest flexibility in grouping at their level. However, partnership groupings must satisfy the appropriate economic unit standard. The partnership must also have the books and records needed to disaggregate.

Partner K-1 Issues

Schedule K-1 shows a great deal of information that affects the partners, but it also includes some questions intended to help the IRS identify significant issues. If the IRS develops a type of AI to identify high audit risk situations, these questions are going to be very important. The K-1 shows the following information:

- The partners' allocable share of profit and loss, partner by partner
- A reconciliation of the capital account (transactional tax basis required)
- Unrecognized Code Sec. 704(c) gain/loss
- Shares of liabilities
  — Recourse
  — Nonrecourse
  — Qualified nonrecourse: Works for at-risk basis. These liabilities must be in connection with the activity of holding real property. The lender must be in the trade or business of lending and not have an interest in the activity.

¶ 409 ALLOCATIONS OF PROFIT AND LOSS

Generally, allocations may be made by agreement. However, allocations by agreement must have "substantial economic effect"; these allocations are governed by Code Sec. 704(b). Allocations that lack substantial economic effect, or allocations made in the absence of any specific agreement, must follow the partners' interests in the partnership.

The regulations state that if a partnership has the right language in its agreement, the IRS will not challenge its allocation. According to the Sec. 704(b) substantial economic effect safe harbor, the correct language includes:

- Capital accounts are maintained per the regulations.
- Liquidating distributions follow the capital accounts.

- There is either (1) a deficit restoration obligation, which states that if the capital account is negative, the partner has to give the partnership money; or (2) a qualified income offset, which states that a taxpayer cannot make the capital account go negative by an allocation, but if it happens to go negative because of something like a distribution, the taxpayer must bring it back up to zero with an allocation of income.

There is also a substantiality test, which is beyond the scope of this chapter.

Target Allocations

If a partnership was liquidating and filed a partnership return just once in the life of the partnership, it would be easy to do allocations that match the economics of the deal. The problem is that partnerships do not liquidate one time and file one return. They liquidate one time but file lots of returns. Basically, a target allocation means that at the end of each year when the partnership has to file its tax return, it should pretend that it liquidated at that year and determine how much each partner would get if it liquidated. The allocation is then made to "target" a capital account balance that matches the distribution from the hypothetical liquidation.

Target allocations exist because the safe harbor agreement does not prescribe distributions upon liquidation. Safe harbor agreements focus on allocations and then use capital balances to determine rights to distributions. In a target agreement, distributions are typically made by agreement. Income or loss is then allocated to hit a target capital account that reflects the distribution "waterfall." The target capital is generally Sec. 704(b) "book"; allocations would then be of book items rather than tax. Book–tax disparities are still governed by Code Sec. 704(c). There is more burden on the preparer; no safe harbor is satisfied. There are many simple agreements where allocations and distributions are made in the same proportions as invested capital. Those simple agreements do not raise issues.

Special Allocations of Nonrecourse Deductions

Nonrecourse deductions are those financed by nonrecourse borrowing. The problem with nonrecourse deductions is that they cannot meet an economic effect test because the principle of economic effect is that that taxpayer will match the tax allocations to the economics.

Therefore, the partnership will allocate income to the partner who received a benefit from that income. It will allocate a deduction to the partner who suffered a detriment that gave rise to that deduction. No partner bears a risk for nonrecourse loans because the non-partner lender bears a potential risk of loss. It is then not possible to match deductions financed by nonrecourse debt to the partner who suffers the economic detriment associated with that deduction. The absence of economic effect means the allocation must follow the partners' interests in the partnership.

However, the regulations state that nonrecourse deductions may be allocated by agreement, if the agreement satisfies the "deemed in accordance with the partners' interests test," which requires certain language to be included in the agreement.

Instead of a qualified income offset or a deficit restoration obligation, the partnership agreement must have a "minimum gain chargeback." Partners can be allocated losses in excess of their Sec. 704(b) capital if those allocations are nonrecourse. The chargeback ensures they will not exit the partnership with a negative capital account. It then functions similar to a qualified income offset for recourse allocations.

Target Allocation Agreement

A target allocation agreement does not meet the safe harbor (liquidating distributions are not based on capital) but generally targets Sec. 704(b) capital. It is often characterized by a reference to target capital based on a hypothetical liquidation at book value. The preparer must determine the target allocation.

To identify a target allocation, look to the agreement, which refers to "hypothetical" items, including hypothetical distributions arising from a hypothetical sale of assets (at book value) followed by a hypothetical liquidation of the partnership. Allocations are those that allow the taxpayer to reach a hypothetical "target" capital equal to the hypothetical distributions.

EXAMPLE: Partner A contributes $100,000 and Partner B contributes $50,000 to the AB Partnership. There is a distribution waterfall:

- Partner A gets 6% preference on his capital first.
- Partner A gets his $100,000 contribution next.
- Partner B gets his $50,000 capital next.
- Partner A gets 50% and Partner B gets 50% of any upside.

Year 1 income = $30,000.

Assets after Year 1 = $180,000 (capital plus income).

Find the "target" capital balances. With $180,000 to distribute,

- Partner A gets $6,000.
- Partner A gets $100,000.
- Partner B gets $50,000.
- Partner A gets $12,000; Partner B gets $12,000.

So, Target A = $118,000; Target B = $62,000.

The $30,000 profit is allocated so that the capital, based on a hypothetical liquidation, matches the target.

- $100,000 plus $18,000 income = $118,000 target.
- $50,000 plus $12,000 income = $62,000 target.

Other Provisions Governing Allocations

Allocations that relate to precontribution gain or loss must take into account the built-in gain or loss at contribution. These allocations are governed by Sec. 704(c). If partners' interests change during the year, the "varying interest rule" of Sec. 706(d) applies. Allocations may be made using an interim close of the books or by proration. The rules for allocations when interests vary are the following:

- Interim close is the default rule.
- Proration must be elected by the signed partner agreement.
- Proration still requires "extraordinary item" tracking by date.

¶ 410 CODE SEC. 704(C) REPORTING

The basic premise of Code Sec. 704(c) precontribution gains or losses is that partnership allocations relate to items of gain and loss that arise while the owners are in a partnership form. Thus, gains and losses that arose before the owners became partners should not be shared by all owners. Instead, the partner who contributed the property should be allocated the gain or loss that arose outside of the partnership. This is now tracked (by amount) on the partners' Schedule K-1 forms.

Code Sec. 704(c) also requires that depreciation or amortization with respect to contributed property consider the difference between fair market value and tax basis. Sec. 704(c) also applies to unrealized gains and losses of the partnership before a new partner is admitted by contribution. Dealing with Sec. 704(c) allocations requires consideration of the following questions:

1. Is there a Sec. 704(c) item?
2. What is the amount of the Sec. 704(c) item?
3. To which partner does it belong?

Questions 1 and 3 can be tracked on Schedule K-1. A box is checked when a partner contributes property with a built-in gain or loss. A second question asking for the unrecognized Sec. 704(c) gain or loss at the beginning and the end of the year was required beginning with the 2019 K-1. Book–tax capital comparisons are the easiest way to deal with the new questions.

Capital Accounts

An essential element of substantial economic effect is the proper maintenance of capital accounts. The Code Sec. 704(b) regulations have specific rules that are neither traditional "book" or "tax." Practitioners call it Sec. 704(b) book, and it often is the same as tax. Special adjustments may be needed for admittance of new partners and distributions of property, including exercise of options and option equivalents.

The 2018 and earlier Schedule K-1 asks how capital accounts are reported:

- GAAP
- Sec. 704(b) book
- Tax
- Other

In 2019, all of these methods were allowed, but a separate statement needed to be attached to identify the method. Starting in 2020, practitioners now need to report tax basis capital for all clients. Nonetheless, many agreements mandate that the partnership also maintain Sec. 704(b) capital. Keeping Sec. 704(b) capital in addition to tax basis can be helpful because:

- Allocations are made using a regulatory safe harbor that requires Sec. 704(b) capital.
- Liquidation distributions often follow book capital, and target allocations are tied to book capital.
- New question on unrecognized Sec. 704(c) gain may be tracked by comparing tax and Sec. 704(b) capital.
- Sec. 199A UBIA is based on book depreciation.

The IRS "threatened" to require one of two fairly complex tax basis capital reporting requirements. But when it asked for comments, practitioners responded that they preferred the "transactional" approach, which the IRS had said would not be allowed. However, the Form 1065 instructions now indicate that the transactional approach is the one to use.

¶ 411 DISTRIBUTIONS

A partnership recognizes no gain or loss as a result of a distribution. The partner may recognize gain or loss, and information reporting is required to assist in determining the tax effect. Gain is recognized when cash is received in excess of the partner's outside basis. Loss may arise if the distribution liquidates the partner's interest, consists solely of money and ordinary-income property, and the basis of the partner's interest cannot be allocated in full to the distributed assets. A partnership Sec. 754 election may also lead to a partnership (Sec. 734) basis adjustment.

The Schedule K-1 capital account reconciliation reports (actual) distributions. It also shows changes in debt shares, which also create deemed distributions if the partner's share is reduced, per Code Sec. 752(b). The K-1 reporting for 2020 and beyond now provides greater information to determine the tax effect. Tax basis capital may approximate the partner's outside basis when adjusted for the share of liabilities. Anti-abuse provisions may also cause a partner to recognize gain; these provisions are not identified by the capital reporting.

¶ 412 PARTNER SHARES OF LIABILITIES

Increases and decreases in partners' "shares" of entity liabilities affect basis. A "share" of a liability is determined using the Reg. § 1.752 rules. Recourse liabilities are shared using economic-risk-of-loss principles, and nonrecourse liabilities are shared in a three-step approach, which is somewhat arbitrary but pro-taxpayer. Schedule K-1 requires that the following be reported:

- Share of recourse debt
- Share of nonrecourse debt
- Share of qualified nonrecourse debt

Qualified nonrecourse debt allows at-risk basis; it applies only to real property activities where the lender is in the business of lending.

STUDY QUESTIONS

4. When reporting liability shares, Schedule K-1 requires each of the following, ***except?***

a. Share of recourse debt
b. Share of nonrecourse debt
c. Share of qualified recourse debt
d. Share of qualified nonrecourse debt

5. Which of the following is the default rule with respect to the varying interest rule?

a. Fair value
b. Interim close
c. Allocation
d. Equity

6. Which of the following statements is correct with respect to capital account reporting?

a. All methods were allowed in 2018, but a separate statement is attached to identify the method.

b. All partnerships must report tax basis capital for each member starting in 2020.

c. Starting in 2021, K-1s ask how capital accounts are reported.

d. Notice 2019-66 deferred 2019 tax basis reporting until the 2022 year.

CPE NOTE: When you have completed your study and review of chapters 1-4, which comprise Module 1, you may wish to take the Final Exam for this Module. Go to **cchcpelink.com/printcpe** to take this Final Exam online.

MODULE 2: TAX DEVELOPMENTS AND UPDATES—Chapter 5: 2023 Mid-Year Tax Update

¶ 501 WELCOME

This chapter provides highlights of recent tax legislation, new court cases and administrative guidance, and other developments including the IRS's proposed spending plan.

¶ 502 LEARNING OBJECTIVES

Upon completion of this chapter, you will be able to:

- Identify important new tax cases
- Recognize how to apply important new IRS guidance
- Identify the impact of new legislation on clients

¶ 503 OVERVIEW

The use of artificial intelligence is increasingly common in the tax world. Cannabis businesses can get the qualified business income deduction. The IRS released its plan for its $80 billion of supplemental funding. (Although in June of 2023, this funding was reduced by Congress and a "gentlemen's agreement" between the White House and Speaker Kevin McCarthy. The total was cut by roughly $20 billion.) These are among the many recent tax developments that will be discussed in this chapter. Also covered are the new clean vehicle credit that began in 2023, new residential energy credits, accounting method changes, and more.

¶ 504 DISABILITY INCOME

Disability income is taxable if the employer pays the premium, according to the Tax Court in *Hailstone v. Commissioner* (TC Summary Opinion 2023-17). The case involved an employer that paid an employee's premiums for a disability policy. Typically, taxpayers do not report their employer's disability insurance premium payments as income at the time the employer pays (Treas. Reg. § 1.106-1). However, if the employee pays the premiums, the employee can exclude the benefits because he pays the premiums with "after-tax" dollars.

However, in this case, the taxpayer did not pay for the premiums; the employer did. The premium payments were not included in the employee's income, so the employee had to pay tax on the disability benefits when the employee became disabled. Note that more favorable rules apply to workers' compensation.

¶ 505 USING ARTIFICIAL INTELLIGENCE IN TAX PRACTICE

ChatGPT-4, a new chatbot released by OpenAI in early 2023, can generate text that is similar to human writing. GPT, which stands for Generative Pre-trained Transformer, is a deep learning technology that uses artificial intelligence (AI) to think and write like a human. According to OpenAI, its new GPT-4 "is more creative and collaborative than ever before. It can generate, edit, and iterate with users on creative and technical writing tasks, such as composing songs, writing screenplays, or learning a user's writing style" (https://openai.com/gpt-4).

In fact, ChatGPT-4 passed the Uniform Bar Exam in 2023 by a significant margin. The chatbot also ranked in the 88th percentile in the Law School Admissions Test (LSAT). Although AI and chatbots are not expected to replace all accountants, one participant at an AI Forum noted that "an accountant with AI experience will replace other accountants without AI experience."

Practitioners should view ChatGPT as another tool that can help them in their work, along with existing tools like the Internal Revenue Code, cases, treatises, and Google articles. The chatbot is a good tool for finding easy-to-understand tax explanations and for drafting client memos.

But while ChatGPT provides clear and convincing answers to queries, they can often be inaccurate. For this reason, ChatGPT can be both helpful and harmful, and it is best used by experienced tax practitioners. In fact, one large accounting firm reported disastrous results when new recruits used ChatGPT. In addition, ChatGPT's answers can be inconsistent.

EXAMPLE: This author asked ChatGPT if S corporations qualify for "first time abatement" of late filing penalties. I got a very good, very concise answer with a link to the irs.gov website. I clicked on the link, it took me directly to the relevant information at irs.gov, and I confirmed the ChatGPT answer. However, when I asked the same question a few minutes later, I didn't get the link. ChatGPT's answers can be inconsistent.

ChatGPT's database can be old; at the time of this writing, its data had been updated through September 2021. For example, the Roth feature for SEP IRAs, part of the SECURE 2.0 Act passed in December 2022, was not in ChatGPT's database.

Users must have a basic familiarity with tax topics to identify blatantly incorrect answers, as ChatGPT sometimes fabricates answers. In fact, AI cofounder Ilya Sutskever has noted that "it has a propensity of making stuff up from time to time" (https://www.forbes.com/sites/craigsmith/2023/03/15/gpt-4-creator-ilya-sutskever-on-ai-hallucinations-and-ai-democracy/?sh=375062e51218). Some experts estimate that ChatGPT makes stuff up roughly 15 percent to 20 percent of the time. However, the technology is always improving.

One trick for getting around ChatGPT's shortcomings is "platform hopping." After you get an authority from ChatGPT, search for that authority in a tax treatise or in a tax research service, or Google it to confirm the information.

To summarize, ChatGPT is a promising technology for tax professionals that needs to be taken with a "grain of salt." It is best used by experienced practitioners who can spot obvious errors. The technology is sure to improve in the future, so practitioners may want to get experience using it now.

NOTE: There is a way to try ChatGPT for free: Google "openai.com." Click on "Sign up" and register for an account. Currently, it's free as long as you use ChatGPT 3.5; there is a fee for ChatGPT 4. However, ChatGPT 4 can be accessed without charge through Bing Chat. Bing Chat is most easily accessed through the Microsoft Edge browser.

¶ 506 DEDUCTIONS

Bonus Depreciation

December 2023 marks the six-year anniversary of the Tax Cuts and Jobs Act (TCJA). That means bonus depreciation began to phase out in 2023. However, Code Sec. 179 and *de minimis* expensing are not phasing out, making it more important than ever to consider making the *de minimis* election.

Property Placed in Service	Bonus Depreciation Percentage*
September 28, 2017–2022	100%
2023	80%
2024	60%
2025	40%
2026	20%
2027	None

* Special rule applies to longer production period property and certain planes.

Research Expenditures (Code Sec. 174)

The IRS provided a method for changing accounting methods to the new TCJA requirement to capitalize Code Sec. 174 research expenditures (Rev. Proc. 2023-11, superseding Rev. Proc. 2023-8). Under that method, the taxpayer does not have to file Form 3115, *Application for Change in Accounting Method*. The cutoff method will be used, so a calendar-year taxpayer will simply start capitalizing research expenditures beginning January 1, 2022.

Taxpayers that paid research expenditures after December 31, 2021, must attach a statement to their 2022 return that includes the following:

- Name and employer identification number (EIN) or Social Security Number (SSN)
- Beginning and ending of tax year (usually calendar year 2022)
- Designated accounting method (#265)
- Description of the type of research expenditures
- Amount of research expenditures in 2022
- Declaration that the taxpayer is changing the method of accounting to capitalize research expenditures (but only for expenditures after December 31, 2021)

To claim the research credit, the expenditures must, among other requirements, be Code Sec. 174 expenditures. That means practically, if taxpayers claim a research credit, they must capitalize and amortize Code Sec. 174 expenditures. However, the Code Sec. 41 research credit has many additional requirements, so taxpayers may still have to capitalize even if they are not able to claim the Code Sec. 41 credit.

Code Sec. 199A and Cannabis

Cannabis businesses are allowed a tax benefit for the cost of goods sold, but they cannot deduct expenses "paid or incurred," according to Code Sec. 280E. Many cannabis businesses have argued that the qualified business income deduction (QBID) under Code Sec. 199A is neither paid nor incurred and therefore should be allowed as a deduction for cannabis businesses.

At a February 10, 2023, American Bar Association meeting, the IRS indicated—informally—that it agrees. It appears that cannabis businesses can deduct the Sec. 199A QBID since it is neither paid nor incurred.

New Clean Vehicle Credit

Federal tax credits are available for electric vehicle (EV) purchases. The credit is up to $7,500 for new vehicles and up to $4,000 for used vehicles. There is a hard way and an easy way to determine the new credit. The hard way is as follows:

- Read the statute.
- Read the proposed regulations.
- Become an expert in electrical batteries.
- Do research to determine if the EV was manufactured in North America.
- Read IRS Notices.

The easy way to determine the credit (for a new EV, not a used EV) includes three steps:

- **Step 1:** Go to www.fueleconomy.gov. Check the appropriate box:
  - — Took delivery of the vehicle from January 1, 2023, but before April 18, 2023.
  - — Took delivery on or after April 18, 2023.
- **Step 2:** Confirm that the client meets the manufacturer's suggested retail price (MSRP) test.
  - — The MSRP is on the vehicle's sticker and includes options, accessories, etc. (but *not* destination fees or taxes).
  - — For most cars, the MSRP limit is $55,000. This is a strictly interpreted "cliff limit." If a car's MSRP is $55,001, clients will not get a credit, even if they negotiate a price of $55,000.
  - — Trucks, sports utility vehicles (SUVs), and vans have a higher MSRP limit ($80,000).
- **Step 3:** Confirm that the client meets the modified adjusted gross income (MAGI) test: For example, for taxpayers who are married filing jointly, MAGI must be less than or equal to $300,000 in the current *or* preceding year. That means in MAGI for 2023 when they claim credit or in 2022, the preceding year.

Filing Status	New EV MAGI Limit
Married filing jointly	$300,000
Head of household	$225,000
Single and other	$150,000

EXAMPLE: Barry and Sue buy a new EV in 2023. Their filing status is married filing jointly, and they have MAGI of $300,000 in 2022 and $7.5 billion in 2023. They pass the MAGI test and may qualify for the EV credit (since they pick the *lower* amount of MAGI for 2022 and 2023).

EXAMPLE: Mohammed and Tiffany, married taxpayers filing jointly, buy a new EV in 2023. Their MAGI is $300,001 in 2022 and $300,001 in 2023. They do not pass the MAGI test because their MAGI is $1 over the limit in both years. Therefore, they do not qualify for the EV credit. This is a strict "cliff limit."

NOTE: There is also a North American manufacture assembly requirement for the credit, so some EVs (e.g., Kia) will not qualify for the credit at all in 2023.

Vehicle manufacturers will report the EV information both to the EV purchaser and to the IRS. They are required to give the buyer this information at the time of sale and must show the buyer the maximum credit available. The IRS issued Form 15400, *Clean Vehicle Seller Report*, in July 2023 for dealers to report this information. Form 15400 is used to report both the new clean vehicle credit and the used clean vehicle credit.

If a taxpayer has a binding contract to purchase an EV before August 16, 2022, none of the new requirements apply. There are no MAGI or MSRP limits. The manufacturer Rivian pushed potential customers to qualify for this grandfathered rule. For these binding contracts, the taxpayer can take the credit on their 2022 tax return even if they receive the vehicle in 2023. This may require amending a 2022 tax return if the delivery of the vehicle occurs after the original return is filed.

Used Clean Vehicle Credit

The used car EV credit applies to EVs priced at or below $25,000 that are placed in service after December 31, 2022. Other requirements include the following:

- The credit cannot exceed 30 percent of the sales price (but the maximum credit is limited to $4,000).
- The credit applies only for the first resale of the vehicle after August 16, 2022, and the EV must be purchased from a dealer that meets reporting requirements.
- The person claiming credit cannot be allowable to another person for the dependent deduction.
- The model year of the EV must be two years earlier than the calendar year in which the buyer acquires it.
  — For example, if a taxpayer buys a used EV in 2023, the EV must be a 2021 model year or earlier.
- A taxpayer can claim the used car EV credit only once every three years.
- The MAGI limits are $150,000 for married filing jointly, $112,500 for head of household, and $75,000 for single taxpayers.
- The EV does not have to comply with "assembled in North America" rules.

Commercial Clean Vehicle Credit

For commercial EVs, there is no MSRP limit and no MAGI limit, and the commercial EV can be manufactured outside North America (IRS Publication 5724-H, *IRS Commercial Clean Vehicle Reference Chart*). To qualify for the credit, the commercial EV must:

- Have a battery capacity of not less than 7 kW hours (15n kW hours if the vehicle weighs 14,000 pounds or more). Almost all EVs meet this requirement.
- Be a plug-in.
  — The credit rate is 30 percent if the EV does not have a gas or diesel engine (15 percent if it does). The credit is limited by the "incremental cost" of the EV over an internal combustion car. See IRS Notice 2023-9 for a safe harbor. Practically, commercial electric vehicles that do not have a gas/diesel gas or diesel engine and have a gross vehicle weight of less than 14,000 pounds get a $7,500 credit.
  — The maximum credit is $7,500 if the EV is less than 14,000 pounds. For heavier EVs, the credit is limited to $40,000.
- Be of a "character subject to depreciation."
  — This means it is used in the trade or business of the taxpayer.

This credit can apply to EVs purchased by S corporations and partnerships. It should also include rideshare vehicles (e.g., Uber).

NOTE: A personal clean vehicle credit takes priority over the commercial EV rules. If the personal clean vehicle credit is allowed, a taxpayer cannot take the commercial EV credit (Code Sec. 45W(d)(3)).

For more details on EV credits, refer to Chapter 2, "Tax Credits for Vehicles."

Residential Energy Credits

As solar capacity is predicted to increase 300 percent over the next five years, there will likely be many more solar panel tax credits in the future. Solar panel costs have dropped at the same time utility costs have increased. The average cost of installing a solar roof varies by state but is generally between $13,000 and $17,000. The cost has been declining as technology is becoming more inexpensive.

Code Sec. 25D Solar Credit Oasis. The Inflation Reduction Act of 2022 amended Code Sec. 25D, increasing the solar credit percentage and extending the credit through 2034. The credit has been increased to 30 percent of expenditures, including sales tax and labor, for solar panel installations completed after December 31, 2021, and that percentage will be in place until December 31, 2032. The credit will then decrease to 26 percent in 2033 and to 22 percent in 2034. It also adds qualified battery storage technology expenditures beginning in 2023. The credit is reduced by subsidies from public utilities but not by state credits (Notice 2013-70).

> **EXAMPLE:** Randy has solar panels installed on his house for a cost of $19,000 (including sales tax and labor). He receives a $1,000 rebate from a public utility. His net expenditures to compute the credit are $18,000 (total costs less the rebate). Therefore, his credit is $5,400 ($18,000 × 30%).

The solar credit is nonrefundable, but any excess can be carried over to future years. No credit cap or MAGI cap is associated with the credit.

> **EXAMPLE:** Jose's MAGI is $1.8 million, and he spends $1,000,000 (including parts and labor) on a solar panel system for his home. He will receive a $300,000 credit.

There are no complicated energy-efficiency requirements for solar panels in regard to the credit; they just have to use solar power to generate electricity. However, there are requirements for solar water heaters and for geothermal and battery storage systems. Note that the solar panel credit applies to principal and second residences (or third residences).

> **EXAMPLE:** Jerry can take the solar credit on both his principal residence and his vacation home, but his rental properties do not qualify for the credit.

The credit applies to new construction with solar panels installed (see Code Sec. 25D(e)(8)(B) and https://www.energy.gov/eere/solar/homeowners-guide-federal-tax-credit-solar-photovoltaics). The solar credit is reported on IRS Form 5695, *Residential Energy Credits*.

Other eligible property (besides solar panels). The following types of property need to meet technical requirements to qualify for a tax credit:

- Solar water heater
- Geothermal heat pump
- Battery storage technology (the credit began in 2023)
- Fuel cell property—usually hydrogen
- For 2022 only, biomass fuel property was allowed (usually wood and wood pellet stoves). The property must meet a 75 percent efficiency standard. The credit for biomass fuel property beginning in 2023 will now be taken as part of the energy credit for homeowners (see below).

Energy credits for homeowners. The 2022 energy-efficiency rules offered very limited credit. The lifetime maximum was $500. However, the 2023 energy-efficiency rules offer a credit of up to $3,200 each year, which can be meaningful.

The residential energy credit is generally 30 percent of expenditures, but there are annual ceilings for specific types of property. The overall ceiling for all property *except* qualifying heat pumps, heat pump water heaters, and biomass stoves is $1,200. The ceiling is increased up to $2,000 per year for the following:

- Qualifying electric and natural gas heat pumps,
- Electrical or natural gas heat pump water heaters, or
- Qualifying biomass stoves.

Taxpayers who purchase a qualifying heat pump or biomass stove can take the $2,000 credit and also claim up to $1,200 for other eligible property. The credit is nonrefundable, and there is no carryover if the taxpayer is unable to use it in the current year. The maximum credit, then, is $3,200 (regular cap $1,200 + $2,000 for heat pump, biomass stove, etc.). There is no high-income phaseout.

Although, as mentioned earlier, the credit is generally 30 percent of expenditures, there are annual subceilings for the following:

- Exterior doors: $250 for the first door, $500 if there is more than one door
- Windows and skylights: $600 total
- HVACs, water heaters, furnaces, boilers: $600
- Home energy audit: $150

EXAMPLE: Andy's only eligible expenditure for the residential energy credit is $8,000 on qualifying windows. His tentative credit is $2,400 ($8,000 × 30%). But this is limited to the subceiling of $600 for windows.

Credits for improvements to a building's envelope—such as exterior windows or skylights, exterior doors, or insulation—are available for one's principal residence only (Code Sec. 25C(c)(1)(A)). According to Code Sec. 25C(d), credits for heating and cooling equipment are available for one's principal and second (or third or fourth) residence. Heating and cooling equipment includes electric or natural gas heat pumps (including heat pumps for a water heater); central air conditioners; natural gas, propane, or oil water heaters; natural gas, propane, or oil furnaces or hot water boilers; biomass stoves; and fuel blend oil furnaces or hot water boilers.

EXAMPLE: Mikio installs qualifying exterior windows on his vacation home. He doesn't get a credit because building envelope expenditures must be for his principal residence to qualify.

EXAMPLE: Mikio installs a qualifying electric or natural gas heat pump in his vacation home. He is credit eligible because heating and cooling equipment on any residence used by the taxpayer as a dwelling qualifies.

New energy efficiency standards. The energy efficiency standards changed in 2023, and the old standards no longer apply. The new standards are outlined in the following chart:

New Energy Efficiency Standards (2023)	
Electric or natural gas heat pumps (and heat pump water heaters); central air conditioners; natural gas, propane, or oil water heaters; and natural gas, propane or oil furnace or hot water boilers.	Highest efficiency tier (not including an advanced tier) established by the Consortium for Energy Efficiency (as in effect the first day of the calendar year item is placed in service).
Biomass stove (usually wood stove or wood pellet stove) or boiler	Thermal efficiency of at least 75% (measured by the higher heating value of the fuel).
Improvements to panelboard, sub-panelboard, branch circuits, or feeders	Installed in a manner consistent with National Electric Code, load capacity of at least 200 amps, and installed in conjunction and enables installation and use of qualifying property.

New Energy Efficiency Standards (2023)	
Exterior window or skylight	Energy Star "most efficient"
Exterior door	Energy Star requirements
Insulation material or system	Prescriptive criteria for such component established by International Energy Conservation Code standard as of the beginning of the calendar year which is two years prior to calendar year in which improvement is placed in service.
Certain fuel blend oil furnaces and hot water boilers	Varies by date placed in service.

There are three ways to determine if energy-efficient improvements qualify for the credit:

- Get the manufacturer's certificate from the manufacturer (make sure it is an updated version reflecting the 2023 standards).

EXAMPLE: As an example, Trane is a major seller of energy-efficient heaters and air conditioners. Its website has a link to 2023 manufacturer's certificates. This certificate will show that a particular model is eligible for the credit.

- Check the Energy Star website at https://www.energystar.gov/about/federal_tax_credits/non_business_energy_property_tax_credits. As of this writing, it has not yet been updated to reflect the 2023 standards, but it will be.
- Ask the contractor who will be installing or has installed the equipment.

Home energy audits. The IRS issued Notice 2023-59, which lists the requirements to claim the home energy audit credit (discussed above). The report has a number of technical requirements, including that it must identify the most cost-effective improvements, be consistent with Department of Energy standards, and be signed by the auditor. Beginning in 2024, the auditor (or a person the auditor supervises) will have to be certified. Since this credit is limited to $125, many preparers will likely just ask the client if they have a signed report.

Research and Development Credit (Code Sec. 41)

The courts are requiring more documentation for R&D credits. In *Little Sandy Coal Company v. Commissioner*, the court ruled that the taxpayer relied too heavily on arbitrary estimates of its R&D expenditures. Little Sandy Coal's CEO estimated the percentage of time spent on research. No credit was extended for the wages paid to the CEO. According to the court, some detailed documentation (emails, etc.) must be provided to claim the R&D credit.

¶ 507 TRUSTS AND ESTATES

Grantor Trusts

Grantor trusts are treated as disregarded entities. The grantor (transferor) is treated as if it still owned the property. The most common type of grantor trust is a revocable trust, in which the grantor retains the right to revoke the trust (take property back). This type of trust is commonly used to avoid probate because property in the trust passes automatically upon the trustor's death. The grantor is treated as the trust's owner and pays tax on the trust's income.

EXAMPLE: Paul puts property in a revocable trust. Paul will pay tax on the trust's income and deduct its expenses (as if the trust did not exist).

Grantor trusts are eligible S corporation shareholders. In *Starer v. Commissioner*, TC Memo 2022-124, Robert and Merle Ann Starer transferred 94 percent of their S corporation stock to grantor trusts. The IRS audited the S corporation and proposed a great deal of tax. Robert and Merle Ann countered that *they* didn't have to pay the tax—the *trust* had to pay it.

However, the Tax Court held that because the Starers agreed that the trust was a grantor trust, they must pay the tax. They are treated as the owners of S corporation stock, and the grantor trust is a disregarded entity.

65-Day Election for Trusts and Estates

Trusts and estates have very compressed tax rates; the top rate and net investment income tax (NIIT) begin at $14,450 for 2023. It is usually better to have beneficiaries pay the tax, and distributions to beneficiaries "carry" the income to the beneficiaries' Forms 1040, because they usually have lower tax rates.

Trusts and estates can make a special election to treat distributions made within the first 65 days of the tax year as if they were made in the preceding year (Code Sec. 663(b)). This is known as the "65-day election." They can make the election by checking Box 6 on page 3 of Form 1041. The election must be made on a timely filed return.

> **EXAMPLE:** ABC Trust has $100,000 of 2023 income and no distributions in 2023. Almost all the income would be taxed at 37 percent. The trust's beneficiaries are in much lower tax brackets. The trust can make an election to treat the distributions made in the first 65 days of 2024 as made in 2023. This carries some or all of the income out to the beneficiaries' returns.

IRS Private Letter Ruling 202303001 concerns an estate that made distributions in the first 65 days but failed to make the election when it filed its tax return. According to Reg. § 1.663-2(b), the election must be filed by the extended due date of the return. However, the IRS granted the taxpayer permission to make a late election.

STUDY QUESTIONS

1. Which of the following statements is correct with respect to ChatGPT?

- **a.** ChatGPT is always helpful.
- **b.** You need tax experience to "smoke out" bad answers.
- **c.** For experienced tax practitioners, it can be dangerous.
- **d.** The data it uses is always real-time and up to date.

2. The bonus depreciation rate for the year 2027 is which of the following?

- **a.** 0 percent
- **b.** 20 percent
- **c.** 60 percent
- **d.** 80 percent

3. Which of the following identifies the first step in claiming the new clean vehicle credit?

- **a.** Confirm client meets the MAGI test.
- **b.** Confirm that the MSRP test is met.
- **c.** Go to www.fueleconomy.gov (click on qualifying EV box).
- **d.** Consider how many miles will be driven each year.

4. Which of the following statements is correct regarding the commercial electric vehicle credit?

a. The vehicle must be of a character subject to depreciation.

b. It must have battery capacity of not less than 10 kW hours to qualify.

c. The commercial vehicle must be manufactured in North America.

d. You can only take some of the commercial EV credit if you are allowed a personal EV credit.

¶ 508 ACCOUNTING METHOD CHANGES

Accounting methods relate to the timing for income and/or deductions. Taxpayers are required to get the IRS's consent when changing accounting methods. Examples include:

- Depreciation (when to take depreciation), and
- The cash versus accrual method (when to report income or take deductions).

To obtain the IRS's consent to change their accounting method, taxpayers must file Form 3115, *Application for Change in Accounting Method*. One copy is attached to the tax return, and another copy is mailed to the IRS. There is no "statute of limitations" when it comes to accounting method changes (see *Graff Chevrolet Co. v. Campbell*, 343 F.2d 568). Both taxpayers and the IRS can correct accounting method mistakes made years ago.

EXAMPLE: ABC LLC bought an apartment building in 2009 and allocated the purchase price to the land and building. It missed allocating a portion to land improvements and personal property, which would have resulted in faster depreciation. This was a mistake. ABC can fix this error on its 2023 tax return.

ABC files Form 3115 with its 2023 Form 1065 and also mails a copy to the IRS. ABC deducts the missed depreciation on its 2023 Form 1065 and increases its beginning accumulated depreciation, even though the statute of limitations closed years ago. The statute of limitations does not apply to accounting method changes.

As mentioned earlier, the IRS can also make accounting method changes even though the statute of limitations is closed.

EXAMPLE: Assume that in the prior example, ABC LLC had taken $60,000 depreciation on the land. The IRS can reverse the depreciation on the land and increase income to $60,000 in 2022, even if the statute of limitations is closed.

In *Starer v. Commissioner*, TC Memo 2022-124, the taxpayer transferred land and received proceeds on that land in 2006. He did not report the sale and did not recognize gain; he reported the sale as a loan. The taxpayer admitted neglecting to report the sale but argued that the statute of limitations was closed for 2006. He stressed that this wasn't a *timing* difference; it was a *permanent* difference—and receipt of a loan is never taxable.

The Tax Court held that the taxpayer was wrong. It *was* an accounting method (timing difference). The taxpayer should have either recognized gain in 2006 or reported a discharge of indebtedness in a later year. The court held that the taxpayer must pay tax on the gain; the statute never closes on a timing difference.

Accounting Methods Recap	
Accounting methods: *Starer v. Commissioner*	• Change in timing (income or deduction) • Statute of limitations doesn't apply. • Both taxpayers and the IRS can fix mistakes made 40 years ago on this year's tax return.
Common examples	• Cash vs. accrual methods • Depreciation
How prior errors are fixed	• Adjust current year's income to cumulatively fix prior years' errors. • If the taxpayer should have taken $50,000 in depreciation in 2008–2022 but only took $20,000, the taxpayer should flush through the missed $30,000 depreciation on its 2023 return. • Taxpayers need to file Form 3115, including one copy with their tax return and mailing or faxing another copy to the IRS.
Issue in *Starer v. Commissioner*	• Was the mistake made in reporting sales proceeds as a loan an accounting method (timing) difference? • Yes, this can be fixed now, even though the statute of limitations is closed.

NOTE: The IRS revised Form 3115 and its instructions in December 2022. The revised form must be used for accounting method changes filed on or after April 18, 2023.

¶ 509 IRS DEVELOPMENTS

New IRS Commissioner

On March 13, 2023, Danny Werfel was sworn in as the new Commissioner of the IRS. Werfel has worked in both the public and private sectors, and has served in the following roles:

- Department of Justice trial attorney
- Acting Commissioner of the IRS (2013)
- Controller, Office of Management and Budget, 2009–2013
- Global leader of Boston Consulting Group's Public Sector practice

The IRS's $80 Billion Spending Plan

The IRS released its long-awaited $80 billion spending plan April of 2023. Although the "Internal Revenue Service Inflation Reduction Act Strategic Operating Plan, FY 2023–2031" is still missing some important details, it includes good ideas for ensuring better service.

The agency has already met some of its promises in the plan, including hiring 5,000 additional customer service representatives and reducing taxpayers' wait time on phone calls.

NOTE: The $80 billion funding amount was reduced in June of 2023. The Fiscal Responsibility Act rescinded $1.4 billion of the original $80 billion in funding. Funding was further reduced by a "gentlemen's agreement" between the White House and House Speaker to cut another $20 billion. The IRS has indicated that these cuts will not affect spending in the next few years.

Enforcement. There is some uncertainty regarding the IRS's promise for "no increase" in audits for taxpayers making less than $400,000 per year, but it appears that the same threshold would apply to both single and married filing jointly taxpayers.

> **EXAMPLE:** Sue, a single woman "earning" $399,999, would *not* be subject to higher audit rates. But Bobbi and Bob, married taxpayers filing jointly and "earning" $400,000, would experience higher audit rates.

Small businesses also will not be subject to increased audit rates. However, "small" has not been defined. The author's best guess is that a small business means one with assets of less than $10 million.

In April 2023, Commissioner Werfel told the Senate Finance Committee that for taxpayers "making less than $400,000," audit rates will not be increased beyond "historical" audit rates. "Historical" refers to audit rates in 2018 ("for at least several years"). The 2018 audit rate for these taxpayers was 1 in 301 (.3 percent), meaning 3 in 1,000 returns were audited. "Making less than" $400,000 will be based on "total positive income." In other words, it appears that losses are added back.

> **EXAMPLE:** Bob has $375,000 in adjusted gross income (itemized deductions have no effect). However, this includes $30,000 in losses (K-1s, Schedule C). It appears that the IRS will treat Bob as "making" $405,000 (adding back the losses). Therefore, he will be subject to the higher audit rate.

Hiring. The IRS is gradually hiring new enforcement personnel. In FY 2023, it hired 1,543 new enforcement employees, while in FY 2024, it plans to hire 7,239 new enforcement employees. New customer service employees are being hired as well. The agency hired 7,394 new customer service employees in FY 2023 and plans to hire 6,489 in FY 2024.

Focus. The IRS's spending plan also focuses on several other areas, including:

- Digitizing all incoming paper documents
- Expanding online Tax Pro accounts
- Conducting high-wealth audits (audits of taxpayers earning $1 million or more)

Audit targets. Areas where audits will be increased include employment taxes, excise taxes, and estate and gifts taxes. With regard to employment taxes, practitioners should have a discussion with clients who have questionable "independent contractors." Practitioners should determine if those clients qualify for the IRS's Voluntary Classification Settlement Program (VCSP). If a taxpayer files Form 8952, *Application for Voluntary Classification Settlement Program*, before the IRS starts an employment tax audit, it can settle $100,000 per year payments to an "independent contractor" for a $1,082 payment.

For a more in-depth look at how the IRS plans to spend the funding it received through the Inflation Reduction Act, see Chapter 8.

IRS Data Book

Published annually, the IRS Data Book contains data on collecting revenue, issuing refunds, enforcing the law, assisting taxpayers, and its budget and workforce. According to its latest Data Book, the popularity of business entities has changed as follows:

- C corporations: +5.5 percent
- S corporations: +4.3 percent
- Partnerships: –2.7 percent

These statistics are a little surprising. S corporations are typically used by service organizations to shield against payroll taxes. It is difficult to make the case that C corporations work well for most small businesses. In addition, partnerships usually provide better tax results, including step-ups on death or sale, usually tax-free liquidations, and larger Sec. 199A deductions.

IRS Audits

Currently, 0.49 percent of individual tax returns are audited, so approximately 5 out of 1,000 returns. The rate is higher (8.5 percent) for individuals with income greater than $10 million.

For C corporation returns, the audit rate is 0.8 percent, or 8 out of 1,000. For large C corporations, the auditor-proposed average tax bill is approximately $1.5 million. For small C corporations (those with less than $250,000 in assets), that tax bill is approximately $48,346; for very large C corporations (those with more than $20 million in assets), it is approximately $27 million.

Audit rates for partnerships have decreased. This might be the result of the IRS getting accustomed to the new Centralized Partnership Audit Rules (CPAR).

The auditor-proposed average tax bill for audited individuals is approximately $20,000 per Form 1040. According to the IRS Data Book, IRS auditors propose additional tax 90 percent of the time. However, only 2 percent of taxpayers challenge this assessment.

EXAMPLE: Rashid and Sue are audited. The IRS auditor disallows some of their business expenses due to a lack of substantiation, and their proposed tax bill is $12,000. But Rashid and Sue have some support for the expenses: credit card receipts and some details where they lack receipts (e.g., Sue buys coffee for her home office every week). Rashid and Sue should consider filing an administrative appeal with the IRS.

Filing an administrative appeal with the IRS is easy to do. Historically (in Seattle), taxpayers reach an agreement with the appeals officer 95 percent of the time, and the average reduction in tax is about 65 percent. If taxpayers cannot agree with the appeals officer, they should consider filing a Tax Court petition. The Tax Court has "fill-in-the blank" forms with instructions on how to file a petition.

IRS Dirty Dozen

In April 2023, the IRS released its "Dirty Dozen" list of tax scams for 2023. It included the following:

- Employee retention credit claims
- Scammers who offer to "help" set up online IRS accounts (getting SSNs, etc.) but are actually trying to get confidential information
- Fake charities (especially after disasters)
- Syndicated conservation easements
- Microcaptive insurance companies (businesses that set up their own private insurance companies).
- Hiding cash or digital assets offshore
- Maltese foreign individual retirement accounts (Taxpayers argue the income is exempt under treaty.)

NOTE: The IRS issued proposed regulations in 2023 that would treat these as listed transactions, subjecting taxpayers, and advisors to reporting requirements and possible penalties.

- Charitable remainder annuity trusts ("CRAT's") that are abusive
  - Taxpayers attempt to avoid gain on the sale of property by improperly claiming that there is a step-up when they contribute property to a CRAT.
  - In 2023, a district court barred several individuals from marketing these tax shelters (***Eickhoff***, DC MO, 131 AFTR 2d, 2023-690).
- Monetized installment sales
  - These involve using an intermediary to accomplish the sale of appreciated property. The seller transfers property to an intermediary in return for an installment note. The intermediary then immediately resells the same property to a third party for cash. The seller then borrows money (so that it is in a similar position as if it had made a cash sale) and uses the installment sales payments from the intermediary to repay the new loan.

NOTE: The IRS issued proposed regulations in 2023 that would treat these as listed transactions in 2023 (see IR-2023-139).

- Offer-in-compromise mills
- "Ghost" tax return preparers (who do not sign returns)
- Preparers who charge for their services based on a percentage of the refund

The IRS is very active in the employee retention credit (ERC) area. It has charged many "ERC mills" with crimes. The IRS director has warned tax professionals to think twice before filing ERC claims. According to an alert from the IRS Office of Professional Responsibility (2023-02), the tax professional's role in ERC claims is as follows:

- Be diligent as to accuracy.
- Be careful not to rely on the advice of ERC "experts."
- Gain in-depth knowledge of the ERC refund claim.

NOTE: An Indiana CPA firm has been sued by a client over the preparation of an ERC refund claim. The client alleges that the CPA firm failed to use due diligence in preparing the refund claim. See *Acer Landscape Services v. Lasiter*, No. 3:23-cv-00531.

See Chapter 6 for further discussion of the Dirty Dozen tax scams.

¶ 510 INFORMATION REPORTING

Form 1099-K Reporting for 2022

With regard to sales on "third-party platforms" (e.g., Etsy, Uber, Lyft, eBay, VRBO, TaskRabbit, Venmo, etc.), taxpayers received a Form 1099-K, *Payment Card and Third Party Network Transactions*, for 2022 transactions if their gross payments were greater than $20,000 and they had more than 200 transactions (IRS Notice 2023-10).

EXAMPLE: eBay doesn't withhold tax on payments to Bob. No 2022 Form 1099-K is provided if Bob has under $20,000 in payments and 200 transactions or less.

But if instead eBay backup withheld on payments to Bob (he did not provide his Social Security number), he would get a 2022 Form 1099-K if his payments were greater than $600.

EXAMPLE: Phil drives for Uber. In 2022, he provided 180 rides and had $9,000 in receipts. He will not receive a Form 1099-K. However, if he receives $601 in 2023 for two rides, he will get a Form 1099-K (see the discussion below).

EXAMPLE: Keiko rents out her vacation home in Miami through VRBO. She has 35 rentals per year and $45,000 in gross receipts. If these figures are for 2022, she would not receive a Form 1099-K because although she was paid more than $20,000, she had fewer than 200 transactions. If the figures are for 2023, however, she will receive a Form 1099-K because her payments were greater than $600.

Form 1099-K Reporting for 2023

For 2023 transactions, taxpayers will receive a Form 1099-K for sales on third-party platforms if their gross payments are greater than $600, even if they made just one transaction. This represents a one-year deferral from the original rules pursuant to Notice 2023-10. The new rules apply to sales of goods and services (Treas. Reg. § 1.6050W-1) but not to cash transfers or payments to friends and family. For example, Venmo payments for gifts or loans to friends and family will not require a Form 1099-K. These rules apply to third-party platform transactions beginning January 1, 2023.

EXAMPLE: A client sells his used portable heater on eBay on January 9, 2023. eBay will report this (if the client's total sales for the year are greater than $600) in January 2024.

NOTE: The IRS has estimated that this new rule will raise almost $8.4 billion over 10 years. Tax practitioners should expect many matching notices from the IRS regarding 2023 Forms 1040.

Most gross sales on eBay should offset significant costs. These will reduce or eliminate gain. However, if a taxpayer has personal losses (e.g., the sale of a used laptop used only for personal purposes), they are not deductible and may not be used to offset personal gains.

EXAMPLE: Barry sells his used laptop on eBay for $601. If Barry paid $800 for the laptop and did not depreciate, he will not have any taxable income.

One third-party platform expects to issue over 10 million Form 1099-Ks for the 2023 tax year. Tax professionals should expect questions from clients early in 2024 as the Form 1099-Ks for 2023 transactions must be issued by January 31, 2024. They should also expect to ask clients more questions, such as, "How much did the football tickets you sold cost you?" The *Cohan* rule (*Cohan v. Commissioner*, 39 F.2d 540 (2d Cir. 1930)), which states that preparers may use estimates if a taxpayer lacks documentation to support items on their tax return, should apply. However, clients should be advised to begin keeping records now.

Note that Form 1099-K reports the *gross* dollar amount of transactions. This means that fees charged by the third-party platform will need to be deducted from the gross payment.

EXAMPLE: Keiko's VRBO rentals are for gross amount of $14,000, so a Form 1099-K will be provided for $14,000. However, she only receives $12,000 after VRBO deducts $2,000 in fees from that amount. She should report $14,000 in gross payments and deduct the $2,000 in fees. She can get details about the fees on the VRBO website.

Will the IRS match Form 1099-K to the taxpayer's return? According to the Form 1099-K Frequently Asked Questions (https://www.irs.gov/newsroom/form-1099-k-frequently-asked-questions), the answer is "Yes, the data from Form 1099-K, Payment Card and Third-Party Network Transactions, will be used for systemic computer matching . . . to identify potential unreported income." The IRS notes that "99% of the information returns were matched to corresponding tax returns." But what if a taxpayer's 1099-K is incorrect?

EXAMPLE: A family member sent Tim $1,000 though Venmo as a gift, but Venmo reports it on Form 1099-K.

According to the IRS, Tim should report this as $1,000 of income on Form 1040 Schedule 1, Line 8z ("Form 1099-K Received in Error").

Tim should also report a $1,000 deduction on Schedule 1, Line 24z ("Form 1099-K Received in Error").

What if a taxpayer has personal losses and personal gains on sales of personal items? The IRS says the taxpayer should report the gains, but not deduct the losses.

EXAMPLE: Raj purchases tickets to a Bruce Springsteen concert for himself and his spouse. Because a family member visits unexpectedly on the day of the concert, they can't go, so he sells the tickets for a $200 loss on Stubhub. He also buys tickets to a Taylor Swift concert for his and his wife's anniversary. Unfortunately, one of their children came down with the flu on that day, so they cannot attend that concert either. Raj sells the tickets for a $200 gain. The loss on his sale of the Springsteen tickets is nondeductible, but he must report the $200 gain from the sale of the Swift tickets; the gain and the loss do not offset each other (IRS FAQ #7).

What if a taxpayer has investment transactions?

EXAMPLE: Manuel purchases two sets of concert tickets as an investment with an expectation that their price will increase. If he can't sell the tickets for a profit, he'll use them to attend the concert with his spouse and friends (but this is not his primary motive). He sells one set of tickets at a $200 gain and the other set at a $200 loss. He reports both but can net the gain and loss to report a net gain. This is because the primary motive was to earn money from sales.

Combined Reporting

The IRS says that taxpayers can combine personal loss items on a single line. See the Form 1099-K Frequently Asked Questions (updated March 22, 2023).

EXAMPLE: Marcia sells 14 personal use items on eBay (combined sales price = $7,200, estimated cost = $11,500). All 14 are sold at a loss.

- She can report a single sales number for all 14 transactions on Schedule 1, Line 8z ($7,200).
- She will also report a single offsetting number ($7,200) on Schedule 1, Line 24z.
- The two numbers will net to zero.

NOTE: Taxpayers are not supposed to net gain transactions and loss transactions.

The IRS also states that taxpayers can combine all amounts reported in *error* on a single line.

EXAMPLE: Peter's mom sends him $1,000 per month on Venmo (gift), a $12,000 total for the year.

These amounts should not have been reported by Venmo (they are not for the sale of services or goods) but are nonetheless reported.

Peter can combine all the amounts received on a single line item:

- "Forms 1099-K received in error" on Schedule 1 Line 8z: $12,000.
- "Forms 1099-K received in error" on Schedule 1, Line 24z: $12,000.

It is possible that Congress will increase the filing threshold. A bipartisan bill, the Red Tape Reduction Act, would raise the reporting threshold from $600 to $10,000.

PLANNING POINTER: Tax practitioners should ensure that their 2023 checklists cover the new Form 1099-K rules. They should also discuss the rules with clients, so they keep good records for their third-party platform transactions.

S Corporation Distributions of Appreciated Property

An S corporation distribution of appreciated property is treated as if the S corporation sold the property (Code Sec. 311(b) via Code Sec. 1371).

EXAMPLE: Lisa owns 100 percent of an S corporation. The S corporation distributes a car to her with a fair market value of $5,000. The tax basis is $2,000, so the S corporation recognizes a $3,000 gain, just as if it sold the car for $3,000. This gain passes through to Lisa on Schedule K-1.

If an S corporation "confers economic benefit on a shareholder" without expectation of reimbursement, it is treated as a "constructive distribution" (*Loftin & Woodward, Inc. v. United States*, 577 F.2d 1206 (5th Cir. 1978)). If the items "constructively distributed" are appreciated property, they are treated as sold and subject to tax.

In *Starer v. Commissioner*, TC Memo 2022-124, the taxpayers transferred appreciated land to their son-in-law's limited liability company (LLC); no price was paid. The S corporation also transferred land to a friend of a shareholder.

The taxpayers argued that they did not transfer the land to their son-in-law, but rather contributed it to a joint venture he managed. They also stressed that the S corporation did not transfer another parcel of the S corporation's land to their friend, but rather they sold it to him on an installment basis. (However, the taxpayers received no payments.)

The Tax Court did not believe that the taxpayers contributed the land to a joint venture. The land went to an LLC, and the son-in-law was the only owner of that entity. The court also did not believe that the taxpayers made an installment sale of the S corporation's land to a friend, noting that the taxpayers never tried to collect the installments receivable.

It held that the transfers to the son-in-law and friend were for the shareholders' benefit and should be treated as distributions to shareholders. The distribution of appreciated property was treated as a sale.

STUDY QUESTIONS

5. Which of the following statements is correct with respect to the Solar Credit Oasis?

- **a.** The credit rate is 25 percent on qualifying expenditures.
- **b.** The credit fully expires after 2032.
- **c.** Solar panel costs have dropped at the same time utilities costs have increased.
- **d.** It is a refundable credit.

6. Which of the following tax forms is used to apply for an accounting method change?

- **a.** Form 990
- **b.** Form 1040
- **c.** Form 1120
- **d.** Form 3115

7. A Form 1099-K is required to be provided beginning in 2023 if payments from a third-party platform exceed what amount?

a. $200
b. $300
c. $500
d. $600

8. Under which of the following rules has the Tax Court concluded that estimates are generally acceptable?

a. *Cohan*
b. *Peterson*
c. *Carlson*
d. *Wilson*

S Corporation Terminations

Last year, the IRS released Rev. Proc. 2022-19, stating that S corporations that were terminated as a result of having two classes of stock could automatically fix the situation (without filing for a Private Letter Ruling or paying a fee). The most common cause of "second class of stock" terminations is LLCs that elected to be taxed as S corporations and have boilerplate language that states, "liquidating distributions are required to be made according to positive capital accounts." This language is useful for partnerships but causes a problem for S corporations. To get automatic relief (without requesting a Private Letter Ruling), an S corporation must satisfy three requirements:

- Have no disproportionate distributions. (Meeting this requirement can be a problem if the amounts of distributions were not proportionate to stock ownership, or if distributions to shareholders didn't occur on the same date.)
- Have filed all of its S corporation returns on time.
- Have prepared corporate and shareholder statements before the IRS became aware of the issue (samples of these statements are provided in Rev. Proc. 2022-19).

Many S corporations that were terminated due to the "two-classes-of-stock rule" (including LLCs that elected to be taxed as S corporations and had the prohibited "boilerplate" language discussed above) had disproportionate distributions and therefore did not qualify for automatic relief. Richard Probst of the IRS Chief Counsel's office said in 2023, "I think there could be a chance to provide additional guidance and clarification there." Many have interpreted this statement to mean the IRS may remove the disproportionate distribution requirement.

Partnerships

Partnerships can make tax-free distributions of profits-only interests. Often, existing partners wish to add new partners, but the potential new partners do not want to pay for the interest in a business. To incentivize new partners who do not want to pay for the partnership interest, existing partners can extract the fair market value of the partnership and then share subsequent profits generated by the newly admitted partners. Rev. Proc. 93-27 provides a way to accomplish this tax-free for a new partner.

Eventually, the original partners will have a gain on distributions greater than their adjusted basis, but they are allowed to recover their basis in the partnership interest first. Also, if the partnership makes a Code Sec. 754 election, the partnership can step-up its basis in its assets under Sec. 734 for this gain that is recognized.

This cannot be done with S corporation stock because an S corporation can only have one class of stock. This is one advantage of choosing the partnership over the S corporation form of entity.

"Sweat Equity"

Rev. Proc. 93-27 offers taxpayers tax-free "sweat equity." Partners can receive a "profits-only" interest in the partnership without paying tax. Existing owners can "cash out" their equity. The "profits-only" interest transferred for services to the partnership can be received tax-free. However, partnerships do not qualify if any of following are true:

- The profits-only interest relates to a substantially certain and predictable stream of income from high-quality debt or a high-quality net lease;
- Within two years of receipt, the new partner disposes of the interest; or
- The interest is in a publicly traded limited partnership.

The profits-only interest cannot be capital interest. If the partnership is liquidated a moment after the profits interest is issued, the new "sweat equity" partner cannot get any liquidation proceeds.

The typical strategy to avoid a capital interest is to write up ("book up") the existing partners' capital accounts (see Treas. Reg. § 1.704-1(b)) to fair market value and also make sure distributions are disproportionately made to existing partner(s). These should be preferred capital account distributions, so the existing partners can "cash out" their interests. The new "profits-only" partner often gets just enough in distributions to pay their taxes on their Schedule K-1 income.

> **EXAMPLE:** Joe and Sol are existing partners in a tax preparation firm. They want to add Lin as a new partner. Lin does not want to pay for the interest but is willing to work for "sweat equity" in the firm. Joe and Sol want to be paid for the equity in the firm. They write their capital accounts up to $1 million (fair market value). Distributions will be made in accordance with these capital accounts. If the assets were sold seconds later, Lin (the service partner) would get $0 in distributions. Joe and Sol would get all $1 million.
>
> If they admit Lin as a new "profits-only" partner (with 33.33 percent of the profits), there is no tax to Lin on the issuance of a profits-only interest. Joe and Sol (with 66.67 percent of the profits) get 90 percent of the distributions, and Lin gets 10 percent of the distributions (enough to pay taxes) and 33.33 percent of the profits.
>
> Over time, Joe's and Sol's capital accounts get reduced (since they are receiving larger distributions), so they are gradually liquidated. They share the profits Lin is working to create. Eventually, this will result in Joe and Sol recognizing gain on the excess of distributions over their adjusted basis in the partnership. However, the partnership can receive a step-up at that time under Code Sec. 734 if it has a Code Sec. 754 election in place.

Sweat equity case. ***ES NPA Holding LLC v. Commissioner*** (TC Memo 2023-55) addresses "profits-only" interests in partnerships. This case is complicated; this section covers it in a simplified manner. Note that in the earlier example of Lin's receiving a partnership interest, the service provider was an individual. This case shows that a partnership can also be eligible to earn a "sweat equity" profits-only interest. The issues in the *ES NPA Holding* case included the following:

- Would the "sweat equity" partner have received a portion of the liquidation proceeds if the partnership were liquidated moments after the profits interest was received?
  - — In other words, was it really an interest in capital? (If so, the receipt would trigger tax.)

- Did the partnership need a formal valuation from an expert to show the fair market value of the partnership's assets?
  - — The IRS's expert said the "sweat equity" partner would have received a distribution if the partnership sold its assets and made distributions moments after it received the "sweat equity" profits-only interest. Therefore, the protection of Rev. Proc. 93-27 was not available. This would have resulted in the "sweat equity" partner reporting income on receipt of the partnership interest.

Just prior to the sale of the "sweat equity" interest, the owner of the partnership sold 70 percent of the business for $21 million. That fixed the total value of the business at approximately $30 million ($21 million ÷ 70%). The "sweat equity" partnership agreement provided that *before* the "sweat equity" partner could receive *any* distributions; the original partners must get $30 million in distributions. In other words, if the business were sold moments after the partner received the "sweat equity" profits interest, the first $30 million would have gone to the original partners and the "sweat equity" partner would have received nothing.

The IRS's expert witness argued that the business was really worth $52 million. If the business was sold for $52 million (moments after the "sweat equity" partner was admitted), the first $30 million would go to the original partners, but the "sweat equity" partner would still get millions.

However, the Tax Court held that the sale of 70 percent of the business for $21 million (just before the "sweat equity" partner was admitted) set 100 percent of the value at $30 million. That partner's interest was a profits-only interest, with no distribution to the "sweat equity" partner if the partnership were immediately thereafter liquidated.

The court agreed with the taxpayer that the best proof of the business's fair market value is its sales price just before the "sweat equity" partner was admitted and that no *tax* was imposed for the receipt of "sweat equity" interest.

Limited Partners and Self-Employment Tax

The general self-employment tax rule under Code Sec. 1402(a) is that a partner must pay self-employment tax on their share of income from a business carried on by a partnership. But according to Code Sec. 1402(a)(13), there is an exception for limited partners: Limited partners do not have to pay self-employment tax on their share of ordinary income. They are only required to pay self-employment tax on their guaranteed payments for services.

The purpose of the limited partner exception was to shut down a tax loophole that idle wealthy taxpayers used back in the 1970s to receive Social Security benefits. At that time, very wealthy people who had not worked would buy limited partnership interests so that they could pay self-employment tax. The Social Security system has a progressive benefit structure (people whose employment earnings are low receive proportionately greater benefits). The self-employment earnings they received from the limited partnership allowed them to pay self-employment tax and receive disproportionately large Social Security benefits. Congress decided to shut down this loophole in 1977, and it changed the law to provide that limited partners generally did not have to pay self-employment tax on their share of the partnership's income (and therefore would not receive large Social Security benefits).

The Internal Revenue Code and legislative history therefore provide a "bright line" exception for limited partners. They do not pay self-employment tax on Schedule K-1, Box 1 income, but only on guaranteed payments for services provided. This is *not* ambiguous.

Many hedge funds and private equity funds have exploited the special rule for limited partners. They set up limited partnerships to operate hedge funds and private equity funds. They argue that their earnings (as limited partners) are not subject to self-employment tax. A case in point is *Soroban Capital Partners LP v. Commissioner*, currently pending in the Tax Court. This case involves hedge fund managers who own a limited partnership and argue that because they are limited partners, they owe no self-employment tax. The IRS has argued that the limited partnership structure does not shield them from self-employment tax. It said that back in 1977 when it closed the loophole that Congress was not trying to shield hedge fund managers from self-employment tax and hedge fund managers simply do not look like real limited partners (and did not pass the "functional" test). In essence, the IRS argues that they do not look like limited partners—they look more like general partners.

Soroban Capital filed a motion for summary judgment asking the court to find that its limited partners are exempt from self-employment taxes under the limited partner exception. If the taxpayers win this case, limited partner self-employment tax "screening" will become even more widespread. No matter who wins this case, look for an appeal.

Two older cases give us insight into the Tax Court's view of this issue. These cases were slightly different in that they did not involve state law limited partnerships, but rather limited liability partnerships (LLPs) and LLCs. In *Renkemeyer, Campbell & Weaver, LLP*, 136 TC No. 7 (2011), the LLP operated a law firm. Troy Renkemeyer was a tax attorney and a member of an LLP that provided tax services. His only investment in the LLP was $110. The court found that all of his income was subject to self-employment tax. The Tax Court commented that the "intent" of Code Sec. 1402(a)(13) was that "mere investors" not actively participating in an LLC's business should not get credits toward Social Security coverage. The intent was not to exclude partners performing services from receiving Social Security benefits. Even though an LLP is significantly different from a limited partnership, the Tax Court appeared to test it as a limited partnership.

The case of *Hardy v. Commissioner*, TC Memo 2017-16, involved Stephen P. Hardy, a plastic surgeon with a medical practice in Missoula, Montana. Dr. Hardy also owned part of surgical center in Missoula that was an LLC. A surgical center is similar to a hospital in that it has operating rooms, supplies, and personnel, but patients don't stay overnight. Doctors bill the patients separately for their services. Dr. Hardy made a significant capital contribution ($163,974) to the surgical center but provided no day-to-day management of it. Although he met with the center's other owners quarterly, he had no input in management decisions. Dr. Hardy generally was not involved in hiring and firing decisions.

The court's holding was that Dr. Hardy was not subject to self-employment tax because he was a "mere investor." Contrasting this case with the 2011 *Renkemeyer* case, the court explained that Renkemeyer's income "derived from legal services *performed* by partners" and that Renkemeyer was not acting as an "investor" in the law firm. However, Dr. Hardy *was* acting as an investor. It is worth noting that Dr. Hardy was not an actual limited partner but rather was an LLC member. The Tax Court treated him as exempt from self-employment tax under the limited partner exception, nonetheless.

¶ 511 E-FILING OF FORMS 1099 AND W-2

On February 21, 2023, the IRS issued final regulations (TD 9972) that require certain filers to e-file a number of forms, beginning with 2023 tax year forms that are due to be filed in 2024. The regulations cover a broad range of return filings:

- Forms 1099 and W-2
- Forms 1065, 1120, and 1120-S (IR-2023-31)
- Certain withholding tax returns, registration statements, disclosure statements, notifications, actuarial reports, and certain excise tax returns

The e-filing rule for Forms 1099, W-2, 1065, 1120-S, and 1120 applies to documents required to be filed in 2024, that is, the 2023 Form 1099 series (1099-INT, 1099-MISC, etc.) and the 2023 Forms W-2. Previously, filers were required to e-file their returns if they filed 250 or more returns in a year, but the new regulations have decreased that number to 10 or more returns.

Taxpayers are required to e-file Forms 1099 and W-2 if they filed "10 or more" 1099s and W-2s (and Forms 1042-S, 1094, 1095, 1098, 3921, 3922, 5498, and 8027) in one year. The final regulations require "aggregation across some returns" to see if the "10 or more" threshold has been exceeded. Note that in testing whether the taxpayer has filed 10 or more forms, the IRS counts all Forms 1099 and W-2 but does not count other forms like Forms 941, income tax returns, etc.

EXAMPLE: An S corporation must file for 2023 four Forms 1099-NEC, two Forms 1099-INT, and two W-2s. It also files four Forms 941 and 1120-S. This is a total of 13 filings. However, for this purpose, the S corporation counts only Forms 1099 and W-2 (Forms 941 and 1120-S are not counted). This results in just eight forms, so the S corporation is not over the "10 or more" requirement. Because the S corporation files fewer than 10 forms 1099 and W-2, it is not required to e-file the forms.

NOTE: There is one other test that can require a partnership to e-file Forms 1099 and W-2 (even if it does not file 10 or more 1099s and W-2s). If a partnership has more than 100 partners during the year, it must e-file its Forms 1099 and W-2, even if those forms total fewer than 10.

In the case of mandatory e-filing Form 1065 (partnerships), Form 1120-S (S corporations), and Form 1120 (C corporations), the calculation is different. More types of returns are aggregated to determine if a filer is filing "10 or more" returns. The e-file requirement test for this purpose includes Forms 940, 941, 1120-S, etc.

EXAMPLE: In 2023, an S corporation was required to file the following returns:

- One 2022 Form 1120-S, *U.S. Income Tax Return for an S Corporation*
- Two Forms W-2, *Wage and Tax Statement*
- Two Forms 1099- DIV, *Dividends and Distributions*
- One Form 940, *Employer's Annual Federal Unemployment (FUTA) Tax Return*
- Four Forms 941, *Employer's Quarterly Federal Tax Return*

Because the S corporation must file 10 or more returns in 2023, it must e-file its 2023 Form 1120-S (Treas. Reg. § 301.6037-2(e)). Taxpayers must be very careful to e-file these returns because a late filing penalty applies to each Schedule K-1 and K-3.

Taxpayers who meet the requirements to e-file but cannot do so should file a hardship waiver request 45 days before the form's due date (roughly December 15 for Forms W-2 and 1099-NEC) using Form 8508, ***Application for a Waiver from Electronic Filing of Information Returns***. An automatic waiver is provided for religious exemptions, and the first time a taxpayer applies for a waiver, it is automatically granted (see Form 8508 instructions).

New IRS E-file Portal

The Information Returns Intake System (IRIS) Taxpayer Portal provides a free online method for taxpayers to electronically file the Form 1099 series.

For many years, the IRS's system to e-file Forms 1099 was the Filing Information Returns Electronically (FIRE) system. Software providers use the IRS's system to submit Forms 1099 to the IRS, operating as the "middleman." Although the FIRE system will be available in 2023, the IRS has implied that it will be shut down in the future.

IRIS is the new IRS Portal to e-file Forms 1099 (IR-2023-14). No special software is required to use IRIS, and it is free. Filers can file their 2023 Forms 1099 using IRIS but still need to mail Forms 1099 to recipients.

IRIS can detect filing errors, for example missing SSNs, and alerts filers so they can correct mistakes on Forms 1099. Through the system, the IRS acknowledges receipt of the forms within 48 hours. IRIS also keeps prior years' Forms 1099 available, so, for example, a taxpayer can review their 2023 Forms 1099 in 2026.

In order to use the new IRIS system, tax professionals must have an "ID.me" account (discussed in the next section).

Recap: Electronic Filing Forms W-2 and 1099	
Requirement	• 10 or more • Only count all 1099s and W-2s (don't count other forms such as 941s, etc.) *Example:* A filer that has five Forms 1099-NEC, four 1099-INT, and one W-2 (10 total) must e-file
Waivers	• File Form 8508 (45 days before due date) • Basis for waivers —Cost —Religious beliefs —First-year waiver

ID.me Account for IRS e-Services and Tax Pro

ID.me is an IRS "partner" that authenticates a tax professional's identity. Beginning May 17, 2023, if tax professionals want to use the following, they need to have an ID.me account:

- e-services (such as IRIS to file Forms 1099 for free), and
- Tax pro accounts (e.g., to ask clients to approve a power of attorney electronically and to respond to IRS notices).

To create an ID.me account:

- Go to irs.gov Your Online Account.
- Click "Sign in to Your Online Account."
- Then click "ID.me create an account."

¶ 512 SOCIAL SECURITY AND DECISION-MAKING

The significance of Social Security benefits and whether they will be reduced in the future are popular concerns today. According to an Associated Press (AP) poll, Americans strongly prefer tax increases over Social Security benefit cuts: 79 percent oppose reducing Social Security benefits while 58 percent support raising taxes on households making over $400,000 per year. Both political parties are opposed to reducing Social Security benefits, and a Congressional subcommittee has agreed on the urgency of addressing the Social Security problem.

Raising payroll taxes *significantly* would fix the problem. A Social Security tax increase beginning 2033 from 12.4 percent (6.2 percent for both employer and employee) to 15.9 percent would largely solve the problem. As an alternative, eliminating the cap on maximum taxable wages (currently $160,200) would also largely fix the problem.

Unlike income taxes, Social Security taxes have a direct benefit. Payroll taxes increase Social Security benefits. On average, Social Security benefits are 40 percent of a taxpayer's pre-retirement income. For many taxpayers, these benefits are more important than their retirement savings. As a result, S corporation owners should consider paying more in wages than the minimum amount of reasonable compensation to increase future Social Security benefits.

> **EXAMPLE:** Jerry is an S corporation shareholder. A reasonable amount of compensation is in the range of $60,000 to $80,000 per year. If he pays wages on the high side ($80,000), the result is $3,060 in extra tax. But this also increases his Social Security benefits by $10,000 in the future. Jerry may want to pay $80,000 in W-2 compensation.

The ultimate question is: What is the relationship between paying more payroll taxes and receiving more Social Security benefits? Taxpayers can use the following computation (simplified on an annual basis) to answer this question.

- **Step 1:** What are your historical Social Security wages?
- **Step 2:** Index the historical wages to get the current dollar equivalent. The index factors are available at www.ssa.gov/oact/cola/awifactors.html.
- **Step 3:** Get the annual average (high 35 years indexed Social Security wages) and divide it by 35.
- **Step 4:** Plug the inflation-adjusted high 35-year wage average into the Average Indexed Monthly Earnings (AIME) table. This is your Social Security benefit at normal retirement age (age 67 if born in 1960 or later). The benefit is decreased if you draw Social Security benefits before your normal retirement age.

> **EXAMPLE: INDEXING HISTORICAL WAGES:** Before Juan determines his Social Security benefits, he needs to index his wages. Juan was born in 1961 and began working in 1983. His W-2 has Social Security wages of $14,249. Indexed for inflation, this amount is $56,637. Juan will use $56,639 to compute his Social Security benefit.

Year	Nominal Earnings	Indexing Factor	Indexed Earnings
1983	$14,249	3.9749	$56,639
1984	$15,134	3.7542	$56,817
1985	$15,828	3.6008	$56,994
1986	$16,349	3.4970	$57,173
1987	$17,446	3.2874	$57,352
1988	$18,362	3.1331	$57,530

Year	Nominal Earnings	Indexing Factor	Indexed Earnings
1989	$19,149	3.0138	$57,710
1990	$20,095	2.8807	$57,887
1991	$20,908	2.7772	$58,066

Note that actual computations are a bit more complex. Taxpayers should index wages for inflation only up to age 60 and "lock into" the formula table in effect the year they turn 62. The actual computation involves average monthly earnings; we have used *annual* earnings to simplify. The example below produces roughly the same result as an actual computation.

Relationship Between Social Security Earnings and Benefits (2023)	
Average *Indexed* Annual Earnings (High 35-Year Average)	**Annual Social Security Benefit (at Full Retirement Age)**
$0–$13,380	90%
$13,381–$80,652	32%
$80,653–$147,000	15%
> $147,000	0%

EXAMPLE: Joe indexes all of his prior years' Social Security earnings for inflation. He computes the best 35-year average (indexed for inflation) of wages as $84,065.

	Rate	Annual Benefit	Comments
First $13,380	90%	$12,042	Great return—Joe paid 6.2% (12.4% for both employer and employee)
$13,381–$80,652	32%	$21,526	Good return—Joe paid 6.2% (12.4% for both employer and employee)
$80,653–$84,065	15%	$512	So-so return, unless Joe's spouse has a low earnings history
Total annual benefit		**$34,080**	At full retirement age.

Long-Term Solvency of the Social Security System

According to the 2023 Social Security Trustee's report issued in April 2023, combined Social Security retirement and disability funds have a current *surplus* (as of December 31, 2022) of $2.8 trillion (combined OASDI trust funds). This surplus will be exhausted in 2034. At that time, the government will be able to pay 80 percent of current benefits. Although Congress will very likely fix this problem before 2034 (so that a cut in Social Security benefits will not be necessary), it will probably not do so in the next few years.

When to Draw Social Security

The best advice is generally to wait until age 70 to draw Social Security, unless you need the money earlier. Think of Social Security as insurance: If you live a long life, your Social Security benefits will continue to be paid. However, your 401(k) and retirement savings may run out.

Income-Related Monthly Adjustment Amount (IRMAA)

Everyone must pay for Medicare benefits: Part B (doctors) and Part D (prescription drugs). There are higher charges for high-income taxpayers. Medicare beneficiaries who earn over $97,000 a year and who are enrolled in Medicare Part B and/or Medicare Part D pay the income-related monthly adjusted amount (IRMAA), which is a surcharge added to the Part B and Part D premiums.

The 2023 IRMAA is based on the Medicare beneficiary's MAGI from 2021. If that MAGI exceeded $97,000 (single) or $194,000 (joint return), the IRMAA is charged. MAGI includes nontaxable Social Security, municipal interest, and excluded foreign earned income. Beneficiaries pay an IRMAA of between $88 and $472 per month for 2023.

> **EXAMPLE:** Jerry is 66 years old and single, and his 2021 MAGI was $100,000. This is over the IRMAA threshold. Jerry's Medicare premium charges increase $937 for 2023 (the tax return filed for two years prior, 2021, is used to calculate the surcharged in 2023).

> **NOTE:** IRMAA can be reduced if a beneficiary experiences a life-changing event such as a marriage, divorce, loss of income, etc. Form SSA-44, *Medicare Income-Related Monthly Adjustment Amount—Life-Changing Event*, should be filed to request the adjustment.

IRMAA is an important consideration. For the year an individual turns 63 and after, income determines the IRMAA at age 65; 2023 income is used to determine IRMAA for 2025. This can lead to an unanticipated Medicare charge increase for clients and should be considered by older clients before they make Roth conversions.

> **EXAMPLE:** Mohammad is age 63 in 2023. He is retired and in a low tax bracket. Mohammad is converting his IRA to a Roth account. His tax professional should discuss IRMAA with him as it affects his 2025 Medicare cost. The same idea holds true if Mohammed were 70 years old.

Medicare Troubles

The Medicare program is under stress. Medicare Part A hospital insurance is funded by Medicare withholding at work (2.9 percent combined). As is true for Social Security, this trust fund will run out soon; projections indicate it will be gone by 2031. Tax collections could fund 89 percent of the cost in 2031. Congress is expected to fix this problem or to fund the difference. No cut in benefits is anticipated. For Medicare Parts B (doctors) and D (prescription drugs), Congress funds any shortfalls. However, due to the aging population, it will become increasingly difficult to come up with the funding, and therefore rates may be raised in the future.

¶ 513 FOREIGN BANK ACCOUNT REPORTING

In *Bittner v. United States,* 131 AFTR 2d 2023-799, the Supreme Court addressed a taxpayer's non-willful failure to file Foreign Bank Account Reports (FBARs). The IRS's position was that if a taxpayer had 50 foreign bank accounts for a year, the $10,000 penalty applies for each account, for a total of $500,000 in penalties.

In this case, the taxpayer asserted that the $10,000 penalty applies just one time per year, no matter how many bank accounts the taxpayer has, since the taxpayer failed to file just one FBAR form. The Supreme Court ruled that the taxpayer was right in the case. A single $10,000 penalty applies for a year, no matter how many foreign bank accounts one has.

STUDY QUESTIONS

9. Which of the following identifies the most common cause of S corporation terminations?

- **a.** Second class of stock
- **b.** More than 100 shareholders
- **c.** Entrance of foreign investor
- **d.** Delay in filing tax return

10. Which of the following identifies one of the relationships Dr. Hardy had with the surgical center in the referenced case?

- **a.** Performed all surgeries at that location
- **b.** Met with other owners quarterly
- **c.** Had a very limited capital contribution
- **d.** Was involved in the hiring and firing process

11. Which of the following statements regarding the new IRS Portal to e-file Forms 1099 is correct?

- **a.** It can detect filing errors.
- **b.** There is a $9.95/month fee for gain access.
- **c.** You no longer need to mail 1099s to recipients.
- **d.** The IRS acknowledges receipt within 24 hours.

12. Which of the following identifies the second step in computing Social Security benefits?

- **a.** Determine monthly average of historical Social Security wages.
- **b.** Adjust historical wages to get current dollars.
- **c.** Determine the amount of historical Social Security wages.
- **d.** Plug the inflation-adjusted high 35-year wage average into the AIME table.

MODULE 2: TAX DEVELOPMENTS AND UPDATES—Chapter 6: The Dirty Dozen Tax Scams: What You Should Know to Protect Your Clients

¶ 601 WELCOME

Compiled annually, the IRS's "Dirty Dozen" list highlights a variety of common tax scams that taxpayers may encounter. This chapter outlines what these scams involve, explains how to help clients avoid being victims of them, and details the consequences of committing such fraud.

¶ 602 LEARNING OBJECTIVES

Upon completion of this chapter, you will be able to:

- Identify the Dirty Dozen tax scams
- Recognize how to educate clients to avoid falling prey to scammers
- Describe the consequences of participating in a tax scam

¶ 603 INTRODUCTION

The Dirty Dozen, according to the IRS, "represents the worst of the worst tax scams." The annual list highlights the top 12 tax scams of which taxpayers and tax professionals should be aware. Although these scams can occur at any time, many peak during filing season as people prepare their returns or hire someone to help with their tax return preparation. Tax practitioners should be able to recognize these scams to protect their clients and keep them informed.

The Dirty Dozen list changes each year, but because many of the scams remain on the list for several years, there is some overlap between the 2022 and 2023 lists. For 2022, the IRS identified the following as the Dirty Dozen:

1. Charitable remainder annuity trusts
2. Foreign individual retirement arrangements
3. Foreign captive insurance
4. Monetized installment sales
5. COVID-related fraud
6. Offer-in-compromise mills
7. Anonymous solicitations
8. Spear phishing
9. Hidden offshore accounts and digital assets
10. High-income non-filers
11. Abusive syndicated conservation easements
12. Abusive micro-captive insurance arrangements

The IRS typically issues several news releases announcing the Dirty Dozen. For example, IR-2022-113, dated June 1, 2022, introduced the first four tax scams for 2022. In its 2022 Dirty Dozen, the IRS focused on the following four transactions that are wrongfully promoted and will likely attract additional agency compliance efforts in the future. These four potentially abusive transactions involve charitable remainder annuity trusts, Maltese individual retirement arrangements, foreign captive insurance, and monetized installment sales.

Many of these schemes are advertised online, promising tax savings that are simply too good to be true and will likely cause taxpayers to legally compromise themselves. Therefore, taxpayers should think twice before including these questionable arrangements on their tax returns.

> **NOTE:** Taxpayers are legally responsible for what is on their tax returns. Tax practitioners should stress this fact to their clients.

¶ 604 THE 2022 DIRTY DOZEN TAX SCAMS

Charitable Remainder Annuity Trusts

In this type of transaction, appreciated property is transferred to a charitable remainder annuity (CRAT). Taxpayers improperly claim the transfer of the appreciated assets to the CRAT, which in and of itself gives those assets a step-up in basis to fair market value, as if the assets had been sold to the trust. Essentially, this is an artificial way of stepping up the basis to fair market value.

The CRAT then sells the property but does not recognize gain due to the claimed step-up in basis. Then, the CRAT uses the proceeds to purchase a single premium immediate annuity (SPIA). The beneficiary reports as income only a small portion of the annuity received. And through a misapplication of the law, the beneficiary treats the remaining payment as an excluded portion, representing a return of investment for which no taxes are due.

Taxpayers seek to achieve this inaccurate result by misapplying the rules under Code Secs. 72 and 664. This scam is designed to be sophisticated, complicated, and technical in nature, in hopes of confusing the IRS and making it more difficult to understand the nature of the transaction.

Maltese Pension Arrangements Misusing Treaty

This scam involves U.S. citizens or U.S. residents attempting to avoid U.S. income tax by making contributions to certain foreign individual retirement arrangements in Malta. The contributions could be made to such arrangements in any foreign country, but the most problematic have been contributions to foreign individual retirement arrangements in Malta. In these transactions, the taxpayers typically lack a local connection—that is, they don't really live in Malta. In addition, local law allows contributions in a form other than cash or does not limit the amount of contributions by reference to income earned from employment or self-employment.

Therefore, by improperly asserting the foreign arrangement as a "pension fund" for U.S. tax treaty purposes, the U.S. taxpayer misconstrues the relevant treaty to improperly claim an exemption from U.S. income tax on earnings and distributions from the foreign arrangement.

Puerto Rican and Other Foreign Captive Insurance

In these transactions, U.S. owners of closely held entities participate in a purported insurance arrangement with a Puerto Rican or other foreign corporation with sell arrangements or segregated asset plans in which the United States owner has a financial interest and the United States–based individual or entity claims a deduction for the cost of insurance coverage provided by a fronting carrier, which reinsures the coverage with a foreign corporation.

The characteristics of the purported insurance arrangements typically include one or more of the following: an implausible risk covered, non–arm's-length pricing, and lack of business purpose for entering into the arrangement.

Monetized Installment Sales

Monetized installment sales are transactions that involve the inappropriate use of the installment sale rules under Code Sec. 453 by a seller who, in the year of the sale, effectively receives the sale proceeds through purported loans.

In a typical transaction, the seller enters into a contract to sell the appreciated property to a buyer for cash, and then purports to sell the same property to an intermediary in return for an installment note. The intermediary then purports to sell the property to the buyer and receives the cash purchase price.

Therefore, through a series of related steps, the seller receives an amount equivalent to the sales price, less various transaction fees, in the form of a purported loan that is nonrecourse and unsecured.

> **NOTE:** Taxpayers who have engaged in any of these transactions or who are contemplating engaging in them should carefully review the underlying legal requirements and consult competent, independent advisors before claiming any of these tax benefits. The hope is that the taxpayer will reach out to a qualified, legitimate, honest tax return preparer to advise them against these particular schemes.
>
> Taxpayers who have already claimed the purported tax benefits of one of these four transactions should consider taking corrective action. They should file an amended return (1040-X, *Amended U.S. Individual Income Tax Return*) and seek advice where appropriate. If the IRS challenges the purported tax benefits from the transactions, it may impose an accuracy-related penalty, which can range from 20 to 40 percent; or a civil fraud penalty, which is 75 percent of the underpayment.
>
> In the worst-case scenario, the IRS may refer the taxpayer's case to the IRS Criminal Investigation Division.

Pandemic-Related Scams

On June 6, 2022, the IRS released IR-2022-117, highlighting another type of tax scam in its Dirty Dozen list: pandemic-related scams. Unfortunately, criminals were still using the COVID-19 pandemic as an opportunity to steal people's money and identity with bogus emails, social media posts, and unexpected phone calls, among other things.

These scams take a variety of forms to steal money and information from taxpayers, including Economic Impact Payment (EIP) and tax refund schemes, unemployment fraud, bogus employment offers, and fake charities. All these efforts can lead to sensitive personal information being stolen, and scammers using that information to file a fraudulent tax return or harm victims in other ways.

Caution and awareness are the best lines of defense against these criminals. Practitioners should educate their clients to verify the information they receive by consulting a trusted website, such as IRS.gov.

Economic Impact Payment (EIP) and tax refund scams. Fraudsters contacting taxpayers about EIPs, also known as stimulus payments, attempt to steal taxpayers' personal information by purporting to be from the IRS and asking for sensitive data.

Tax refund scams are similar; they can involve communications that seem to be from the IRS and are designed to mislead taxpayers into believing they are owed a refund or to ask for personal information in regard to a refund.

EIP and tax refund scams are a continuing threat to individuals. Taxpayers should watch out for the tell-tale signs of these scams: a text message, unexpected phone call, or email from the "IRS" requesting an individual's personal identifiable information (PII) such as Social Security Number or bank account information.

> **NOTE:** The IRS does *not* initiate contact with taxpayers by phone, email, text, or social media. Taxpayers should *never* click a link in a text or an email to verify their data. The best practice is to delete such texts or emails without opening them.

Keep in mind that the IRS has issued all EIPs, so most eligible people have already received theirs. Those who are missing a payment or received less than the full amount could claim a recovery rebate credit on their return.

Unemployment fraud leading to inaccurate Form 1099-Gs. As a result of the pandemic, many taxpayers lost their jobs and received unemployment compensation from their state. Scammers, however, took advantage of the pandemic by filing fraudulent claims for unemployment compensation using stolen personal information of individuals who had not filed claims. The payments made on these fraudulent claims went to the identity thieves. Unfortunately, the person whose identity was stolen received Form 1099-G, *Certain Government Payments*, to report the unemployment compensation. But they did not apply for or receive unemployment benefits.

The IRS urges victims of this scam to contact their appropriate state agency for a corrected form, and if a corrected form cannot be obtained from the state so that the taxpayer can file a timely tax return, the taxpayer should complete their return, claiming only the unemployment compensation and/or other income they actually received.

The U.S. Department of Labor also provides information on reporting unemployment identity fraud at https://www.dol.gov/agencies/eta/UIIDtheft. The site includes links and phone numbers for each U.S. state.

Fake employment offers posted on social media. Another COVID-related scam involves fake employment offers posted on social media. Because of the pandemic, many newly unemployed people were eager to seek new employment, and scammers saw them as easy targets. The fake job posts enticed victims to provide their personal financial information used to file fraudulent tax returns or in some other criminal endeavor, such as applying for a credit card or a bank loan.

Fake charities. This type of scam is always a problem but tends to be a bigger threat when there is a national crisis, like a pandemic. Fake charities are especially prevalent after a natural disaster, such as a devastating hurricane, earthquake, tsunami, blizzard, or tornado.

Taxpayers who give money or goods to a qualified charity may be able to claim a deduction on their federal tax return. To determine whether an organization is a legitimate qualified charity for purposes of the deduction, taxpayers can use the Tax Exempt Organization Search Tool on the IRS website at https://www.irs.gov/charities-non-profits/search-for-tax-exempt-organizations

Individuals should never let any caller from a charity pressure them. A legitimate charity will be happy to get a donation at any time, so there is no rush. Donors are encouraged to take time to do their research. Potential donors should ask the fundraiser for the charity's exact name, web address, and mailing address so it can be confirmed. Also, individuals should make donations by credit card or check, not gift cards or wires.

Avoid Offer in Compromise Mills

Offer in compromise (OIC) mills is yet another example involving unscrupulous tax preparers. IR-2022-119, issued on June 7, 2022, advises "taxpayers with pending tax bills to contact the IRS directly and not go to unscrupulous tax companies that use local advertising and falsely claiming they can resolve unpaid taxes for pennies on the dollar." These claims are usually made in television and radio ads.

An OIC is an agreement between a taxpayer and the IRS to resolve a tax debt. Taxpayers should be wary of any entity that uses local advertising to claim that it can resolve their tax debt at a low price. The IRS asserts that nobody can get a better deal for a taxpayer than the taxpayer can usually get for themselves by working directly with the IRS to resolve their tax debt.

Taxpayers can check online at IRS.gov for their best offer-in-compromise deal, or they can call a specialized collection line where they can get fast service by using voice and chat bots or options to speak with a live phone assister. This service has been tremendously improved with the recent addition of 5,000 new employees at the IRS. Those who feel they need help can also contact a reputable tax professional.

While OIC mills are a problem all year long, they tend to be more visible right after the filing season is over and taxpayers are trying to resolve their tax issues, perhaps after receiving a balance due notice in the mail.

The IRS has the authority to settle, or compromise, federal tax liabilities by accepting less than the full amount under certain circumstances. However, some promoters are inappropriately advising indebted taxpayers to file an OIC with the IRS, even though they know the person will not qualify. Therefore, before taxpayers start investing time to do the paperwork necessary to submit an offer, they should check out the IRS's Offer in Compromise Pre-Qualifier tool at irs.treasury.gov/oic_pre_qualifier/ to make sure they are eligible to file one. Note that even though individuals and businesses can submit an offer, the tool is currently only available to individuals.

The IRS has also created an OIC video playlist (https://www.irsvideos.gov/Business/PostFilingIssues/OfferInCompromise) that leads taxpayers through a series of steps and forms to help them calculate an appropriate OIC based on their assets, income, expenses, and future earnings potential.

> **NOTE:** The IRS reminds taxpayers that under the first-time penalty abatement policy, they can go directly to the IRS for administrative relief from a penalty that would otherwise be added to their tax debt.

"Ghost" preparers and inflated refunds. Taxpayers need to be wary of unscrupulous "ghost" preparers and aggressive promises of manufacturing a bigger refund. By law, anyone who is paid to prepare or assist in preparing federal tax returns must have a valid preparer tax identification number (PTIN). And paid preparers must provide their signature and their PTIN on the return.

If a taxpayer mentions to his tax practitioner that a preparer handled his prior year Form 1040, but the form itself indicates "self-prepared," that is an indication that a "ghost" preparer might be involved. It is likely that something on that prior-year return is fabricated, false, nondeductible, or omitted. If that is the case, the practitioner should encourage the client to amend that return and should keep notes of any discussions with the client. These notes can help confirm facts if issues arise in the future.

When it comes to promising a taxpayer a big refund or charging fees based on the size of the refund (both of which are inappropriate), not signing the return is a red flag that the paid preparer may be looking to make a quick profit. Unscrupulous tax return preparers might also require payment in cash only and not provide a receipt. In addition, they may invent income to qualify their clients for tax credits.

EXAMPLE: Mr. Abbot, an unscrupulous tax return preparer, charges a fee for tax preparation that equals 30 percent of the client's refund. His client would normally receive a $500 refund, but he exaggerates the client's Schedule C net profit, which does not even exist—the client does not even have a company. Abbot ensures the phony company is a cash-intensive business that would have no Form 1099s.

Abbot puts the perfect amount of net profit on the client's return to maximize the earned income credit. Or maybe he prepares a fake W-2 with federal income tax withheld and that generates earned income and qualifies for the credit—plus the bogus withholding, plus the child tax credit—and his client receives a $15,000 refund. Abbot does all this because he gets 30 percent of the refund.

NOTE: Taxpayers are legally responsible for the contents of their tax returns even if the returns are prepared by someone else.

Taxpayers who are looking for someone to prepare their tax return must use caution and steer clear of unscrupulous preparers, including the ones who claim fake deductions to boost the size of the refund. To choose a reputable tax professional, they can consult the IRS's guidance at https://www.irs.gov/tax-professionals/choosing-a-tax-professional.

Scammers Using Tricks to Steal Identities

Identity theft is the focus of IR-2022-121, dated June 8, 2022. Although the IRS notes it has had much success in preventing and reducing tax-related identity theft, it remains a serious threat to taxpayers and tax practitioners who do not adequately protect Social Security numbers (SSNs) and other personal information.

For example, criminals can quickly file a fake tax return using a stolen SSN in the hope that it has not already appeared on another filed return. And people frequently do not realize they are a victim of identity theft until they are notified by the IRS of a possible issue with their tax return, or their return is rejected because the SSN appears on a return already filed.

Tax practitioners must be especially careful to safeguard the information they have, as they typically have more people's personal identifiable information (PII) than other professions. For example, they may know more financial information about the husband of a married filing couple than the wife knows and vice versa. Tax practitioners should walk through their offices, ensuring that sensitive information is securely locked away and no PII can easily be obtained by the wrong people.

Common identify theft scams include text messaging, email phishing, and phone scams.

Text message scams. There are many types of text message scams. For example, a text might be sent asking the recipient to confirm a purchase or answer a question about a purchase by clicking on a link. Other scam texts might reference things such as COVID-19 stimulus payments or IRS refunds but contain bogus links claiming to be the IRS or some type of online tool.

Other than IRS Secure Access, the IRS does not use text messages to discuss personal tax issues, including bills or refunds. The IRS also does not send taxpayer messages via social media platforms. If a taxpayer receives an unsolicited text that appears to be from either the IRS or a program closely linked to it, the taxpayer should take a screenshot of the text and include it in an email to phishing@irs.gov. The email should include the date, time, and time zone in which the text message was received and the phone number that received the text message.

> **NOTE:** Never click on a link or open an attachment in an unsolicited, suspicious, or unexpected text message.

Email phishing scams. These are similar to text message scams, but the taxpayer is contacted through email. Often, the email requests an individual's personal or financial information. Remember, the IRS initiates most contacts through regular mail, not through email. If a taxpayer receives an unsolicited fraudulent email that appears to be from the IRS, they should report it to the IRS by sending the email as an attachment to phishing@irs.gov.

Phone scams. The IRS does not leave taxpayers prerecorded urgent or threatening messages such as the following:

- "You owe money."
- "We're sending the sheriff right now."
- "You need to pay the balance due."

In one of the many variations of the phone scam, victims are told that if they do not call back, a warrant will be issued for their arrest. Other verbal threats might mention law enforcement agencies, deportation, or revocation of licenses. Criminals can fake or spoof caller ID numbers to appear to be from anywhere in the country—including an IRS office, a sheriff's office, the state department of motor vehicles, and federal agencies—preventing taxpayers from being able to verify the caller's true number.

The IRS, and authorized private collection agencies of the IRS, will never call to demand immediate payment using a specific payment method such as a prepaid debit card, gift card, or wire transfer. The agency will never threaten to immediately bring in local police or law enforcement or threaten arrest. The IRS will not demand that taxes be paid without giving the taxpayer the opportunity to question or appeal the amount. Nor will the IRS ask for a credit or debit card number over the phone. Remember, the IRS will first mail a bill to a taxpayer who owes money, and all tax payments should be made payable only to the United States Treasury.

> **NOTE:** The best advice for anyone who receives scam calls is to *hang up immediately*.

Spear Phishing Attack

In IR-2022-122, released on June 9, 2022, the IRS reiterated warnings to tax practitioners and other businesses of dangerous spear phishing attacks. Spear phishing is an email scam that attempts to steal the computer system credentials of any small business with a client database. Tax practitioners are popular targets. Thieves are trying to steal client data and tax preparers' identities in an attempt to file fraudulent tax returns for refunds. However, spear phishing can be tailored to attack any type of business or organization.

A recent phishing email includes the IRS logo. It uses a variety of subject lines, for example, "Action required: Your account has been put on hold." The IRS has observed similar bogus emails that claim to be from a tax preparation application provider, and one such variation offers an unusual activity report and a solution link for the recipient to restore their account.

The scam email will send the user to a website that shows the logos of several popular tax software preparation providers, and clicking on one of those logos will prompt a request for tax preparer account credentials. Again, individuals are warned not to respond or take any of the steps outlined in the emails. The emails include malicious links or attachments that are set up to steal information or download malware onto their computer.

Hidden Offshore Accounts and Cryptocurrency

Also issued in June 2022, IR 2022-125 warns taxpayers to avoid being misled into using bogus tax avoidance strategies. International tax compliance is a top priority for the IRS, with a focus area being taxpayers who attempt to avoid taxation by concealing assets in offshore accounts. Some taxpayers are using foreign trusts, employee-leasing schemes, private annuities, and structured transactions to try to conceal the true ownership of accounts or insurance plans. A key point to remember is that U.S. taxpayers are taxed on their *worldwide* income—being offshore does not put income out of the U.S. tax system's reach.

The improper reporting of digital assets is another IRS focus area. Digital assets, such as cryptocurrency, are being adopted by many mainstream organizations, creating challenges for tax administration. Some unscrupulous scammers are spreading false information that digital assets are undetectable and that taxpayers can easily conceal their cryptocurrency. However, this is far from the truth. Individuals who attempt to conceal their digital assets can face civil fraud penalties and criminal charges.

High-Income Individuals Non-Filers

Also discussed in IR-2022-125 are high-income non-filers. As part of its mission, the IRS is focused on high-income taxpayers, especially those earning more than $100,000 per year, who engage in various types of tax violations, including the most basic—failure to file a return. The failure to file penalty is much greater than failure to pay penalty. If the failure to file is deemed fraudulent, the maximum penalty increases from 25 percent to 75 percent.

Fraudulent tax avoidance strategies are promoted to unsuspecting individuals with "too good to be true" promises of reducing taxes or avoiding taxes altogether. Taxpayers should not assume that they can hide from the IRS. The IRS continues to focus on these deals, and people who engage in them face steep civil penalties and or criminal charges.

Abusive Syndicated Conservation Easements

The IRS is also taking a close look at sophisticated transactions involving the abuse of syndicated conservation easements (IR-2022-125). It has stepped up its efforts on abusive schemes in recent years, and as part of the wider IRS effort, is hiring additional attorneys to help the agency combat abusive syndicated conservation easements and micro-captive transactions, as well as other abusive schemes.

In abusive syndicated conservation easement schemes, promoters twist a provision of the tax law allowing for conservation easements by using inflated appraisals of undeveloped land and partnership agreements devoid of a legitimate business purpose. They grossly inflate tax deductions and generate high fees for themselves. When it comes to these scams, taxpayers should be aware that if it sounds too good to be true, it probably is.

Abusive Micro-Captive Insurance Arrangements

IR-2022-125 also mentions that the IRS has conducted thousands of examinations and investigations of promoters who use potentially abusive offshore captive insurance companies. In this scam, promoters persuade owners of closely held entities to participate in schemes that lack many attributes of insurance. For example, the coverage may "insure" implausible risks, such as a hurricane in Arizona or an avalanche in Florida. The premiums are excessive and are used to skirt the law. Investigation of these transactions is a high priority for the IRS.

STUDY QUESTIONS

1. Which of the following IRS news releases includes information about tax avoidance strategies?

a. IR-2022-113

b. IR-2022-117

c. IR-2022-122

d. IR-2022-125

2. Which of the following types of trusts is likely to attract additional agency compliance efforts?

a. Charitable remainder annuity trusts

b. Grantor trust

c. Testamentary trust

d. Spendthrift trust

3. Which of the following is ***not*** one of the telltale signs of an Economic Impact Payment (EIP) scam?

a. Text message

b. Unexpected phone call

c. Written correspondence from the IRS

d. Email

¶ 605 NEW SCAMS IN THE 2023 DIRTY DOZEN

Some of the tax scams the IRS included in its 2022 Dirty Dozen list remain for 2023. However, a few new ones made the 2023 Dirty Dozen list:

- Employee retention credit claims (IR-2023-49)
- Scammers offering to "help" set up an online account (IR-2023-54)
- False fuel tax credit claims (IR-2023-55)
- Tax advice on social media is bad news (IR-2023-61)

The remaining 2023 Dirty Dozen tax scams, with their relevant IRS news releases, are as follows:

- IR-2023-51, Filing season scammers
- IR-2023-57, Fake charities
- IR-2023-59, Shady tax preparers
- IR-2023-62, Spear phishing
- IR-2023-63, Offer in compromise "mills"
- IR-2023-65, Charitable remainder annuity trusts
- IR-2023-67, Abusive tax avoidance schemes
- IR-2023-71, Scams and schemes

Employee Retention Credit Claims

For the start of the annual Dirty Dozen list of tax scams for 2023, the IRS spotlighted employee retention credits (ERCs) following blatant attempts by promoters to con ineligible people to claim the credit. Renewing several earlier alerts, the IRS highlighted schemes from promoters who have been blasting ads on radio and the internet touting refunds involving ERCs. These promotions can be based on inaccurate information related to eligibility for and computation of the credit.

"The aggressive marketing of these credits is deeply troubling and a major concern for the IRS," said IRS Commissioner Danny Werfel. "Businesses need to think twice before filing a claim for these credits. While the credit has provided a financial lifeline to millions of businesses, there are promoters misleading people and businesses into thinking they can claim these credits. There are very specific guidelines around these pandemic-era credits; they are not available to just anyone. People should remember the IRS is actively auditing and conducting criminal investigations related to these false claims. We urge honest taxpayers not to be caught up in these schemes."

The IRS is stepping up enforcement action involving these ERC claims, and people considering filing for these claims—only valid during the pandemic for a limited group of businesses—should be aware they are ultimately responsible for the accuracy of the information on their tax return. The IRS Small Business/Self-Employed division has trained auditors examining these types of claims, and the IRS Criminal Investigation Division is on the lookout for promoters of fraudulent claims for credits.

Scammers Offering to Help Set Up an Online Account

The IRS Online Account provides valuable tax information for people. But this information in the wrong hands can provide important information to help an identity thief try to submit a fraudulent tax return in the person's name in hopes of getting a big refund. People should watch out for these scam artists offering to help set up these accounts because these are identity theft attempts to run off with the taxpayer's personal or financial information.

"Scammers are coming up with new ways all the time to try to steal information from taxpayers," said IRS Commissioner Danny Werfel. "An Online Account at IRS.gov can help taxpayers view important details about their tax situation. But scammers are trying to convince people they need help setting up an account. In reality, no help is needed. This is just a scam to obtain valuable and sensitive tax information that scammers will use to try stealing a refund. People should be wary and avoid sharing sensitive personal data over the phone, email, or social media to avoid getting caught up in these scams."

In this scam targeting individuals, swindlers pose as a "helpful" third party and offer to help create a taxpayer's IRS Online Account at IRS.gov. People should remember they can set these accounts up themselves. But third parties making these offers will try to steal a taxpayer's personal information this way. Taxpayers can and should establish their own Online Account through IRS.gov.

These scammers often ask for the taxpayer's personal information including address, Social Security number or Individual Taxpayer Identification Number (ITIN), and photo identification. The criminal then sells this valuable information to other criminals. Criminals can also use the sensitive information to file fraudulent tax returns, obtain loans, and open credit accounts.

The IRS urges people to watch out for these "helpful" criminals. The only place individuals should go to create an IRS Online Account is IRS.gov. People should not use third-party assistance, other than the approved IRS authentication process through IRS.gov, to create their own IRS online account.

False Fuel Tax Credit Claims

"People should watch out for erroneous fuel tax credit claims and the scammers that promote them," said IRS Commissioner Danny Werfel. "These scammers will often charge a hefty fee for these bogus claims, and participants also face the possibility of identity theft. This is another example that people should always remember: Be wary if a tax deal sounds too good to be true."

Improper credits continue to be an important area of focus for the IRS. The fuel tax credit is meant for off-highway business and farming use and therefore is not available to most taxpayers. However, unscrupulous tax return preparers and promoters are enticing taxpayers to inflate their refunds by erroneously claiming the credit. The IRS has seen an increase in the promotion of filing certain refundable credits using Form 4136, *Credit for Federal Tax Paid on Fuels*.

In this scam, a third party convinces a taxpayer to fraudulently claim the credit with promises of a windfall refund. But the promoters are focused on their own gain, taking advantage of the taxpayer with inflated fees, refund fraud, and identity theft.

Taxpayers contemplating participating in any questionable tax scheme such as this should be aware the IRS has increased its compliance efforts related to falsely claiming these credits. IRS processing systems, including new identity theft screening filters, are now stopping a significant number of suspicious fuel tax credit refund claims.

Before taking the bait on a dubious credit claim, taxpayers should seek advice from a legitimate source. Returns filed by individuals and tax preparers who knowingly claim a credit to which they are not entitled may face fines and even be subject to federal criminal prosecution and imprisonment.

Tax Advice on Social Media Is Bad News

Social media can circulate inaccurate or misleading tax information, and the IRS has recently seen several examples. These can involve common tax documents like Form W-2 or more obscure ones, like Form 8944, that are aimed at a very limited, specialized group. Both schemes encourage people to submit false, inaccurate information in hopes of getting a refund.

"There are many ways to get good tax information, including from a trusted tax professional, tax software and IRS.gov. But people should be incredibly wary about following advice being shared on social media," said IRS Commissioner Danny Werfel. "The IRS continues to see a lot of inaccurate information that could get well-meaning taxpayers in trouble. People should remember that there is no secret way to fill out a form and simply get a larger refund that they aren't entitled to. Remember, if it sounds too good to be true, it probably is."

Social media can connect people and information from all over the world. Unfortunately, sometimes people provide bad advice that can lure good taxpayers into trouble. The IRS warns taxpayers to be wary of trusting internet advice, whether it's a fraudulent tactic promoted by scammers or a patently false tax-related scheme trending across popular social media platforms.

The IRS is aware of various filing season hashtags and social media topics leading to inaccurate and potentially fraudulent information. The central theme involves people trying to use legitimate tax forms for the wrong reason. Here are just two of the recent schemes circulating online:

Form 8944 fraud. A recent example of bad advice circulating on social media that could lead to fraudulent form filing involves Form 8944, *Preparer e-file Hardship Waiver Request.* There are wildly inaccurate suggestions being made about this form. Posts claim that Form 8944 can be used by taxpayers to receive a refund from the IRS, even if the taxpayer has a balance due. This is false information. Form 8944 is for tax practitioner use only.

Although Form 8944 is a legitimate IRS tax form, it is intended for a targeted group of tax return preparers who are requesting a waiver so they can file tax returns on paper instead of electronically. It is not in any way a form the average taxpayer can use to avoid tax bills. Taxpayers who intentionally file forms with false or fraudulent information can face serious consequences, including potentially civil and criminal penalties.

Form W-2 fraud. This scheme, which is circulating on social media, encourages people to use tax software to manually fill out Form W-2, *Wage and Tax Statement*, and include false income information. In this scheme, scam artists suggest people make up large income and withholding figures as well as the employer they are coming from. Scam artists then instruct people to file the bogus tax return electronically in hopes of getting a substantial refund.

The IRS, along with the Security Summit partners in the tax industry and the states, are actively watching for this scheme. In addition, the IRS works with payroll companies and large employers—as well as the Social Security Administration—to verify W-2 information.

The IRS and Summit partners warn people not to fall for this scam. Taxpayers who knowingly file fraudulent tax returns potentially face significant civil and criminal penalties.

> **NOTE:** Taxpayers should always keep in mind that if something sounds too good to be true, it probably is. IRS.gov has a forms repository (at https://www.irs.gov/forms-instructions) with legitimate and detailed instructions for taxpayers on how to fill out the forms properly. Taxpayers should use IRS.gov, official IRS social media accounts, or other government sites to fact-check information.

¶ 606 RECOGNIZING ILLEGAL TAX AVOIDANCE SCHEMES

IRS Publication 3995, *Recognizing Illegal Tax Avoidance Schemes* (revised in March 2023), includes important tips for taxpayers who might be targets of such illegal schemes. These often include language that sounds too good to be true, such as:

- "I can get you the earned income tax credit."
- "Put your money in a trust and never pay taxes again."
- "Use a charitable trust to eliminate income."
- "I don't pay taxes—Why should you?"
- "Do not pay taxes on capital gains."
- "Deduct personal expenses."
- "The IRS does not want you to know about this."
- "I can get you a big refund."

The publication includes information to discount what is being promoted. For example, regarding the "I don't pay taxes, why should you?" scheme, promoters may talk about how they don't file or pay taxes and then charge people a fee to share their secret. The secret they don't reveal is that many of them actually do file and pay taxes;

they just don't publicly admit it. Taxpayers should consider whether a promoter or preparer is asking them to do any of the following:

- Underreport income
- Intentionally omit income
- Overstate the amount of deductions
- Create new entities
- Make false entries in their books and records
- Claim personal expenses as business expenses
- Claim false deductions
- Put false information on tax return
- Hide or transfer assets or income

Publication 3995 also provides arguments taxpayers can use if they are entertaining one of these "too good to be true" schemes. Taxpayers must always remember the following:

- Taxpayers are responsible and liable for the content of their tax return.
- Anyone who promises a taxpayer a bigger refund without knowing the tax situation could be misleading the taxpayer.
- Taxpayers should never sign a tax return without looking it over to make sure it is honest and correct.

¶ 607 TIPS FROM THE IRS ON CHOOSING A TAX PREPARER

There are various types of tax return preparers, including certified public accountants, enrolled agents, attorneys, and many others who do not have a professional credential. The IRS's advice for those who are choosing a tax preparer includes the following:

- Look for a tax return preparer who is available year-round.
- Review the preparer's history by checking the following:
  - — Better Business Bureau
  - — State Board of Accountancy
  - — State Bar Association
  - — IRS
- Ask about service fees.
- Ensure that the preparer offers e-filing.
- Ensure that the preparer provides records and receipts.
- Understand the preparer's credentials and qualifications.
- Never sign a blank or incomplete return.
- Review the tax return before signing it.

Taxpayers expect their preparer to be skilled in tax preparation and accurately file the tax return. They also trust their preparers with their most personal information, including details about their marriage and children, Social Security numbers, and financial life.

To get information about preparers, taxpayers can visit https://www.irs.gov/tax-professionals/choosing-a-tax-professional. The web page has a link to the IRS Directory of Federal Tax Return Preparers with Credentials and Select Qualifications, which can help them find preparers in their area who have professional credentials recognized by the IRS, or who hold an Annual Filing Season Program Record of Completion.

¶ 608 REPORTING SUSPECTED ABUSIVE TAX PROMOTIONS OR PREPARERS

The IRS is warning tax practitioners to look out for promoters who peddle false hopes of large tax deductions from abusive arrangements, make false claims, or charge high fees. Tax scams are generally marketed aggressively by unscrupulous promoters who are constantly looking for ways to cheat the system. Taxpayers who participate are just playing the audit lottery, hoping they do not get caught.

The IRS is relying on the return preparer community to identify promoters who offer tax tips that are "too good to be true." If a tax practitioner encounters any tax schemes, such as the ones discussed in this chapter, they should report them by submitting Form 14242, *Report Suspected Abusive Tax Promotions or Preparers*, and supporting materials to the IRS Lead Development Center at the following address:

IRS LDC

Stop MS5040

24000 Avila Road

Laguna Niguel CA 92677-3405

The LDC will follow up on each referral and forward it for further IRS action, including the IRS Criminal Investigation Division. Referrals may lead to:

- Injunctions against abusive tax promoters or preparers
- Monetary penalties
- Suspension or revocation of their electronic filing identification number (EFIN)
- Criminal prosecution
- Referral to the Office of Professional Regulation (OPR)

¶ 609 TIPS TO FIGHT FRAUD

The Social Security Administration (SSA) and the Office of the Inspector General designated March 9, 2023, as "National Slam the Scam Day," an initiative centered on raising public awareness of government imposter scams and preventing scammers from succeeding in their crimes.

The Federal Trade Commission (FTC) has estimated that consumer fraud cost $8.8 billion in 2022, a 44 percent increase from 2021. A whopping $2.6 billion of that figure involves imposter scams. They are the most common form of fraud, second only to investment scams.

The FTC offers the following tips to fight fraud:

- Block unwanted calls and filter unwanted text messages.
- Don't give personal or financial information in response to an unexpected request.
  - Honest organizations do not call, email, text, or ask for personal information such as Social Security, bank account, or credit card numbers.
  - Never click on any links asking for information.
- Resist pressure to act immediately.

Scammers often request payment by cryptocurrency, wire transfer, or gift card. Those who encounter suspected fraud should stop and talk to someone they trust. They should also contact the FTC. The SSA provides information on Social Security–related scams at https://identitytheft.gov/ssa. Fraudulent calls can be reported at https://oig.ssa.gov/report or by phone at 800-269-0271.

Other helpful resources include the following:

- Publication 4557, *Safeguarding Taxpayer Data*
- Publication 5293, *Protect Your Clients; Protect Yourself: Data Security Resource Guide for Tax Professionals*
- Publication 5199, *Tax Preparer Guide to Identity Theft*
- The National Institute of Standards and Technology (NIST) *Small Business Information Security: The Fundamentals*

STUDY QUESTIONS

4. Which of the following is something you'd likely ***not*** do in response to a text message scam?

a. Take a screenshot

b. Open attachments

c. Email to phishing@IRS.gov

d. Avoid clicking any links

5. Which of the following statements is correct with respect to consumer fraud?

a. $2.6 billion involves imposter scams.

b. It cost $4.6 billion in 2022.

c. There was a 22 percent increase from 2021.

d. It is the third most common type of fraud.

6. Which of the following IRS publications relates to safeguarding taxpayer data?

a. Publication 4557

b. Publication 5293

c. Publication 5199

d. Publication 502

MODULE 2: TAX DEVELOPMENTS AND UPDATES—Chapter 7: Cryptocurrency and Taxes Update

¶ 701 WELCOME

This chapter provides the reader with a basic understanding of cryptocurrency. It covers the history of virtual currencies and explains how they work. Some of the legal issues involved with virtual currencies are discussed, as well as the advantages and disadvantages of using virtual currencies. The chapter also reviews the IRS rules for tracking and reporting cryptocurrency transactions for tax purposes.

¶ 702 LEARNING OBJECTIVES

Upon completion of this chapter, you will be able to:

- Describe cryptocurrency
- Recognize how virtual currencies work
- Identify the tax implications of using cryptocurrency

¶ 703 OVERVIEW OF CRYPTOCURRENCY

Cryptocurrency is a type of virtual currency. Virtual currency can be defined as virtual money. It is issued by its developers and used within a given virtual community. The European Banking Authority defines virtual currency as "a digital representation of value that is neither issued by a central bank or a public authority, nor necessarily attached to a fiat currency, but is accepted by natural or legal persons as a means of payment and can be transferred, stored or traded electronically."

The Financial Crimes Enforcement Network (FinCEN), a bureau of the U.S. Treasury, has defined virtual currency as "a medium of exchange that operates like a currency in some environments, but does not have all the attributes of real currency." In particular, virtual currency does not have legal tender status in any jurisdiction.

You should also note that the IRS defines virtual currency as property, not as currency. There are several types of virtual currencies, including closed, single-flow, and convertible.

- **Closed virtual currencies** are used in a closed community, most commonly multiplayer online games. The currency is fictional and has no value outside of the game. Game rules often prohibit players from buying and selling the currency outside of the game.
- **Single-flow virtual currencies** are similar to coupons. Common examples are frequent flyer miles with airlines and Amazon Coin. The currency can be purchased, or provided with a purchase, and can be used to purchase goods and services from a provider, but it cannot be purchased or exchanged on an open market.
- **Convertible virtual currencies** can be purchased and sold on exchanges and used to complete transactions with individuals, businesses, and governments. Bitcoin is the most well-known convertible virtual currency.

What Is Cryptocurrency?

Cryptocurrency is a digital currency using cryptography to secure transactions and to control the creation of new currency units. Not all virtual currencies use cryptography, so cryptocurrencies are a subset of virtual currencies. There are many types of cryptocurrency, including the following:

- **Payment coins** are crypto assets that can be used to facilitate transactions for goods and services on the internet. Examples include Bitcoin (BTC), Litecoin (LTC), and Dogecoin (DOGE).
- **Fiat stable coins** are crypto assets tied to a traditional fiat currency such as the U.S. dollar or the Euro. Examples include Tether (USDT), USD Coin (USDC), and Binance USD (BUSD).
- **Central bank coins** are a type of cryptocurrency designed and issued by a central government as alternatives to fiat currencies. Examples include Sand Dollar (Bahamas), JAM-DEX (Jamaica), and eNaira (Nigeria).

NOTE: In March 2022, President Biden signed an executive order asking the U.S. Treasury to explore the creation of a U.S.-issued cryptocurrency.

- **Utility coins** are crypto assets used to access services on a given blockchain protocol. Typically, a user will have to acquire the crypto asset and hold it to gain the privileges other asset holders enjoy, including governance, trading fee discounts, and start-up investment rounds (also called IDO or Initial DEX Offering). Examples include Ether (ETH), Binance Coin (BNB), Golem (GNT), OX (ZRX), and OmiseGo (OMG).
- **Meme coins** are cryptocurrencies that are created to take advantage of social media memes. Although their origins were considered to be a joke, some meme coins have gone on to become legitimate cryptocurrencies. Examples include Dogecoin (DOGE) and Shiba Inu (SHIB).
- **Privacy coins** are cryptocurrencies that are designed to provide users with additional privacy over and above what traditional crypto coins offer. Examples include Zcash (ZEC), Dash (DASH), and PIVX (PIVX).

Advantages and Disadvantages of Using Cryptocurrency

Advantages of using cryptocurrency include, but are not limited to, the following:

- **No intermediary.** All of a person's cryptocurrency transactions are on the blockchain, and all of their cryptocurrency is in their wallet.
- **Anonymity.** A person does not have to show any identification to give somebody else cryptocurrency, like they would have to with a check or a credit card transaction.
- **Transparency.** Because all cryptocurrency transactions are recorded on the blockchain, everybody knows what is going on.
- **Low fees.** Fees such as per-check fee or a percentage fee for a credit card transaction do not apply to cryptocurrency.
- **Irreversible transactions.** This is a big advantage for sellers. People cannot dispute a cryptocurrency payment they made, and they cannot ask for a refund like they can with a credit card payment. A stop payment cannot be issued for cryptocurrency like it can for a check.
- **Worldwide use and access.** Cryptocurrency can be used anywhere where there is internet access, including places that do not accept U.S. dollars.

- **Limited tracking.** Although law enforcement is getting better at tracking cryptocurrency, tracking efforts are still limited as compared to tracking money in bank accounts.
- **No third-party seizure.** Because there is no central authority for cryptocurrency, it cannot be garnished by a third party.

However, there are also several disadvantages of using cryptocurrency. These include, but are not limited to, the following:

- **Volatility and risk.** This is the biggest disadvantage, as volatility in price can be extreme.

EXAMPLE: In early 2017, one could purchase a Bitcoin for $600. By the end of 2021, it was selling for $68,000. However, at the end of 2022, the price decreased to approximately $17,000. These kinds of fluctuations are common.

- **Hacking and theft.** Blockchain and exchanges can be hacked and crypto can be stolen.
- **Growth industry.** Because crypto is a growth industry, bugs in the software are an issue.
- **Wallets can be stolen.** It is possible for criminals to steal people's crypto wallets if they are not appropriately protected.
- **No buyer protections.** For example, if a buyer pays for an item with cryptocurrency and that item is never shipped, the buyer has no recourse.
- **No guarantee of value.** The value of cryptocurrency can decrease to zero or increase by millions. It is not guaranteed to retain a certain value.
- **No physical form.** Cryptocurrency exists solely as numbers on a computer. A person cannot hold cryptocurrency in their hand.

Crypto Tokens

Crypto tokens are a type of virtual currency that represents fungible and tradable assets or utilities that reside on their own blockchains. Crypto tokens are new and are a very niche product. They can be based on copyrighted art or give someone the use of a vacation home, a timeshare, or other assets. There are several types of crypto tokens:

- **Exchange tokens.** Exchange tokens are cryptocurrencies associated with or issued by cryptocurrency exchanges. These could be centralized (CEX) or decentralized exchanges (DEX), but both can create native tokens that are used to power their ecosystems. Examples include the Cronos.org chain token (CRO), Huobi token (HT), KuCoin Shares (KCS), and Uniswap DEX tokens (UNI).
- **Security tokens.** Security tokens are digital equivalents of traditional securities existing on a blockchain. Think of any regulated conventional financial security, such as equity shares or property rights. These can be represented on the blockchain. Examples include Spice VC, Science Ventures, and Sia Funds.
- **Wrapped tokens.** Wrapped tokens are alternate versions of a given cryptocurrency enabling its value to be ported over to another blockchain. This is usually done because of issues with the coding or security of the original blockchain. Examples include renBTC, renDOGE, and Wrapped Ether.

Blockchain

Virtual currencies are based on a technology known as blockchain. Each cryptocurrency has its own blockchain. Blockchains are lists of records held on diverse computers (nodes) that are used to record and verify data.

There are both public and private blockchains. Public blockchains are open source, meaning anybody can conduct transactions with them; no special access is needed. Bitcoin, Dogeoin, and Ethereum are examples of public blockchains.

Private blockchains are maintained on closed or private networks, which limits who can access them. For example, a bank could offer a blockchain that is only available to the bank's customers. Another use for a private blockchain is smart contracts, where only the parties to the contract have access to what is on the blockchain so the information can be secured.

Cryptocurrency goes in the original block on the blockchain, and every time there is a transaction, another block is added. Think of it like a puzzle: every time a transaction occurs, another piece is added to the puzzle. The key point is that a block cannot be changed once it is on the blockchain. That means data recorded on the blockchain is there forever. One cannot adjust a block that has already been added. To make an adjustment, one would have to do another transaction on the block. A block also cannot be deleted. A reversing transaction can be made, but the original block will remain.

Data on the blockchain is secured by using cryptography. Cryptography secures who can view and access the data. Both a public key and a private key are needed to access the blockchain. When the public key is matched to the private key, a digital signature is created, allowing another block to be added to the blockchain.

These digital keys are long, complicated strings of uppercase and lowercase letters, numbers, and special symbols that would take more than a lifetime to hack. Although there are cases where a private key has been stolen, there are none where someone was able to guess, or hack, someone else's private key.

Virtual Currency Wallets

A virtual currency wallet is needed to buy, store, and use virtual currencies. A "wallet" is a software program that stores private and public keys and interacts with the virtual currencies blockchain. The "wallet" does not store the virtual currencies or coins; it only maintains the information that allows the users to access the information for their transactions on the blockchain.

When a virtual currency transaction occurs, nothing is actually transferred. When an individual sends a virtual currency to someone, they are signing over the ownership of the Bitcoin. As described in the previous section, public and private keys are compared, and if they match, the ownership is transferred, and the transaction is recorded on the blockchain.

There are many different types of virtual currency wallets. A person could store their private key on a piece of paper, which obviously would be the safest from online hacking. But if that paper "wallet" is lost or destroyed, the private key will be gone too. A virtual wallet can be kept on a desktop computer, a server, or an external jump drive. Many people keep their virtual wallet on their mobile devices, such as cell phones or tablets.

¶ 704 BITCOIN

Bitcoin, released in 2009, was the first cryptocurrency. Today, there are thousands of different types of crypto coins on the market, and new ones are created every day. Some notable events in the history of Bitcoin are summarized on the next page.

History of Bitcoin: Highlights

- September 24, 2012: The U.S. Securities and Exchange Commission (SEC) announces an investigation of Bitcoin Savings and Trust after allegations were made that a Ponzi scheme decreased the value of Bitcoins by as much as 30 percent.
- May 2, 2013: The first Bitcoin ATM in the world debuts in San Diego, California.
- May 18, 2013: PrimeDice.com launches an online casino platform that accepts Bitcoin wagers.
- August 6, 2013: Bitcoin is ruled to be a currency by a Texas judge. The ruling was in response to a claim by the founder of Texas-based Bitcoin Savings and Trust that Bitcoins are not real money, in an attempt to sidestep SEC charges of misappropriation of funds.
- October 2, 2013: The FBI shuts down Silk Road, the infamous online drug marketplace, seizing $3.6 million of Bitcoins.
- July 2016: Researchers publish a paper showing that by November 2013, Bitcoin commerce was no longer driven by "sin" activities but instead by legitimate enterprises (https://www.researchgate.net/publication/322791983_The_evolution_of_the_Bitcoin_economy_extracting_and_analyzing_the_network_of_payment_relationships).
- June 2018: According to a study from the University of Texas in Austin, the cryptocurrency boom is driven by a motivated campaign of price manipulation, not market demand (https://www.nysscpa.org/news/publications/the-trusted-professional/article/study-suggests-cryptocurrency-boom-driven-by-manipulation-not-demand-061318).
- December 2020: NFL offensive tackle Russell Okung receives half of his $13 million NFL salary in Bitcoin (https://fortune.com/2020/12/30/russell-okung-nfl-salary-bitcoin/).
- June 2021: El Salvador announces that it will adopt bitcoin as legal tender, making it the first country to do so (https://www.cnn.com/2021/06/06/investing/bitcoin-el-salvador/index.html).
- July 2021: Wyoming is the first state in the United States to legally recognize a Decentralized Autonomous Organization (DAO), which is an entity that uses blockchain to provide a secure digital ledger to track digital interactions across the internet (https://www.prnewswire.com/news-releases/the-american-cryptofed-dao-is-legally-recognized-by-the-state-of-wyoming-as-the-first-decentralized-autonomous-organization-dao-in-the-united-states-301325384.html).
- October 2021: Texas governor Greg Abbott announces that the state is poised to be a leader in digital currencies and blockchain technology (https://www.forbes.com/sites/jasonbrett/2021/10/02/texas-poised-to-be-a-world-leader-in-bitcoin-and-blockchain/?sh=7284a328715b).

Important Terms to Know

Hard fork. A hard fork refers to a radical change to the protocol of a blockchain network that effectively results in two branches, one that follows the previous protocol and one that follows the new version. In a hard fork, holders of tokens in the original blockchain will be granted tokens in the new fork as well, but miners must choose which blockchain to continue verifying. A hard fork can occur in any blockchain, and not only Bitcoin (where hard forks have created Bitcoin Cash and Bitcoin SV, among several others, for example).

Soft fork. A soft fork is a fork in a blockchain protocol where previously valid transactions become invalid. A soft fork is backwards-compatible, as the old nodes running the old protocol will still consider new transactions valid, rather than disregarding them. For a soft fork to work, a majority of the miners powering the network will need to upgrade to the new protocol.

Airdrop. An airdrop occurs when you have free crypto coins sent to your wallet. You did not purchase or earn the coins. Airdrops are usually taxed as ordinary income.

Staking—farming. A "Proof of Stake" is a consensus technique that allows blockchain networks to use less energy while retaining a reasonable level of decentralization on the internet. This is taxed as ordinary income.

Sign messages. Sign messages, wallet signing, and digital signatures constitute a digital way to verify documents and digital messages. Sign messages is a kind of ID system to prove the ownership of Bitcoin or cryptocurrency address. Without revealing your private keys, you can prove ownership by sharing your wallet signature.

STUDY QUESTIONS

1. Airline frequent flyer miles are an example of which of the following?
- **a.** A closed virtual currency
- **b.** A single-flow virtual currency
- **c.** A convertible virtual currency
- **d.** A public virtual currency

2. In May of 2013, Bitcoins were first used in which of the following?
- **a.** Online casinos
- **b.** Money laundering
- **c.** Illegal online purchases
- **d.** Terrorist funding

3. Which of the following occurs when you have free crypto coins sent to your wallet?
- **a.** Exchange token
- **b.** Soft fork
- **c.** Hard fork
- **d.** Airdrop

¶ 705 LEGAL ISSUES ASSOCIATED WITH VIRTUAL CURRENCIES

Virtual currencies are not immune to fraud and other legal issues. For example, in November 2022, the U.S. Department of Justice (DOJ) announced that it had seized over $3 million in Bitcoin that had been stolen from the Silk Road Marketplace. At that time, it was the government's second largest seizure of cryptocurrency.

In another fraud case from 2022, a man was convicted by a federal jury of money laundering, tax evasion, and other charges related to his exchange of U.S. dollars for Bitcoin to launder more than $10 million in proceeds from his internet fraud schemes.

In the same year, FTX, once one of the largest cryptocurrency exchanges in the world, collapsed, causing the price of Bitcoin to plummet, and affecting the entire cryptocurrency industry. The DOJ, suspecting that mismanagement and fraud could have played a role in FTS's bankruptcy, called for an independent investigation into the matter.

¶ 706 INITIAL COIN OFFERINGS

Bitcoins are not the only cryptocurrency being used on the internet. There are a multitude of initial coin offerings (ICOs) being sold to investors. An ICO is a popular way to raise funds, including funds to launch a token or cryptocurrency. Many organizations are looking to profit from the popularity of cryptocurrency, and investors hope they will get rich quick with the new virtual currency.

However, there are risks associated with ICOs. They can be part of a fraud scheme. For example, on May 29, 2018, the U.S. Securities and Exchange Commission (SEC) announced it was suing Titanium Blockchain Infrastructure Services Inc., for a $21 million ICO fraud. The ICO was based on social media marketing that deceived investors with purely fictional claims (http://thehill.com/policy/technology/389786-sec-charges-ico-company-that-raised-21-million-with-fraud). And in January 2022, the SEC charged Craig Sproule and his company, Metavine Inc., and its subsidiaries Crowd Machine Inc. and Crowd Machine SEZC, with raising "more than $33 million from hundreds of investors in the United States and abroad through a fraudulent and unregistered [ICO] of digital asset securities" (www.sec.gov/files/litigation/complaints/2022/comp-pr2022-3.pdf).

According to the SEC, most ICOs should be treated as securities. On June 8, 2018, SEC Chairman Jay Clayton announced that the SEC would consider "all tokens or digital assets that were used to raise funds for a venture or company with an expectation of profit, either given by the company formed or exchangeable on a secondary market," as securities, meaning that most ICOs would fall under the definition of securities (https://cryptocoin.news/videos/breaking-news-sec-chairman-declares-all-icos-as-securities-15119/).

¶ 707 VIRTUAL CURRENCIES AND TAXES

As mentioned earlier in this chapter, for federal tax purposes, virtual currency is treated as property. According to the IRS, general tax principles applicable to property transactions apply to transactions using virtual currency. Virtual currency cannot be reported as a currency transaction, and no foreign currency gain or loss can be claimed on a U.S. tax filing.

A taxpayer who receives virtual currency as payment for goods or services must, in computing gross income, include the fair market value of the virtual currency, measured in U.S. dollars, as of the date that the virtual currency was received. See IRS Publication 525, *Taxable and Nontaxable Income*. The basis of virtual currency that a taxpayer receives as payment for goods or services is the fair market value of the virtual currency in U.S. dollars as of the date of receipt. See IRS Publication 551, *Basis of Assets.*

Currently, the IRS considers single-flow virtual currency transactions (e.g., award programs from hotels or airlines) to be taxable, and therefore taxes are due when points are awarded or exchanged for trips or other awards. However, the IRS has not pursued a tax enforcement program with respect to promotional benefits such as frequent flyer miles because of the issue of valuing and reporting the awards.

Taxpayers must choose a valuation methodology for record keeping when determining the tax basis for virtual currencies.

- First in, first out (FIFO)
- Last in, first out (LIFO)

- Specific identification (the IRS's preferred method)
- Average cost
- Highest in, first out (HIFO)

For U.S. tax purposes, transactions using virtual currency must be reported in U.S. dollars. Therefore, taxpayers are required to determine the fair market value of virtual currency in U.S. dollars as of the date of payment or receipt.

If a virtual currency is listed on an exchange and the exchange rate is established by market supply and demand, the fair market value of the virtual currency is determined by converting the virtual currency into U.S. dollars (or into another real currency which in turn can be converted into U.S. dollars) at the exchange rate, in a reasonable manner that is consistently applied.

If the fair market value of property received in exchange for virtual currency exceeds the taxpayer's adjusted basis of the virtual currency, the taxpayer has taxable gain. The taxpayer incurs a loss if the fair market value of the property received is less than the adjusted basis of the virtual currency.

See Publication 544, *Sales and Other Dispositions of Assets*, for information about the tax treatment of sales and exchanges, such as whether a loss is deductible.

The character of the gain or loss generally depends on whether the virtual currency is a capital asset in the hands of the taxpayer. A taxpayer generally realizes capital gain or loss on the sale or exchange of virtual currency that is a capital asset in the hands of the taxpayer. For example, stocks, bonds, and other investment property are generally capital assets.

A taxpayer generally realizes ordinary gain or loss on the sale or exchange of virtual currency that is not a capital asset in the hands of the taxpayer. Inventory and other property held mainly for sale to customers in a trade or business are examples of property that is not a capital asset.

See Publication 544 for more information about capital assets and the character of gain or loss.

Cryptocurrency capital gains and losses are reported on Line 7 of Form 1040, *U.S. Individual Income Tax Return*. The Digital Assets section on the form asks the taxpayer to indicate whether he or she received, sold, exchanged, gifted, or otherwise disposed of a digital asset or a financial interest in a digital asset. Crypto mining, hard forks, and interest income are reported on Form 1040, Schedule 1, *Additional Income and Adjustments to Income*.

Capital gains and losses related to cryptocurrency are reported in more detail on Form 8949, *Sales and Other Dispositions of Capital Assets*. The details of each transaction should be entered in the appropriate section of the form. Short-term capital gains and losses are reported in Part 1; long-term are reported in Part 2.

Capital gains and losses are also reported on Schedule D of the following forms: Form 1040; Form 1065, *U.S. Return of Partnership Income*; Form 1120, *U.S. Corporation Income Tax Return*; or Form 1120-S, *U.S. Income Tax Return for an S Corporation*.

Note that short-term assets are assets that have been owned for less than one year. These are taxed at ordinary income tax rates. Long-term assets, those owned for longer than one year, are taxed at capital gains tax rates. The capital gains tax rates for 2023 are shown in the following chart:

Individual 2023 Long-Term Capital Gains Tax Rates				
	Taxable Income			
Capital Gains Tax Rate	Single	Married Filing Separately	Head of Household	Married Filing Jointly
0%	$0–$44,625	$0–$44,625	$0–$59,750	$0–$89,250
15%	$44,626–$492,300	$44,626–$276,900	$59,751–$523,050	$89,251–$553,850
20%	Over $492,300	Over $276,900	Over $523,050	Over $553,850

Taxpayers will owe the 3.8 percent net investment income tax (NIIT) if they have net investment income and also have modified adjusted gross income over the following thresholds:

Filing Status	Threshold Amount
Married filing jointly	$250,000
Married filing separately	$125,000
Single	$200,000
Head of household (with qualifying person)	$200,000
Qualifying widow(er) with dependent child	$250,000

The NIIT is reported on Form 8960, *Net Investment Income Tax—Individuals, Estates, and Trusts.*

Common Questions About Virtual Currencies and Taxes

Many taxpayers ask if wash sales apply to cryptocurrency. A wash sale occurs when someone sells a security at a loss for the tax benefits but then turns around and buys the same or a similar security. Currently, wash sales apply only to securities, and cryptocurrency is not considered a security. Therefore, if a taxpayer sells a Bitcoin and then buys a Bitcoin the next day, that is considered a sale and a purchase, not a wash sale.

Another frequently asked question is whether cryptocurrency transactions can be considered Code Sec. 1031 exchanges. According to the Tax Cuts and Jobs Act of (2017), the answer is no, as Sec. 1031 exchanges are only allowed for real property. Keep in mind, however, that the TCJA has a sunset provision, and it is unclear whether Congress will decide to retain the TCJA tax cuts in the future.

Exchanging one cryptocurrency asset for another is a taxable event. When a taxpayer successfully "mines" virtual currency (e.g., uses computer resources to validate Bitcoin transactions and maintain the public Bitcoin transaction ledger), the fair market value of the virtual currency as of the date of receipt is includible in gross income. See IRS Publication 525 for more information on taxable income.

If a taxpayer's "mining" of virtual currency constitutes a trade or business, and the "mining" activity is not undertaken by the taxpayer as an employee, the net earnings from self-employment (generally, gross income derived from carrying on a trade or business less allowable deductions) resulting from those activities constitute self-employment income and are subject to the self-employment tax. Self-employment income includes all gross income derived by an individual from any trade or business carried on by the individual as other than an employee.

Consequently, the fair market value of virtual currency received for services performed as an independent contractor, measured in U.S. dollars as of the date of receipt, constitutes self-employment income and is subject to the self-employment tax. Net earnings from self-employment income are reported on Form 1040, Schedule SE, *Self-Employment Tax.*

When compensating employees, the medium in which remuneration for services is paid is immaterial to the determination of whether the remuneration constitutes wages for employment tax purposes. The fair market value of virtual currency paid as wages is subject to federal income tax withholding, Federal Insurance Contributions Act (FICA) tax, and Federal Unemployment Tax Act (FUTA) tax and must be reported on Form W-2, *Wage and Tax Statement*.

A payment made using virtual currency is subject to information reporting to the same extent as any other payment made in property. For example, a person who in the course of a trade or business makes a payment of fixed and determinable income using virtual currency with a value of $600 or more to a U.S. non-exempt recipient in a taxable year is required to report the payment to the IRS and to the payee on Form 1099. Examples of payments of fixed and determinable income include rent, salaries, wages, premiums, annuities, and compensation.

A person, or business, who in the course of a trade or business makes a payment of $600 or more in a taxable year to an independent contractor for the performance of services is required to report that payment to the IRS and to the payee on Form 1099-MISC, *Miscellaneous Income*. Payments of virtual currency required to be reported on Form 1099-MISC should be reported using the fair market value of the virtual currency in U.S. dollars as of the date of payment. The payment recipient may have income even if the recipient does not receive a Form 1099-MISC.

Payments made using virtual currency are subject to backup withholding to the same extent as other payments made in property. Therefore, payors making reportable payments using virtual currency must solicit a taxpayer identification number (TIN) from the payee. The payor must backup withhold from the payment if a TIN is not obtained prior to payment or if the payor receives notification from the IRS that backup withholding is required.

Form 1099-NEC, *Nonemployee Compensation*, is used for paying workers who are not classified as employees, such as gig workers or independent contractors. Any type of nonemployee compensation, including cryptocurrency, must be reported on the form, as well as any taxes withheld. Form 1099-K, *Payment Card and Third-Party Network Transactions*, is used by entities such as credit card companies and financial services companies to report payments made to third parties. Starting in 2023, third-party payment platforms must report transactions totaling $600 or more to the IRS, regardless of the number of transactions they made. The threshold was previously $20,000.

Penalties

Taxpayers may be subject to penalties for failure to comply with tax laws. For example, underpayments attributable to virtual currency transactions may be subject to penalties, such as accuracy-related penalties under Code Sec. 6662. In addition, the failure to timely or correctly report virtual currency transactions when required to do so may be subject to information reporting penalties under Code Secs. 6721 and 6722.

STUDY QUESTIONS

4. The IRS considers virtual currencies to be which of the following?

a. Nontaxable

b. Property

c. Currency

d. Securities

5. Even though the IRS does not enforce compliance, it considers transactions in which of the following types of virtual currencies to be taxable?

a. Closed virtual currencies

b. Single-flow virtual currencies

c. Convertible virtual currencies

d. Cryptocurrencies

6. Which of the following valuation methodologies is preferred by the IRS for reporting gains or losses on virtual currencies?

a. LIFO

b. FIFO

c. Specific identification

d. Average cost

MODULE 2: TAX DEVELOPMENTS AND UPDATES—Chapter 8: The Inflation Reduction Act: What the IRS Is Doing with $80 Billion

¶ 801 WELCOME

This chapter discusses the Inflation Reduction Act funding for the IRS, which offers a transformational opportunity for the future of tax administration. This once-in-a-generation investment, totaling approximately $80 billion in funding over the next decade, is designed to provide the resources the IRS needs to dramatically change the way it serves taxpayers; harness the power of contemporary technology; invest in and grow its public servants with new tools, skills, and capabilities; and address the drivers of the tax gap.

¶ 802 LEARNING OBJECTIVES

Upon completion of this chapter, you will be able to:

- Describe the IRS Inflation Reduction Act's transformational opportunities for future tax administration
- Recognize what is true and not true about the $80 billion expenditure
- Identify resources to seamlessly help taxpayers and paid preparers

¶ 803 INTRODUCTION

Signed into law by President Joe Biden on August 16, 2022, the Inflation Reduction Act of 2022 (IRA) focuses on curbing inflation, lowering prescription drug prices, and investing in domestic energy production, among other provisions. It also provides for $80 billion in funding to the IRS over the next decade for increased tax enforcement, operations support, business system modernization, and taxpayer services.

> **NOTE:** A tentative deal to raise the debt ceiling limit includes up to $21.4 billion of IRS budget cuts, slashing part of the nearly $80 billion in agency funding from the IRA.

The IRS has been significantly underfunded over the past decade, with a budget reduction of 22 percent in real terms from 2010 to 2021, leaving the agency with outdated technology and a shrinking workforce in the face of an increasingly complex tax environment where it must administer the U.S. tax code. That lack of investment led to low levels of service; the IRS simply did not have the manpower to provide a high-quality experience to taxpayers.

The IRA's funding for the IRS provides a historic opportunity to transform both the administration of the tax system and the services provided to taxpayers. These resources will also ensure the fairness of the tax system by addressing the tax gap. The tax gap is the difference between taxes due and taxes paid, and most recently that gap was estimated to be $496 billion.

Shortly after the IRA's enactment, the Department of the Treasury and the IRS initiated an effort to develop a strategic operating plan, identifying the highest priority opportunities to deliver transformational changes for taxpayers. The planning process leveraged prior IRS planning efforts, including the Taxpayer First Act Report to Congress, new thinking around best practices and available technology capabilities, and current and past input from a wide range of stakeholders in tax administration.

The IRS released its "Inflation Reduction Act Strategic Operating Plan," detailing how it plans to use the IRA funding to transform its services, on April 6, 2023. The full text of the SOP is available at www.irs.gov/pub/irs-pdf/p3744.pdf.

¶ 804 THE IRS STRATEGIC OPERATING PLAN

The IRS SOP is a comprehensive plan that will impact fiscal years 2023 through 2031. The plan outlines how the IRS will deploy the IRA funding to better serve taxpayers, tax professionals, and the broader tax ecosystem. It details how the IRS will improve the taxpayer experience through better customer service, clearer guidance on how to correctly file taxes, increased options for filing electronically, and robust online accounts to take care of business quickly and independently. Although it will take years to fully implement, there will be some immediate accomplishments.

Congress gave the IRS the responsibility to administer—as effectively and efficiently as possible—more than 150 credits, deductions, and other tax preferences in the new tax law, often referred to as "incentives" throughout the SOP.

We know that many factors drive unintentional noncompliance and prevent taxpayers from claiming incentives for which they are eligible. So, the IRS will be making significant improvements in the services it provides and tailor its compliance work in new ways. Taxpayers will have the tools, information, and assistance needed to get their tax filings right, both in paying what they owe and claiming the incentives for which they are eligible.

Employees will likewise have the data analytics and tools to ensure compliance and fairness in the tax system. The work to improve service must also be coupled with efforts to improve compliance by those who choose not to meet their obligations. The IRA acknowledges that an adequately funded federal tax administration will generate significant revenue for the country.

The IRS will also devote resources to enforcing tax laws against taxpayers who attempt to avoid paying their tax obligations, and all compliance efforts will be consistent with the Secretary of the Treasury's August 10, 2022, directive that IRA resources are not used to increase the share of small businesses or households earning $400,000 or less that are audited relative to historical levels.

The money will be used for additional resources provided under the IRA to address high-dollar noncompliance issues such as those related to complex partnership structures, large corporations, and high-income individuals.

The Congressional Budget Office estimates that the additional $80 billion provided to the IRS by the IRA will increase federal revenue by more than $180 billion in the decade ahead, considering only direct enforcement revenue based on additional staffing.

To improve taxpayer services and compliance, the IRS must deliver technology capabilities at a faster pace and on a bigger scale than ever before. This investment in new technology, building on contemporary foundational platforms with modern architectures designed to meet their future needs, will require careful coordination between delivering new capabilities and modernizing or retiring legacy platforms.

The IRS will also work to attract and retain the best talent as it transitions to being a modern, digitally capable, customer-centric agency. For example, there is a huge need for data scientists because the technology exists to do work faster, more effectively, and more efficiently using the knowledge of such professionals. Therefore, as the IRS develops and supports a workforce that has modern tools to do its job effectively, broad knowledge of complex tax issues, and analytical capabilities to work efficiently and effectively, the organizational culture should deliver much more effectively.

The SOP envisions a modernized IRS that is focused on the customer experience, prefers digital to manual processes, and prioritizes compliance efforts. The five components of the SOP are as follows:

- Part I: Executive Summary
- Part II: Objectives and Initiatives
- Part III: Managing the Transformation
- Part IV: Case Study
- Part V: Context and Background

Part I: Executive Summary

The IRS's SOP will deliver the following:

- IRA Transformation Vision
  — "We will make it easier for taxpayers to meet their tax responsibilities and receive tax incentives for which they are eligible. We will adopt a customer-centric approach that dedicates more resources to helping taxpayers get it right the first time, while addressing issues in the simplest ways appropriate. We will address noncompliance, using data and analytics to expand enforcement in certain segments. We will become an employer of choice across government and industry. These changes will enable us to serve all taxpayers more equitably and in the ways they want to be served."
- IRA Transformation Objectives
  — Dramatically improve services to help taxpayers meet their obligations and receive the tax incentives for which they are eligible.
  — Quickly resolve taxpayer issues when they arise.
  — Focus expanded enforcement on taxpayers with complex tax filings and high-dollar noncompliance to address the tax gap.
  — Deliver cutting-edge technology, data, and analytics to operate more effectively.
  — Attract, retain, and empower a highly skilled, diverse workforce and develop a culture that is better equipped to deliver results for taxpayers.
- IRA Transformation Outcomes
  — World-class service experience
  — Digital-first organization
  — Improved take-up of tax incentives by eligible taxpayers
  — Effective enforcement
  — Employer of choice within government and industry

NOTE: Actions the IRS has already taken to assist taxpayers include the hiring of more than 5,000 new customer service representatives to process correspondence and answer phone inquiries. It has also started the process of hiring approximately 650 new employees to work in taxpayer assistance centers across the country.

The SOP will be the guide that IRS leadership and project managers turn to when making decisions. Detailed planning and execution efforts will be coordinated by the IRS Transformation and Strategy Office (TSO).

Part II: Objectives and Initiatives

Each of the IRS's five transformation objectives includes specific initiatives designed to achieve the objective. There are 42 initiatives in total. For each initiative, the SOP includes the following sections: Where We Are Heading, What Success Would Look Like, Key Projects, and, if relevant, specific Milestones by fiscal year. The objectives and initiatives in Part II of the SOP are listed below.

Objective #1: Dramatically improve services to help taxpayers meet their obligations and receive the tax incentives for which they are eligible.

- Initiative 1.1: Improve the availability and accessibility of customer service:
  - — Taxpayers will be able to receive on-demand customer service or schedule service ahead of time.
- Initiative 1.2: Expand digital services and digitalization:
  - — Taxpayers will be able to file documents securely and exchange correspondence electronically.
- Initiative 1.3: Ensure employees have the right tools:
  - — Employees will have the right tools and information to quickly and effectively meet the needs of taxpayers.

NOTE: The IRS currently has hundreds of systems and tools that employees access. The plan is to provide a more streamlined, holistic view so that an employee does not have to access multiple platforms to help answer a taxpayer's question. Doing so will involve the use of chat bots, live assisters, online self-service experiences, etc.

- Initiative 1.4: Improve self-service options:
  - — Taxpayers will have access to secure online accounts where they can view their account and profile information, make changes, interact with the IRS, and manage preferences for payments, refunds, and communications.
- Initiative 1.5: Explore direct file:
  - — The IRS will explore providing taxpayers the option to file certain tax returns directly with the IRS online.
- Initiative 1.6: Enable taxpayers to access their data:
  - — Taxpayers will be able to access, download, and seamlessly share their tax data and IRS history.
- Initiative 1.7: Provide earlier legal certainty:
  - — Taxpayers will have greater upfront clarity and certainty additional guidance on tax issues.
- Initiative 1.8: Deliver proactive alerts:
  - — Taxpayers will be able to receive alerts to help them meet filing and payment obligations, understand opportunities to claim certain incentives, and learn about life changes that could impact their taxes.

NOTE: A key project associated with Initiative 1.8 includes building the capability for taxpayers to inform the IRS of major life changes and receive educational content to enable taxpayers to update their life changes through their channels of choice, allowing the IRS to inform them of potential impacts to tax obligations, credits, and deductions.

- Initiative 1.9: Help taxpayers understand and claim appropriate credits and deductions:
  - — Taxpayers, including individuals and small businesses, will receive education and assistance in claiming available incentives.
- Initiative 1.10: Make payments easy:
  - — Taxpayers will be able to make payments more easily and seamlessly through all service channels.
- Initiative 1.11: Build status-tracking tools for taxpayers:
  - — Taxpayers will be able to use new status-tracking tools to see real-time status updates, next steps, and estimated time to process documents and resolve issues.
- Initiative 1.12: Streamline multichannel customer assistance:
  - — Taxpayers will be able to quickly, securely, and accessibly get the help they need; resolve more issues in a single contact; and experience minimal delays during interactions with the IRS.

Objective #2: Quickly resolve taxpayer issues when they arise.

- Initiative 2.1: Identify issues during filing:
  - — The IRS will send taxpayer notifications about potential issues as they file returns to help them correct errors and claim credits and deductions.

NOTE: A key project associated with Initiative 2.1 includes enhancing systemic checks for return completeness and consistency to identify issues at the point of filing such as math errors, missing forms, or missing income reported by third parties to reduce the need to file amended returns, for example.

- Initiative 2.2: Deliver early and appropriate treatments for issues:
  - — The IRS will provide taxpayers with timely and tailored post-filing treatments to resolve issues and omissions on their tax returns.
- Initiative 2.3: Develop taxpayer-centric notices:
  - — The IRS will send taxpayers notices they can understand, delivered in ways they prefer, with clear explanations of issues and steps to resolution.
- Initiative 2.4: Expand tax certainty and issue resolution programs:
  - — Taxpayers will be able to resolve potential compliance issues up front through expanded pre-filing and tax certainty programs.
- Initiative 2.5: Offer proactive debt resolutions:
  - — The IRS will proactively offer taxpayers appropriate options for past-due payment resolution.

NOTE: A key project associated with Initiative 2.5 includes creating processes for real-time identification of taxpayers who miss payments and contacting them through the channel of their choice (e.g., phone, email, text, or letter).

- Initiative 2.6: Expand engagement with non-filers:
  - — The IRS will provide early, tailored outreach to taxpayers who do not file on time.

- Initiative 2.7: Use improved data and analytics to tailor timely collections contacts:
  - The IRS will provide early, tailored contacts to all taxpayers with past-due balances and will only escalate to more intensive treatments when appropriate.

Objective #3: Focus expanded enforcement on taxpayers with complex tax filings and high-dollar noncompliance to address the tax gap.

- Initiative 3.1: Employ centralized, analytics-driven, risk-based methods to aid in the selection of compliance cases:
  - The IRS will use improved analytics to aid in the selection of cases predicted to be at risk of noncompliance, choosing enforcement treatments that maximize opportunities to improve and sustain taxpayer compliance while ensuring fairness in selection.
- Initiative 3.2: Expand enforcement for large corporations:
  - The IRS will increase enforcement activities to help ensure tax compliance for large corporate taxpayers.
- Initiative 3.3: Expand enforcement for large partnerships:
  - The IRS will increase enforcement activities to help ensure tax compliance for large partnerships.
- Initiative 3.4: Expand enforcement for high-income and high-wealth individuals:
  - The IRS will increase enforcement activities to help ensure tax compliance of high-income and high-wealth individuals.
- Initiative 3.5: Expand enforcement in areas where audit coverage has declined to levels that erode voluntary compliance:
  - The IRS will increase enforcement activities in other key areas where audit coverage has declined while complying with Treasury's directive not to increase audit rates relative to historical levels for small businesses and households earning $400,000 per year or less.
- Initiative 3.6: Pursue appropriate enforcement for complex, high-risk, and emerging issues:
  - The IRS will enhance detection of noncompliance and increase enforcement activities for complex, high-risk, and novel emerging issues, including digital assets, listed transactions, and certain international issues.
- Initiative 3.7: Promote fairness in enforcement activities:
  - The IRS will help promote fairness for all taxpayers by addressing noncompliance appropriately in a balanced manner.

NOTE: Regarding Objective #3, the IRS aims to better leverage technology, data analytics, and centralized operations to improve enforcement and risk identification.

Objective #4: Deliver cutting-edge technology, data, and analytics to operate more effectively.

- Initiative 4.1: Transform core account data and processing:
  - The IRS will modernize the systems used to access and process taxpayer data.

- Initiative 4.2: Accelerate technology delivery:
  - — The IRS will deliver faster and better results by accelerating design, development, and delivery of user-centered technology by shifting to a "product and platform" operating model that incorporates business and technology perspectives.
- Initiative 4.3: Improve technology operations:
  - — The IRS will enhance core technology processes and platforms to support the delivery of expanded capabilities for taxpayers and employees.
- Initiative 4.4: Continue to ensure data security:
  - — The IRS will continue to protect taxpayer data and IRS systems from cyber threats as it transforms.
- Initiative 4.5: Maximize data utility:
  - — The IRS will improve the storage and management of data to support improved taxpayer services and enforcement.
- Initiative 4.6: Apply enhanced analytics capabilities to improve tax administration:
  - — IRS employees will use data and insights to enhance delivery of tax administration and improve the taxpayer experience.
- Initiative 4.7: Strategically use data to improve tax administration:
  - — The IRS will use enhanced data and explore additional innovative analytic techniques to improve strategic planning, decision making, and compliance measurement.
- Initiative 4.8: Partner to expand insights:
  - — The IRS will engage with external partners to develop new insights to generate value for taxpayers and policymakers.

COMMENT: Regarding Objective #4, the IRS plans to retire legacy applications and adopt modern systems. Currently, IRS employees and taxpayers use more than 600 applications, many of which are more than 20 years old. Most of the applications are custom-built and loosely integrated, requiring employees to use multiple systems for similar tasks.

Objective #5: Attract, retain, and empower a highly skilled, diverse workforce and develop a culture that is better equipped to deliver results for taxpayers.

- Initiative 5.1: Redesign hiring and onboarding:
  - — The IRS will implement fast, streamlined hiring processes that address challenges known today, use data to match capabilities to the right jobs, and deliver more effective onboarding programs.
- Initiative 5.2: Attract a talented and diverse workforce:
  - — The IRS will build a new talent pipeline and attract a workforce that reflects the diversity of the people it serves.
- Initiative 5.3: Improve the employee experience:
  - — The IRS will improve the employee experience by offering more flexibility, building a more collaborative team culture, and having better equipped personnel.

- Initiative 5.4: Help employees grow and develop:
  — The IRS will deliver growth and learning opportunities by developing attractive career pathways for all employees, integrating training and skill-building, and ensuring it has better equipped managers to lead high-performing talent.
- Initiative 5.5: Develop a data-savvy workforce:
  — The IRS will create hiring and training programs to build a data-savvy workforce that uses the improved data environment to serve taxpayers and meet mission goals more effectively.
- Initiativc 5.6: Elevate workforce planning strategy:
  — The IRS will leverage workforce planning best practices to forecast and meet hiring demand more effectively to avoid disruption and satisfy business needs.
- Initiative 5.7: Improve organizational structures and governance:
  — The IRS will implement new organizational structures and distribute transparent decision processes to support more collaborative, effective, and efficient tax administration.
- Initiative 5.8: Build a culture of service and continuous improvement:
  — The IRS will build a customer-centric culture by empowering employees and leaders to put the customer first and rewarding outstanding service.

Part III: Managing the Transformation

The IRS obviously faces many challenges in making its SOP vision a reality and delivering on its 42 initiatives. The work requires collaborating across the organization and engaging in disciplined and transparent accountability.

To manage this transformation, the IRS created a new division called the Transformation and Strategy Office (TSO), headed by the Chief Transformation and Strategy Officer (CTSO), who reports directly to the Commissioner of the IRS. Faced with the daunting task of transforming the IRS, for example, the TSO must coordinate efforts and drive the progress across all 42 initiatives, setting key performance indicators and facilitating problem solving, including risk identification and response.

The TSO plans to update the SOP annually considering progress made and lessons learned. Its actions will be made available to the public.

> **NOTE:** The SOP includes a High-Level Roadmap listing its initial target milestones over the next five years. The milestones are organized into two timeframes: FY 2023–FY 2024 and FY 2025–FY 2028.

According to its SOP, the IRS expects to allocate the $80 billion in IRA funding to the SOP transformation objectives as shown in the following chart:

Estimated Allocation of Funds	
Objective 1: Dramatically improve services to help taxpayers meet their obligations and receive the tax incentives for which they are eligible	$4.3 billion
Objective 2: Quickly resolve taxpayer issues when they arise.	$3.2 billion
Objective 3: Focus expanded enforcement on taxpayers with complex tax filings and high-dollar noncompliance to address the tax gap.	$47.4 billion
Objective 4: Deliver cutting-edge technology, data, and analytics to operate more effectively.	$12.4 billion

Estimated Allocation of Funds	
Objective 5: Attract, retain, and empower a highly skilled, diverse workforce and develop a culture that is better equipped to deliver results for taxpayers.	$8.2 billion
Energy Security	$3.9 billion

The SOP outlines how the IRS will transform to significantly improve service for the American taxpayer. However, many other stakeholders will be affected by the plan. The SOP impacts all people who are served by the IRS, including individuals; families; businesses, both large and small; charities and other tax-exempt organizations; international taxpayers; federal, state, and local governments; tribal nations; tax professionals; and others who serve taxpayers.

Part IV: Case Study

This section of the SOP explains how the IRS is working to implement the IRA's "approximately 20 new or revised energy security and clean energy-related tax incentives, along with several new cross-cutting provisions that impact the administration of multiple incentives." According to the IRS, this work will require significant investments.

Part V: Context and Background

This section includes a chart aligning the IRA's five transformation objectives with Goals 1, 2, 3, and 5 of the U.S. Treasury's Strategic Plan. It also discusses the context and trends that shaped the development of the SOP.

STUDY QUESTIONS

1. In what year did Congress enact the Inflation Reduction Act?

a. 2020

b. 2021

c. 2022

d. 2023

2. Based on the IRS's Strategic Operating Plan, the IRS will deliver each of the following, ***except?***

a. IRA Transformation Vision

b. IRA Transformation Mission

c. IRA Transformation Objectives

d. IRA Transformation Outcome

3. Which of the following identifies one of the initiatives related to dramatically improving services to help taxpayers meet their obligations and receive the tax incentives for which they are eligible?

a. Improve the availability and accessibility of customer service.

b. Expand enforcement for large corporations.

c. Deliver early and appropriate treatments for issues.

d. Expand tax certainty and issue resolution programs.

4. Which of the following identifies one of the ways the IRS is planning to expand enforcement on taxpayers with complex tax filings and high-dollar noncompliance to address the tax gap?

a. Transform core account data and processing.

b. Attract a talented and diverse workforce.

c. Improve the availability and accessibility of customer service.

d. Expand enforcement for high-income and high-wealth individuals.

5. Which of the following identifies one of the IRS initiatives for attracting, retaining, and empowering a highly skilled, diverse workforce?

a. Transform core account data and processing.

b. Expand tax certainty and issue resolution programs.

c. Develop a data-savvy workforce.

d. Expand enforcement of partnerships.

6. Which of the following objectives has the most funds allocated to it?

a. Quickly resolve taxpayer issues when they arise.

b. Focus expanded enforcement on taxpayers with complex tax filings and high-dollar noncompliance to address the tax gap.

c. Deliver cutting-edge technology, data, and analytics to operate more effectively.

d. Attract, retain, and empower a highly skilled, diverse workforce.

¶ 805 PROGRESS TOWARD SOP OBJECTIVES

On July 14, 2023, the IRS issued a news release that gives an update on its progress in implementing its SOP objectives. The IRS states it has delivered dramatically improved service for filing season 2023, including the following achievements:

- Achieved 87 percent level of service
- Answered three million more calls
- Reduced phone wait times from 38 minutes to three minutes
- Served 140,000 more taxpayers in-person
- Digitized eighty times more returns than in 2022
- Cleared backlog of unprocessed 2022 individual tax returns with no errors
- Launched two new digital tools
- Enabled new direct-deposit refund option for amended returns

NOTE: The full text of the IRS News Release, IR-2023-26, is available at https://www.irs.gov/newsroom/building-on-filing-season-2023-success-irs-continues-to-improve-service-pursue-high-income-individuals-evading-taxes-modernize-technology.

To improve taxpayer service and help taxpayers "get it right the first time," the IRS is implementing community assistance visits designed to give taxpayers from underserved areas an opportunity to meet in-person with IRS customer service representatives. The first of such events was held in June 2023 in Paris, Texas, in a joint effort with the United Way, and seven additional locations for community assistance visits have been chosen.

In addition, the IRS has opened or reopened 35 Taxpayer Assistance Centers (TACs). The new centers include two in Puerto Rico and one in Greenville, Mississippi.

Online Accounts

The IRS is working to ensure taxpayers' online accounts offer the same functionality they have come to expect from their online banking accounts. Within the next five years, it plans to offer taxpayers the ability to:

- File returns securely,
- Respond to notices online, and
- Access and download data and account history.

IRS projects are underway to provide the following services for individual, tax professional, and business online accounts. (Note that some services are already available.)

Individual accounts:

- Enhanced capabilities
- Secure messaging, live chat, and virtual assistant
- Bank account validation (will launch by end of September 2023)
- Virtual assistant (available since May 2023)
- Live chat (available since May 2023)

Tax professional accounts:

- Enhanced capabilities
- Account authorization management (will launch by end of September 2023)
- Payment viewing (will launch by end of September 2023)
- Live chat (will be available FY24)
- Secure two-way messaging (will be available FY24)

Also, Business Online Accounts (BOAs) will be launched, enabling businesses to:

- View outstanding businesses
- Make payments online
- Conduct a business tax check

NOTE: According to the news release, BOAs will be available for sole proprietors by the end of September 2023.

IRS.gov Improvements

The IRS notes that the following improvements to its website are scheduled to be completed by filing season 2024:

- Ability to access and find information
- Home page updates
- Filing season content updates
- More intuitive global site navigation

Application-to-Application Launch for Form 1099 Filing

This IRS initiative will allow bulk filers, third-party transmitters, and software developers to:

- Transmit from their systems to the IRS Information Return Intake System (IRIS)
- Transmit hundreds of thousands of Forms 1099 at once via the new platform

Although this tool launched in January 2023, its features continue to be expanded and improved upon.

Responding to Notices Online

The IRS has already achieved some of its goals in this area. Currently, taxpayers can respond online to 10 of the most common notices, such as notices for the earned income credit and health insurance credits. The ability to respond online rather than by mail saves taxpayers both time and money. The IRS expects that by the middle of August 2023, taxpayers will be able to respond online to more than 53 other IRS notices and letters.

Submission of Mobile-Friendly Forms

According to the IRS news release, for filing season 2024, taxpayers will be able to submit the following forms in a mobile-friendly format:

- Forms 941-X, 943-X, 945-X
- Forms 4626, 7203, 7205, 7207, 7208, 7210, 8332, 8985, 8986
- Form 1116 Schedule B and Form 1116 Schedule C
- Form 1118 Schedule L
- Form 1120-S Schedule B1
- Form 8936 Schedule A

The IRS stressed that it is important to offer mobile-friendly forms because 15 percent of Americans rely only on their mobile phones for Internet access.

Ensuring High-Income Taxpayers Pay Taxes Owed

The IRS is making delinquent millionaire taxpayers pay their fair share, noting it has recovered $38 million over the past several months by closing 175 delinquent tax cases involving high-income taxpayers. It plans to continue to aggressively pursue these delinquencies using the resources it received from the Inflation Reduction Act.

In addition, its Criminal Investigation group has closed many cases in which high-income taxpayers were sentenced for crimes like money laundering, tax evasion, and filing false tax returns. It also identified wealthy individuals hoping to avoid paying tax through fraudulent activity such as a high-dollar scheme in Puerto Rico and pension arrangements in Malta.

Modernizing Technology

The IRS has also made inroads in replacing its out-of-date technology with modern equipment and systems. For example, it is currently replacing old mail-sorting machines with newer versions that will allow it to process paper tax returns and deliver refunds more quickly. To process large volumes of incoming paper more efficiently, the agency is also replacing hundreds of old scanners with newer models.

Its digitization efforts are also well underway. The IRS states that as of the filing season, it had scanned 480,000 forms, and in the three months since, it scanned over 250,000 more. Regarding its efforts in all these areas, the IRS notes that it "is continuing to build on this progress focusing on critical work across the agency."

CPE NOTE: When you have completed your study and review of chapters 5-8, which comprise Module 2, you may wish to take the Final Exam for this Module. Go to **cchcpelink.com/printcpe** to take this Final Exam online.

¶ 10,100 Answers to Study Questions

¶ 10,101 MODULE 1—CHAPTER 1

1. a. *Incorrect.* The SECURE 2.0 Act was not even passed until 2022 and has no retroactive provisions.

b. *Incorrect.* Most SECURE Act provisions were effective for tax years beginning January 1, 2020.

c. *Correct.* **Most SECURE 2.0 Act provisions are effective for tax years beginning January 1, 2023.**

d. *Incorrect.* Most of the SECURE 2.0 Act provisions are applicable for tax years that begin prior to January 1, 2024.

2. a. *Incorrect.* The combined amount is greater than $7,500.

b. *Incorrect.* This is the maximum elective deferral amount for individuals under age 50.

c. *Incorrect.* This is the combined amount for those between the ages of 50 and 59.

d. *Correct.* **Participants who are between the ages of 60 and 63 may contribute a maximum of $32,500 to an employer-sponsored 401(k) plan.**

3. a. *Incorrect.* The saver's credit is effective after 2026.

b. *Correct.* **Starting in 2027, taxpayers earning between $41,000 and $71,000 for married, filing joint taxpayers (and between $20,500 and $35,500 for single taxpayers) will be eligible for a federal retirement saver's match.**

c. *Incorrect.* The saver's match will already be effective in 2030.

d. *Incorrect.* The effective date for the saver's match occurs prior to 2033.

4. a. *Incorrect.* This is the 401(k)-plan elective deferral limit for 2023.

b. *Incorrect.* This is the maximum amount a 60-year-old may contribute to a 401(k) plan in 2023.

c. *Correct.* **No more than $35,000 in a 529 plan may be rolled over to a Roth IRA during a beneficiary's lifetime.**

d. *Incorrect.* The maximum amount that may be rolled over is less than $40,000.

5. a. *Incorrect.* Employers have more time than this to amend their plan documents.

b. *Incorrect.* Prior to the adoption of the SECURE 2.0 Act, the deadline was January 1, 2022.

c. *Incorrect.* The date by which employers must amend their plans to comply with these laws is not January 1, 2023.

d. *Correct.* **Employers have until the end of the first plan year beginning on or after January 1, 2025, to amend their plans to comply with these laws.**

6. a. *Correct.* **Taxpayers age 70½ or older may make charitable contributions directly from an IRA without being required to include such amounts in taxable income so long as such amounts do not exceed $100,000 per year.**

b. *Incorrect.* The maximum charitable contribution amount that can be made tax-free from an IRA is not $125,000.

c. ***Incorrect.*** $200,000 is not the amount shielded from taxation in this context.

d. ***Incorrect.*** The tax-favored amount is less than $250,000.

¶ 10,102 MODULE 1—CHAPTER 2

1. a. ***Correct.*** **The general rule is that taxpayers can choose which method to use.**

b. ***Incorrect.*** There are two ways to calculate the deduction.

c. ***Incorrect.*** The standard mileage rate method may not be used by those operating five or more vehicles at the same time.

d. ***Incorrect.*** Parking and tolls are separately deductible and are not factored into the standard mileage rate.

2. a. ***Incorrect.*** The amount Regina may deduct is higher than $7,320.

b. ***Correct.*** **Regina may take a deduction in the amount of $12,120 (which is 60 percent of $20,200).**

c. ***Incorrect.*** The capped amount for Regina is not $20,200.

d. ***Incorrect.*** The amount that Regina may deduct in year 1 is less than $72,000.

3. a. ***Incorrect.*** This was the standard mileage rate for 2018.

b. ***Incorrect.*** In 2020, this was the applicable rate.

c. ***Incorrect.*** The applicable rate for the second half of 2022 was 62.5 cents per mile.

d. ***Correct.*** **The standard mileage rate for 2023 is 65.5 cents per mile.**

4. a. ***Incorrect.*** Medical purpose driving includes driving to pharmacies.

b. ***Incorrect.*** The cost of driving for medical purposes may be based on the total of actual expenses incurred, but this is not the only option for calculating deductible expenses for medical driving.

c. ***Incorrect.*** If a taxpayer itemizes deductions, total medical expenses must exceed 7.5 percent of adjusted gross income to be deductible.

d. ***Correct.*** **The standard rate for 2023 is 22 cents per mile.**

5. a. ***Incorrect.*** The maximum amount exceeds $2,500.

b. ***Incorrect.*** $5,000 is not the amount of the credit.

c. ***Correct.*** **The maximum credit amount for 2023 is $7,500.**

d. ***Incorrect.*** The maximum amount of the credit is less than $10,000.

6. a. ***Incorrect.*** The SALT cap is more than $7,500.

b. ***Correct.*** **The SALT cap is $10,000.**

c. ***Incorrect.*** $12,500 is not the amount of the SALT cap.

d. ***Incorrect.*** The cap is less than $15,000.

¶ 10,103 MODULE 1—CHAPTER 3

1. a. *Incorrect.* The business factor is one of the five domicile factors. For this factor, it's important to assess what you do, not just where you do it.

b. *Correct.* **Forwarding address is not one of the five domicile factors presented. Instead, the five domicile factors include home, business, time, near and dear, and family.**

c. *Incorrect.* "Near and dear items" is one of the five domicile factors. Another one of the five domicile factors is the family factor.

d. *Incorrect.* The time factor is one of the five domicile factors. It's important to note that this does not relate to the 183-day test.

2. a. *Incorrect.* California is not sourced to the employer's home state. Instead, California is sourced to the employee's home state. A state that is sourced to the employer's home state is New York.

b. *Correct.* **Mississippi is sourced to the employer's home state. Another state that is sourced to the employer's home state is Georgia.**

c. *Incorrect.* Oregon is not sourced to the employer's home state. Instead, a state that is sourced to the employer's home state is Rhode Island.

d. *Incorrect.* Minnesota is not sourced to the employer's home state. Instead, Minnesota is sourced to the employee's home state.

3. a. *Correct.* **Wisconsin is sourced to the employee's home state. Another state that is sourced to the employee's home state is North Carolina.**

b. *Incorrect.* New York is not sourced to the employee's home state. Instead, New York is a state that is sourced to the employer's home state.

c. *Incorrect.* Rhode Island is not sourced to the employee's home state. Another state that was sourced to the employer's home state is Nebraska (until July 30, 2021).

d. *Incorrect.* Mississippi is not sourced to the employee's home state. Instead, Mississippi is a state that is sourced to the employer's home state.

4. a. *Correct.* **Pennsylvania is among the states that have this rule. In general, if the employee works from home for their own convenience, broadly defined, the workdays at home will be treated as days worked at the assigned work location if that is one of the six states for nonresident income allocation and withholding purposes.**

b. *Incorrect.* Florida is not one of the six states with a "convenience rule." Instead, one of the six states to have this rule is New York.

c. *Incorrect.* Hawaii is not one of the six states with a "convenience rule." Employers need to be careful about nexus and convenience rule issues when employees are no longer required to work from home.

d. *Incorrect.* Missouri is not one of the six states with a "convenience rule." Instead, one of the six states to have this rule is Connecticut.

5. a. *Incorrect.* Income/loss from real property qualifies as income from in-state sources. It's important to note that double taxation is possible for dual residents.

b. *Correct.* **Income from in-state sources includes wages for services performed in-state, income/loss from real property, and income/loss from in-state business.**

c. *Incorrect.* Wages for services performed in-state qualify as income from in-state sources. Note that not all income has a source.

d. *Incorrect.* Income/loss from in-state business qualifies as income from in-state sources. Also, it's important to note that states generally allow their residents a credit for taxes paid to other states.

6. a. *Incorrect.* This is not the term used for this type of agreement. Note that this type of agreement is not applicable to income earned in a third state that is not party to the agreement.

b. *Correct.* **However, reciprocal tax agreements typically exist only between neighboring states, and not all neighboring states have them.**

c. *Incorrect.* This is not the term used for this type of agreement. Note that this is applicable to local taxing jurisdictions.

d. *Incorrect.* This is not the term used for this type of agreement. Note that there are several considerations for employers with telecommuters. One of these is unemployment insurance.

¶ 10,104 MODULE 1—CHAPTER 4

1. a. *Incorrect.* Guaranteed payments can be for capital or for services. Said another way, it is not always clear what is a guaranteed payment.

b. *Correct.* **Guaranteed payments are determined without regard to income. In other words, they are not entrepreneurial risk-type payments.**

c. *Incorrect.* This is an incorrect statement. Instead, they are deductible to a partnership. Additionally, they are separately reported as ordinary income to the partner.

d. *Incorrect.* This is an incorrect statement. Instead, they are treated as if made to a non-partner, not a partner.

2. a. *Incorrect.* Sec. 754 is not an account-level election. Also note that Sec. 743 adjustments are designed to equate the "inside" and "outside" basis.

b. *Incorrect.* Sec. 754 is not a partner-level election. However, note that it affects two different transactions.

c. *Correct.* **Sec. 754 is an entity-level election. It affects two transactions: sale or exchange of an interest and distributions of money or property from the partnership.**

d. *Incorrect.* Sec. 754 is not a transaction-level election. One of the transactions that is affected by Sec. 754 is a distribution of money or property from the partnership.

3. a. *Incorrect.* While one of the requirements for a mandatory adjustment is that it is negative, it is not mandatory if it exceeds $50,000. The amount that it must exceed in order to be mandatory is higher.

b. *Incorrect.* In this situation, the adjustment would not be mandatory. For example, one of the requirements is that it must be negative, not positive.

c. *Incorrect.* Generally, Code Sec. 734 and 743 adjustments are not made unless a Sec. 754 election is in effect.

d. *Correct.* **A mandatory adjustment applies to both Code Sec. 734 and Code Sec. 743. It is required if it is negative and exceeds $250,000.**

4. a. ***Incorrect.*** The share of recourse debt is a component that is required by Schedule K-1. Also note that increases and decreases in partners' "shares" of entity liabilities affect basis.

b. ***Incorrect.*** The share of nonrecourse debt is a component that is required by Schedule K-1. It's important to note that nonrecourse liabilities are shared in a three-step approach, which is somewhat arbitrary.

c. ***Correct.*** **Instead, Schedule K-1 requires the share of recourse debt, share of nonrecourse debt, and share of qualified nonrecourse debt.**

d. ***Incorrect.*** The share of qualified nonrecourse debt is a component that is required by Schedule K-1. Note that qualified nonrecourse debt allows at-risk basis.

5. a. ***Incorrect.*** This is not one of the two methods offered by the Treasury. Instead, the two methods are the interim closing method and the proration method.

b. ***Correct.*** **Code Sec. 706(d) says if partners' interests change, distributive shares are to be determined using any method prescribed by the Secretary that takes into account the varying interests.**

c. ***Incorrect.*** This is one of the methods used with respect to varying interest. The proration method is less accurate but administratively simple and must be elected by agreement.

d. ***Incorrect.*** This is not one of the two methods offered by the Treasury. One of the methods is the proration method, but it is not the preferred method.

6. a. ***Incorrect.*** This is an incorrect statement. Instead, in 2019 (not 2018) all methods are allowed, but a separate statement is attached to identify the method.

b. ***Correct.*** **This is a correct statement. Additionally, note that Notice 2019-20 deferred 2018 negative basis reporting until March 15, 2020.**

c. ***Incorrect.*** This is an incorrect statement. Instead, the 2018 and earlier K-1 asks how capital accounts are reported.

d. ***Incorrect.*** While Notice 2019-66 deferred 2019 tax basis reporting, it did not defer it until the 2022 year. Instead, it deferred it until the 2020 year.

¶ 10,105 MODULE 2—CHAPTER 5

1. a. ***Incorrect.*** While ChatGPT can be helpful, it can also be harmful.

b. ***Correct.*** **Also note that ChatGPT sometimes fabricates answers. In fact, some experts estimate that ChatGPT makes stuff up roughly 15 percent to 20 percent of the time.**

c. ***Incorrect.*** Instead, for experienced tax practitioners, it's another tool that can help. For new practitioners, it can be dangerous.

d. ***Incorrect.*** Instead, the database is old. In fact, it usually does not address 2022 or 2023 tax developments.

2. a. ***Correct.*** **The bonus depreciation rate for the year 2027 is 0 percent. This compares to 40 percent for the year 2025 and 60 percent for the year 2024.**

b. ***Incorrect.*** 20 percent is not the bonus depreciation rate for the year 2027. Instead, 20 percent is the bonus depreciation rate for the year 2026.

c. ***Incorrect.*** 60 percent is not the bonus depreciation rate for the year 2027. Instead, 60 percent is the bonus depreciation rate for the year 2024.

d. ***Incorrect.*** 80 percent is not the bonus depreciation rate for the year 2027. Instead, 80 percent is the bonus depreciation rate for the year 2023.

3. a. ***Incorrect.*** This is not the first step in claiming the new clean vehicle credit. Instead, this is the second step in the process.

b. ***Incorrect.*** This is not the first step in claiming the new clean vehicle credit. Instead, this step is performed only after you confirm that your client meets the MAGI test.

c. ***Correct.*** **This is the first step in the process. This is an easy process, whereas reading the statute and proposed regs is a harder way to determine eligibility.**

d. ***Incorrect.*** This is not the first step in claiming the new clean vehicle credit. However, this may be a more general qualitative consideration but not necessarily specific to the clean vehicle credit.

4. a. ***Correct.*** **As a result, it needs to be used in the trade or business of the taxpayer and be similar to EVs purchased by S corporations and partnerships.**

b. ***Incorrect.*** This is an incorrect statement. Instead, you need battery capacity of not less than 15 kW hours.

c. ***Incorrect.*** Unlike the personal use clean vehicle credits, the commercial clean vehicle credit does not require North American manufacturing.

d. ***Incorrect.*** Based on Code Sec. 45W(d)(3), if the personal EV credit is allowed, you can't take the commercial EV credit.

5. a. ***Incorrect.*** This is the incorrect credit rate percentage. Instead, the credit rate on qualifying expenditures is 30 percent.

b. ***Incorrect.*** Instead, the credit starts to phase down after 2032. It doesn't fully expire until 2034.

c. ***Correct.*** **Note that Solar capacity is predicted to increase 300 percent over 5 years. As a result, we're likely to see many more solar panel tax credits in the future.**

d. ***Incorrect.*** It is not a refundable credit (but the excess can be carried over to future years). Note that the Energy Efficient Home Improvement Credit is also not refundable.

6. a. ***Incorrect.*** Organizations exempt from income tax must report their activities to the IRS each year. Annual reporting is done on Form 990, *Return of Organization Exempt from Income Tax.*

b. ***Incorrect.*** Form 1040 is used by U.S. taxpayers to file an annual income tax return. Starting in tax Year 2018, you will no longer use Form 1040A or Form 1040EZ, but instead will use the redesigned Form 1040.

c. ***Incorrect.*** Form 1120 (officially the *U.S. Corporate Income Tax Return*) is one of the IRS tax forms used by corporations (specifically, C corporations) in the United States to report their income, gains, losses, deductions, and credits and to figure out their tax liability.

d. ***Correct.*** **This form is used to request a change in either an overall method of accounting or the accounting treatment of an item. It is available on the IRS's website.**

7. a. ***Incorrect.*** This is the incorrect amount. Note that the threshold amount was reduced from 2021.

b. ***Incorrect.*** This is the incorrect amount. Note that the new rules apply to sales of goods and services.

c. ***Incorrect.*** This is the incorrect amount. Note that the new rules apply to sales of goods and services but not cash transfers to friends and family payments.

d. ***Correct.*** **Note that this reporting was originally supposed to start in the year 2022 but was delayed one year.**

8. a. ***Correct.*** **Even if the taxpayer lacks receipts, a deduction is allowed if, among other requirements, there is a reasonable basis to support the estimate.**

b. ***Incorrect.*** This is not the correct rule. Note that courts bear heavily "upon the taxpayer whose inexactitude is of [her] own making."

c. ***Incorrect.*** This is not the correct rule. Note that estimates are not allowed in some areas, though.

d. ***Incorrect.*** This is not the correct rule. However, estimates are not allowed for travel, gifts, listed property (business autos), and charitable contributions.

9. a. ***Correct.*** **S corporations that were terminated as result of having two classes of stock could have been automatically fixed (without filing PLR or any fee) based on Rev. Proc. 2022-19.**

b. ***Incorrect.*** Having more than 100 shareholders is not the most common cause for S corporation terminations. Note that for LLCs that elected to be taxed as S corporations, most have "boilerplate" liquidating distributions required to be made according to positive capital accounts.

c. ***Incorrect.*** Entrance of a foreign investor is not the most common cause for S corporation terminations. On the topic of automatic relief, many S corporations (including LLCs that elected to be taxed as S corporations) had disproportionate distributions and do not qualify for automatic relief.

d. ***Incorrect.*** The delay in filing a tax return is not the most common cause for S corporation terminations. With respect to automatic relief, certain requirements must be met.

10. a. ***Incorrect.*** Dr. Hardy performed some surgeries there, not all. However, the case does not mention if the LLC was member managed.

b. ***Correct.*** **In addition to only meeting with other owners quarterly, he also had no day-to-day management, was generally not involved in hiring and firing decisions, and had no input in management decisions.**

c. ***Incorrect.*** Instead, Dr. Hardy actually had a significant capital contribution in the amount of $163,974.

d. ***Incorrect.*** He was not involved in the hiring and firing process. The key issue of the case was whether Dr. Hardy was subject to self-employment tax on his distributive share of the surgical center's earnings.

11. a. ***Correct.*** **The new IRS portal to e-file Forms 1099 can detect filing errors. It can also alert filers.**

b. ***Incorrect.*** The new IRS portal to e-file Forms 1099 is not $9.95/month. Instead, the service is provided for free.

c. ***Incorrect.*** This is an incorrect statement. Instead, it's important to note that you still need to mail 1099s to recipients.

d. ***Incorrect.*** This is the incorrect period of time. Instead, note that the IRS acknowledges receipt within 48 hours, not 24 hours.

12. a. ***Incorrect.*** Determining the monthly average of historical Social Security wages is not the second step in the process. Instead, this step should be performed after the historical wages are adjusted to get current dollars.

b. ***Correct.*** **Adjusting historical wages to determine the current dollars is the second step in the process. The first step in the process is to determine what are your historical Social Security wages.**

c. ***Incorrect.*** This is the first step in the process of calculating the cost of lost Social Security benefits. Once this step is performed, then you should adjust the historical wages to get current dollars.

d. ***Incorrect.*** Plugging the inflation-adjusted high 35-year wage average into the AIME table is not the second step in the process. Instead, this is the last step in the process.

¶ 10,106 MODULE 2—CHAPTER 6

1. a. ***Incorrect.*** This news release does not relate to tax avoidance strategies. Instead, it includes information about the 2023 Dirty Dozen.

b. ***Incorrect.*** This news release does not relate to tax avoidance strategies. Instead, it includes information about pandemic-related scams.

c. ***Incorrect.*** This news release does not relate to tax avoidance strategies. Instead, it includes information about spear phishing attacks.

d. ***Correct.*** **In its release, the IRS warned taxpayers to watch out for promoters peddling these schemes.**

2. a. ***Correct.*** **A CRAT is a type of gift transaction in which a donor contributes assets to an irrevocable trust that then donates to one or more charities while also paying a fixed income to one or more designated noncharitable beneficiaries in the form of an annuity.**

b. ***Incorrect.*** A grantor trust is a type of trust where the grantor retains ownership of trust's assets for income tax purposes.

c. ***Incorrect.*** A testamentary trust is a trust contained in a last will and testament. It provides for the distribution of all or part of an estate and often proceeds from a life insurance policy held on the person establishing the trust.

d. ***Incorrect.*** A spendthrift trust is a trust designed so that the beneficiary is unable to sell or give away her equitable interest in the trust property.

3. a. ***Incorrect.*** Text messages are one of the signs of an EIP scam. It's important to remember that the IRS does not initiate contact by text message.

b. ***Incorrect.*** Unexpected phone calls are one of the signs of an EIP scam. Note that the IRS does not initiate contact by phone.

c. ***Correct.*** **This is not one of the telltale signs of an EIP scam. Instead, signs of an EIP scam include text messages, emails, and unexpected phone calls.**

d. ***Incorrect.*** Emails are one of the signs of an EIP scam. When this occurs, you should not click a link to verify data and you should delete it without opening.

4. a. ***Incorrect.*** This is a best practice when receiving unsolicited SMS/text. You should also remind clients that they remain responsible for the contents of their tax returns even if prepared by someone else.

b. *Correct.* You should never open an attachment from one of these text messages. Unsolicited SMS/texts may reference things such as COVID-19, stimulus payments, and refunds.

c. *Incorrect.* This is a best practice when receiving unsolicited SMS/text. When emailing this information, you should include the date, time, and time zone of the text message.

d. *Incorrect.* This is a best practice when receiving unsolicited SMS/text. These links can often be bogus links claiming to be from the IRS or an online account.

5. a. *Correct.* This is a correct statement with respect to consumer fraud. Also note that consumer fraud cost $8.8 billion in 2022.

b. *Incorrect.* This is the incorrect amount. Instead, it cost $8.8 billion in 2022.

c. *Incorrect.* This is the incorrect percentage increase. Instead, the increase was 44 percent from 2021.

d. *Incorrect.* It is not the third most common type of fraud. Instead, it is the most common form of fraud, second only to investment scams.

6. a. *Correct.* This IRS publication relates to safeguarding taxpayer data. You should also be aware of the NIST's Small Business Information Security guide about the fundamentals.

b. *Incorrect.* This IRS publication does not relate to safeguarding taxpayer data. Instead, it includes a data security resource guide.

c. *Incorrect.* This IRS publication does not relate to safeguarding taxpayer data. Instead, it includes a preparer guide to identity theft.

d. *Incorrect.* This IRS publication does not relate to safeguarding taxpayer data. Instead, it includes information on medical expenses. Specifically, what can be deducted tax-free.

¶ 10,107 MODULE 2—CHAPTER 7

1. a. *Incorrect.* Closed virtual currencies have value in online games but not in the real world.

b. *Correct.* Airline frequent flyer programs are examples of a single-flow virtual currency.

c. *Incorrect.* Convertible virtual currencies can be purchased and sold on the open market.

d. *Incorrect.* There is no such thing as a public virtual currency.

2. a. *Correct.* Bitcoins were used for online betting at PrimeDice.com on May 18, 2013.

b. *Incorrect.* The Financial Action Task Force issued warnings of money laundering using virtual currencies in 2010.

c. *Incorrect.* Silk Road was established in 2011, and Bitcoins were used to purchase illegal drugs.

d. *Incorrect.* The government warned of terrorists using virtual currencies to fund operations in 2010.

3. a. ***Incorrect.*** Exchange tokens are cryptocurrencies associated with or issued by cryptocurrency exchanges.

b. ***Incorrect.*** A soft fork is a fork in a blockchain protocol where previously valid transactions become invalid.

c. ***Incorrect.*** A hard fork refers to a radical change to the protocol of a blockchain network that effectively results in two branches.

d. ***Correct.*** **An airdrop happens when free coins, that is, coins that you did not purchase or earn, appear in your wallet. Airdrops are usually taxed as ordinary income.**

4. a. ***Incorrect.*** The IRS has ruled that virtual currency transactions create taxable events.

b. ***Correct.*** **The IRS considers virtual currencies to be property.**

c. ***Incorrect.*** Even though a Texas judge ruled Bitcoins to be a currency, the IRS does not consider them to be currency.

d. ***Incorrect.*** Virtual currencies are not considered to be securities by the IRS even though the SEC considers them securities.

5. a. ***Incorrect.*** Closed virtual currencies have no value outside of a gaming environment and are not taxable.

b. ***Correct.*** **Even though the IRS considers this to be taxable income if received for business purposes, it does not enforce compliance because of issues with mixing personal and business awards in one account.**

c. ***Incorrect.*** Convertible virtual currencies are taxable.

d. ***Incorrect.*** Cryptocurrencies are a subset of convertible virtual currencies, which are taxed.

6. a. ***Incorrect.*** LIFO is legal even though the IRS does not prefer its use.

b. ***Incorrect.*** Even though the IRS does not prefer FIFO, it allows taxpayers to use the FIFO method.

c. ***Correct.*** **The IRS prefers that taxpayers use the specific identification method.**

d. ***Incorrect.*** Even though the IRS will accept the average cost method, which many taxpayers use, it is not the method the IRS prefers.

¶ 10,108 MODULE 2—CHAPTER 8

1. a. ***Incorrect.*** This is the incorrect year when Congress enacted the Inflation Reduction Act. Instead, it was enacted after 2020.

b. ***Incorrect.*** This is the incorrect year when Congress enacted the Inflation Reduction Act. Note that it included $80 billion worth of funding over the next 10 years.

c. ***Correct.*** **This is the correct year when Congress enacted the Inflation Reduction Act. It represents a historic opportunity to transform the administration of the tax system.**

d. ***Incorrect.*** This is the incorrect year when Congress enacted the Inflation Reduction Act. Instead, it was enacted before the year 2023.

2. a. ***Incorrect.*** This is one of the aspects of the Strategic Operating Plan that the IRS will deliver. Note that the plan will serve as a "guide" for decision-making by IRS leadership and project managers.

b. ***Correct.*** **Based on the IRS's Strategic Operating Plan, the IRS will deliver IRA Transformation vision, objectives, and outcome.**

c. ***Incorrect.*** This is one of the aspects of the Strategic Operating Plan that the IRS will deliver. Note that the Transformation and Strategy Office (TSO) will coordinate detailed planning and execution efforts.

d. ***Incorrect.*** This is one of the aspects of the Strategic Operating Plan that the IRS will deliver. Note that the IRS will deploy the IRS investment by following five different objectives.

3. a. ***Correct.*** **Another initiative related to this objective is to expand digital services and digitalization.**

b. ***Incorrect.*** This initiative relates more specifically to expanding enforcement on taxpayers with complex tax filings and high-dollar noncompliance to address the tax gap.

c. ***Incorrect.*** This initiative relates more specifically to quickly resolving taxpayer issues when they arise.

d. ***Incorrect.*** This initiative relates more specifically to quickly resolving taxpayer issues when they arise, not to dramatically improving services to help taxpayers.

4. a. ***Incorrect.*** This initiative relates more specifically to delivering cutting-edge technology, data, and analytics to operate more effectively.

b. ***Incorrect.*** This initiative relates more specifically to attracting, retaining, and empowering a highly skilled, diverse workforce and developing a culture that is better equipped to deliver results for taxpayers.

c. ***Incorrect.*** This initiative relates more specifically to dramatically improving services to help taxpayers meet their obligations and receive the tax incentives for which they are eligible.

d. ***Correct.*** **Another initiative is to employ centralized, analytics-driven, risk-based methods to aid in the selection of compliance cases.**

5. a. ***Incorrect.*** This initiative relates more specifically to delivering cutting-edge technology, data, and analytics to operate more effectively.

b. ***Incorrect.*** This initiative relates more specifically to quickly resolving taxpayer issues when they arise, not specifically related to attracting, retaining, and empowering a highly skilled, diverse workforce.

c. ***Correct.*** **Another way the IRS seeks to accomplish this objective is to improve organizational structures and governance.**

d. ***Incorrect.*** This initiative relates more specifically to expanding enforcement on taxpayers with complex tax filings and high-dollar noncompliance to address the tax gap.

6. a. ***Incorrect.*** This objective does not have the most funds allocated to it. Instead, it has the least amount of funds allocated to it (~$3.2 billion).

b. ***Correct.*** **Of the five objectives discussed, the focus on expanded enforcement on taxpayers with complex tax filings and high-dollar noncompliance to address the tax gap has the highest amount of funds allocated to it. It has approximately $47.4 billion allocated to it.**

c. ***Incorrect.*** This objective does not have the most funds allocated to it. However, it does have the second highest amount of funds allocated to it.

d. ***Incorrect.*** This objective only has ~$8.2 billion allocated to it. There are other objectives that have more funds allocated to them.

Index

References are to paragraph (¶) numbers.

¶ 10,200 Glossary

Analytics: A field of computer science that uses math, statistics, and machine learning to find meaningful patterns in data.

Bitcoin: A type of virtual currency.

Blockchains: Lists of records held on diverse computers (Nodes) that are used to record and verify data.

C Corporation: A legal structure that businesses can choose to organize themselves under to limit their owners' legal and financial liabilities. C corporations are an alternative to S corporations, where profits pass through to owners and are only taxed at the individual level, and limited liability companies, which provide the legal protections of corporations but are taxed like sole proprietorships.

Cannabis: A psychoactive drug from the Cannabis plant used primarily for medical or recreational purposes.

Captive Insurance: An alternative to self-insurance in which a parent group or groups create a licensed insurance company to provide coverage for itself.

Central Bank Coins: A type of cryptocurrency designed and issued by a central government as alternatives to fiat currencies.

Charitable Remainder Annuity Trust (CRAT): A type of gift transaction in which a donor contributes assets to an irrevocable trust that then donates to one or more charities while also paying a fixed income to one or more designated noncharitable beneficiaries in the form of an annuity.

Closed Virtual Currencies: Virtual currencies used in a closed community, most commonly multi-player online games. The currency is fictional and has no value outside the game.

Cohan Rule: Allows taxpayers, when unable to produce records of actual expenditures, to rely on reasonable estimates provided there is some factual basis for it.

Coronavirus Aid, Relief, and Economic Security (CARES) Act of 2020: Legislation that provided economic assistance for American workers and families and small businesses, and preserved jobs for American industries.

COVID-19: An infectious disease caused by a newly discovered strain of coronavirus which is a type of virus known to cause respiratory infections in humans.

Cryptocurrency: A digital currency using cryptography to secure transactions and to control the creation of new currency units.

Data Breach: The release or taking of data from a secure source to an unsecured third-party location (computer).

Data Utility: A measure of how useful a data set is for a given task.

Depreciation: A measurement of the useful life of a business asset to determine the multiyear period over which the cost of that asset can be deducted from taxable income.

Diverse Workforce: Similarities and differences among employees in terms of age, cultural background, physical abilities and disabilities, race, religion, gender, and sexual orientation.

Domicile: The country that a person treats as their permanent home or lives in and has a substantial connection with.

Economic Impact Payment: A key provision of the Coronavirus Aid Relief, and Economic Security (CARES) Act legislation that Congress passed to help reduce the financial burden of COVID-19 on individuals and their families.

Fiat Stable Coins: Crypto assets tied to a traditional fiat currency such as the U.S. dollar or Euro.

Form 1099: One of several IRS tax forms used in the United States to prepare and file an information return to report various types of income other than wages, salaries, and tips.

Form 1120: The tax form C corporations (and limited liability companies filing as corporations) use to file their income taxes.

Generally Accepted Accounting Principles (GAAP): The accounting principles and standards accepted by consensus among professional accountants.

I-9: A form used to document an employee's legal right to work in the United States.

Inflation Reduction Act of 2022: A landmark U.S. law that aims to curb inflation by reducing the deficit, lowering prescription drug prices, and investing into domestic energy production while promoting clean energy.

Initial Coin Offering (ICO): A way to raise funds, including funds to launch a token or cryptocurrency.

Installment Sale: A sale of property where you receive at least one payment after the tax year of the sale.

Internal Revenue Service (IRS): The revenue service for the U.S. federal government which is responsible for collecting U.S. federal taxes and administering the Internal Revenue Code, the main body of the federal statutory tax law.

Limited Liability Company: The U.S.-specific form of a private limited company. It is a business structure that can combine the pass-through taxation of a partnership or sole proprietorship with the limited liability of a corporation.

Liquidation: The process of liquidating a business.

Money Laundering: Taking funds from an illegal source, hiding the source of funds, and making the funds available for use without legal restrictions or penalties.

Nonrecourse Deduction: The payment source is borrowing from a source for which the lender has no recourse if the partnership cannot pay.

Partnership: A type of business organization in which two or more individuals pool money, skills, and other resources, and share profit and loss in accordance with terms of the partnership agreement.

Payment Coins: Crypto assets that can be used to facilitate transactions for goods and services on the internet.

Permanent Place of Abode: A residence (a building or structure where a person can live) that you maintain, whether you own it or not, and that is suitable for year-round use.

Qualified Charitable Distribution (QCD): A tax-free donation from an individual retirement account (IRA) owned by a person who is age 70-1/2 or older that is paid to a qualified charity.

Required Minimum Distribution (RMD): The minimum amount that must be withdrawn from certain retirement accounts each year.

Residency: Usually the official place of residence.

S Corporation: Any corporation that is taxed separately from its owners. A C corporation is distinguished from an S corporation, which generally is not taxed separately.

Safe Harbor: A provision of a statute or a regulation that specifies that certain conduct will be deemed not to violate a given rule.

Saver's Match: Starting in 2027, taxpayers earning between $41,000 and $71,000 for married, filing jointly and $20,500 to $35,500 for single taxpayers will be eligible for a federal retirement savings "match" of up to 50 percent of employee's own contributions (up to $2,000 per year).

Schedule K-1: A federal tax document used to report the income, losses, and dividends of a business's or financial entity's partners or an S corporation's shareholders.

Section 199A: Section of the Internal Revenue Code that provides for a qualified business income deduction of up to 20 percent of qualified business income, applied at the individual level, and subject to certain limitations.

Securing a Strong Retirement Act of 2021: Legislation designed to improve the retirement savings system for U.S. workers. Commonly referred to as "SECURE Act 2.0."

Setting Every Community Up for Retirement Enhancement (SECURE) Act of 2019: Legislation signed into law in December 2019 that made many changes to the retirement plans used in the United States.

Single Premium Immediate Annuity: Purchased with a lump sum and starts paying out periodic income payments almost immediately or within the year.

Spear Phishing: The fraudulent practice of sending emails ostensibly from a known or trusted sender in order to induce targeted individuals to reveal confidential information.

Statutory Resident: A person who is not domiciled in New York State but maintains a "permanent place of abode" in the state, and who spends more than 183 days of the taxable year in the state.

Substantial Economic Effect: The economic effect of an allocation (or allocations) where there is a reasonable possibility that the allocation (or allocations) will affect substantially the dollar amounts to be received by the partners from the partnership, independent of tax.

Tax Cuts and Jobs Act of 2017 (TCJA): A congressional revenue act originally introduced in Congress that amended the Internal Revenue Code of 1986. Major elements of the changes include reducing tax rates for businesses and individuals; a personal tax simplification by increasing the standard deduction and family tax credits but eliminating personal exemptions and making it less beneficial to itemize deductions.

Transformation & Strategy Office: The office within the IRS responsible for coordinating detailed planning and execution efforts of IRA funding.

Virtual Currency: A currency that only exists in cyber space. There is no physical or tangible item to represent the currency.

Workday: Typically includes travel days, days worked from home, and days worked on weekends, and excludes holidays, vacations, sick days, and weekends.

¶ 10,300 Final Exam Instructions

To complete your Final Exam go to **cchcpelink.com/printcpe,** click on the title of the exam you wish to complete and add it to your shopping cart (you will need to register with CCH CPELink if you have not already). Click **Proceed to Checkout** and enter your credit card information. Click **Place Order** to complete your purchase of the final exam. The final exam will be available in **My Dashboard** under **My Account**.

This Final Exam is divided into two Modules. There is a grading fee for each Final Exam submission.

Online Processing Fee: $192.00 for Module 1 $240.00 for Module 2 $432.00 for both Modules	**Recommended CPE:** 8 hours for Module 1 10 hours for Module 2 18 hours for both Modules
IRS Program Numbers: Module 1: 4VRWB-T-04978-23-S Module 2: 4VRWB-T-04979-23-S	**Federal Tax Law Hours:** 8 hours for Module 1 10 hours for Module 2 18 hours for both Modules
CTEC Program Numbers: Module 1: 1075-CE-3261 Module 2: 1075-CE-3262	

Instructions for purchasing your CPE Tests and accessing them after purchase are provided on the **cchcpelink.com/printcpe** website. **Please note, manual grading is no longer available for Top Federal Tax Issues. All answer sheets must be submitted online for grading and processing.**

Recommended CPE credit is based on a 50-minute hour. Because CPE requirements vary from state to state and among different licensing agencies, please contact your CPE governing body for information on your CPE requirements and the applicability of a particular course for your requirements.

Expiration Date: September 30, 2025

Evaluation: To help us provide you with the best possible products, please take a moment to fill out the course Evaluation located after your Final Exam.

Wolters Kluwer, CCH is registered with the National Association of State Boards of Accountancy (NASBA) as a sponsor of continuing professional education on the National Registry of CPE Sponsors. State boards of accountancy have final authority on the acceptance of individual courses for CPE credit. Complaints regarding registered sponsors may be submitted to the National Registry of CPE Sponsors through its website: www.learningmarket.org.

Additional copies of this course may be downloaded from **cchcpelink.com/printcpe.** Printed copies of the course are available for $15.00 by calling 1-800-344-3734 (ask for product 10024491-0011).

¶ 10,301 Final Exam Questions: Module 1

1. Prior to the SECURE 2.0 Act, the required beginning date was April 1 of the calendar year following the later of: (i) the calendar year in which the employee attains age 70½; or (ii) the calendar year in which the employee retires. The SECURE 2.0 Act changed the 70½ age to which of the following starting in 2033?

a. 72
b. 73
c. 74
d. 75

2. The SECURE 2.0 Act provides for a significant reduction in the required minimum distribution (RMD) withdrawal penalty if the taxpayer withdraws the previously un-withdrawn amounts during the correction window, which ends on the earlier of: (a) the date a notice of deficiency is mailed; (b) the date the taxpayer addresses the penalty; or (c) the last day of the ________ year after the penalty is imposed.

a. First
b. Second
c. Third
d. Fourth

3. With respect to SIMPLE plans, in 2025 the catch-up contribution amount for those aged 60 to 63 is increased to the greater of $5,000 (adjusted for inflation) or what percentage of the regular catch-up contribution amount?

a. 100 percent
b. 125 percent
c. 150 percent
d. 200 percent

4. The SECURE 2.0 Act provides for linked emergency savings accounts in a retirement account that will not be subject to an early withdrawal penalty, including allowing taxpayers to make a one-time withdrawal of up to what amount per year for unforeseeable or immediate financial needs related to personal or family emergency expenses?

a. $1,000
b. $2,000
c. $3,000
d. $5,000

5. The SECURE 2.0 Act adds a new Code Sec. 414A, which requires new retirement savings plans to include mandatory automatic enrollment and escalation terms. Under these new provisions, a participant's savings rate must automatically increase by 1 percent annually up to no more than which of the following?

a. 10 percent
b. 12 percent
c. 14 percent
d. 15 percent

6. Which of the following was codified in the SECURE 2.0 Act in accordance with the IRS ruling in Private Letter Ruling 201833012?

- **a.** Student loan matching
- **b.** Expanded catch-up contributions
- **c.** Repeal of IRA contribution age limit
- **d.** Delayed required beginning date

7. The SECURE 2.0 Act increases part-time employee participation in retirement plans by providing that part-time employees who complete how many of the following hours of service in two consecutive years must be permitted to participate?

- **a.** 250
- **b.** 500
- **c.** 1,000
- **d.** 2,000

8. The Department of Labor is required to create a "Retirement Savings Lost and Found" database by the end of which of the following years?

- **a.** 2023
- **b.** 2024
- **c.** 2025
- **d.** 2026

9. Which of the following statements regarding the changes to the RMD rules under the SECURE 2.0 Act is true?

- **a.** The RMD required beginning date in 2033 is based on attaining age 78.
- **b.** Further delaying the RMD required beginning date was a gift to taxpayers.
- **c.** In order to minimize tax to one's heirs, RMDs should be taken starting at age 75.
- **d.** If a taxpayer does not withdraw their RMD, the penalty is 25 percent of the amount that should have been withdrawn.

10. Which of the following was part of the SECURE 2.0 Act?

- **a.** Roth matching opportunities
- **b.** Repeal of IRA contribution age limit
- **c.** Small business retirement plan credits
- **d.** IRA beneficiary withdrawal period changes

11. Which of the following is ***not*** a factor that impacts the tax rules applicable to vehicles?

- **a.** Whether the vehicle is owned
- **b.** Whether the vehicle is driven for personal purposes
- **c.** Whether the vehicle is a fuel cell vehicle that is powered by fossil fuels
- **d.** Whether the vehicle costs more than $30,000

12. Assume a car was purchased by Max for business use in 2020 and he used the standard mileage rate to determine the amount of his deduction. Also assume that Max drove the car for business purposes for 10,000 miles each year. At the beginning of 2022, Max sells the car. The basis of the car should be reduced by the amount of the deemed depreciation of the car. By what amount should the car's basis be reduced?

a. $2,700
b. $5,200
c. $7,900
d. $10,700

13. Assume a taxpayer buys a $50,000 pickup truck for its business. The taxpayer puts $10,000 down and finances the rest. The taxpayer uses the vehicle as follows: 70 percent for business, and 30 percent for personal use. Depreciation in year 1 should be calculated on which amount?

a. $10,000
b. $15,000
c. $35,000
d. $50,000

14. If a vehicle is placed in service in 2022 and uses 100 percent bonus depreciation, the taxpayer must calculate depreciation going forward using the safe harbor method and the applicable depreciation table found in Appendix A of which of the following?

a. Notice 2023-03
b. IRS Publication 15-B
c. IRS Publication 463
d. IRS Publication 946

15. Certain vehicles are exempt from the dollar limits on depreciation and the substantiation requirements. Which of the following vehicles is exempt from these limits?

a. Delivery trucks with seating only for the driver or with a fold-out jump seat
b. Vehicles with an interior cargo bed length of more than 6 feet
c. Luxury sedans used exclusively for business
d. Passenger vans that seat more than 10 people behind the driver's seat

16. Which of the following statements regarding substantiation is correct when a taxpayer uses the standard mileage rate?

a. Substantiation does not require identifying total mileage for the year.
b. Substantiation means keeping contemporaneous records noting specifics regarding the use of the vehicle, such as dates of driving and business destination.
c. Using the standard mileage rate relieves the taxpayer of all recordkeeping obligations.
d. The IRS has stated that the use of apps is treated as written for substantiation purposes.

17. For 2023, the fixed and variable rate (FAVR) method may only be used if an employee's vehicle cost does ***not*** exceed which of the following?

a. $45,872

b. $56,100

c. $60,800

d. $135,000

18. Which of the following statements regarding when a taxpayer may take a deduction for personal use of a vehicle on behalf of a charitable organization is correct?

a. Substantiation is not required.

b. The taxpayer may not add parking and tolls to the deduction.

c. The taxpayer may only deduct actual expenses.

d. The taxpayer may deduct 14 cents per mile.

19. Which of the following statements regarding the available methods of calculating the value of an employee's personal use of a company vehicle is correct?

a. The commuting rule must be used for control employees.

b. The fleet-average valuation rule applies to employers with a fleet of at least 20 vehicles.

c. One of the safe harbors under the actual FMV rule is based on using the manufacturer's suggested retail price minus 4 percent of the cost of the vehicle.

d. Under the ALV method, the fair market value of the car on the date it is put into service by the employer is used to calculate the value of the personal use.

20. Which of the following statements regarding the alternative fuel refueling property credit is correct?

a. The credit runs through 2032.

b. The same rules apply to consumers and businesses.

c. Individuals can claim a tax credit of the lesser of 30 percent of the property's cost or $2,000.

d. Starting in 2023, the maximum credit for businesses is $150,000.

21. The most common statutory residency test involves an assessment of the permanent place of abode plus more than how many days?

a. 150 days

b. 161 days

c. 183 days

d. 210 days

22. Which of the following identifies the number of primary domicile factors considered for New York residency?

a. 4

b. 5

c. 6

d. 9

23. If an employee is a resident of the state where they work, then 100 percent of their compensation income is subject to that state's tax, and an employer must withhold ______ state tax.

a. 50 percent
b. 75 percent
c. 90 percent
d. 100 percent

24. A workday typically includes each of the following, ***except?***

a. Travel days
b. Days worked from home
c. Sick days
d. Days worked on weekends

25. Which of the following identifies the number of approaches to pandemic-related teleworker withholding?

a. 1
b. 2
c. 3
d. 4

26. How many states have a "convenience rule"?

a. 6
b. 7
c. 9
d. 13

27. Regarding equity awards, which of the following is the date on which the employee actually buys the stock?

a. Grant date
b. Vest date
c. Exercise date
d. Sale date

28. Unless a Code Sec. 83(b) election is made, the taxable amount of restricted stock equals the difference between the amount paid (if any) and the __________ at the time of vesting.

a. Fair market value
b. Book value
c. Replacement cost
d. Premium paid

29. States __________ allow their residents a credit for taxes paid to other states.

a. Generally
b. Always
c. Never
d. Rarely

30. Which of the following statements about reciprocal tax agreements is true?

- **a.** Every state in the United States has one.
- **b.** They can apply to income earned in a third state that is not a party to the agreement.
- **c.** Typically, they exist between neighboring states.
- **d.** Typically, they exist only in "convenience rule" states.

31. Partners need separate reporting for anything that might impact their ______ reporting.

- **a.** Basis
- **b.** Capital
- **c.** Tax
- **d.** Fair value

32. Recent tax law changes have generally ________ the required information to be reported.

- **a.** Reduced
- **b.** Significantly reduced
- **c.** Increased
- **d.** Neither increased nor decreased

33. Guaranteed payments are treated as if made to a non-partner and are deductible to which of the following?

- **a.** The partnership only
- **b.** The partner only
- **c.** Neither the partnership nor the partner
- **d.** Both the partnership and the partner

34. Which of the following types of payments to partners is intended to be matched with an allocation of income?

- **a.** Guaranteed payments
- **b.** Variable returns
- **c.** Preference distributions
- **d.** Fixed payments

35. What portion of a guaranteed payment is eligible for the qualified business income deduction (QBID)?

- **a.** 0 percent
- **b.** 25 percent
- **c.** 50 percent
- **d.** 100 percent

36. The Code Sec. 754 election is what type of election?

- **a.** Partner-level
- **b.** Entity-level
- **c.** Both entity- and partner-level
- **d.** Neither entity- nor partner-level

37. Which of the following statements is correct with respect to positive Sec. 734 adjustments?

- **a.** The distributee's basis in property is more than the carryover from the partnership.
- **b.** A loss is recognized by the distributee.
- **c.** They cannot occur upon liquidation.
- **d.** Gain is recognized by the distributee.

38. If the Code Sec. 734 or 743 adjustment would exceed $250,000, a mandatory adjustment occurs when it is which of the following?

- **a.** Negative only
- **b.** Positive only
- **c.** Either positive or negative
- **d.** Able to be estimated

39. Partnership allocations relate to items of gain and loss that arise while the owners are in a partnership form. Which Internal Revenue Code Section deals with allocations of items that arise before the partnership is formed?

- **a.** Code Sec. 704(a)
- **b.** Code Sec. 704(b)
- **c.** Code Sec. 704(c)
- **d.** Code Sec. 704(d)

40. Regarding capital accounting reporting, practitioners must now use what type of approach?

- **a.** Tax adjustment method
- **b.** Book, which may be GAAP or Sec. 704(b)
- **c.** Transactional tax basis method
- **d.** Fair value accounting

¶ 10,302 Final Exam Questions: Module 2

1. Which of the following types of technology is used by ChatGPT 4?

a. Artificial intelligence
b. Macros
c. Algorithms
d. Neurolink

2. Which of the following describes the impact of ChatGPT 4 on new practitioners?

a. It can be fully relied on to provide tax advice.
b. It can be dangerous.
c. It is never inaccurate.
d. It is difficult to understand and use.

3. Bonus depreciation begins to phase out in what year?

a. 2023
b. 2024
c. 2025
d. 2026

4. Which of the following identifies the bonus depreciation rate in 2026?

a. 0 percent
b. 20 percent
c. 40 percent
d. 60 percent

5. Which of the following referenced businesses has argued that the qualified business income deduction (Code Sec. 199A) is neither paid nor incurred?

a. Technology
b. Cannabis
c. Plumbers
d. Geologists

6. To qualify for the clean vehicle credit, the manufacturer's suggested retail price (MSRP) of the car must ***not*** exceed which of the following amounts?

a. $55,000
b. $59,000
c. $63,000
d. $65,000

7. If a client qualifies for the new clean vehicle credit based on the MSRP test and the MAGI test, and the vehicle is manufactured in North America and both of the battery tests are met, the tentative credit is which of the following amounts?

a. $2,500
b. $5,000
c. $7,500
d. $9,000

8. To qualify for the used electric vehicle (EV) credit, the sales price of the car must ***not*** exceed which of the following amounts?

a. $25,000

b. $30,000

c. $35,000

d. $40,000

9. Which of the following identifies the MSRP limit with respect to the *commercial* EV credit?

a. $50,000

b. $100,000

c. $150,000

d. There is no limit.

10. The 2023 energy efficiency rules can produce meaningful credits of up to what amount per year?

a. $1,000

b. $3,200

c. $5,000

d. $10,000

11. Which of the following identifies the most common type of grantor trust?

a. Nonrevocable trust

b. Testamentary trust

c. Revocable trust

d. Compensating trust

12. The $10,000 penalty for failure to file Foreign Bank Account Reports (FBARs) is imposed on a/an _________ basis.

a. Per-account

b. Annual

c. Weekly

d. Monthly

13. What is the income-related monthly adjusted amount (IRMAA)?

a. A penalty for paying Medicare premiums late

b. A penalty for withdrawing from the Medicare Program

c. A surcharge added to Medicare Part B and Part D premiums

d. A surcharge added to the Medicare Part A hospital insurance premium

14. The IRS has confirmed that audit rates won't be increased above historical levels if a taxpayer's income is less than which of the following amounts?

a. $400,000

b. $500,000

c. $750,000

d. $850,000

15. Based on the IRS Data Book, the number of new partnerships has done which of the following?

a. Significantly decreased

b. Slightly increased

c. Dramatically increased

d. Slightly decreased

16. Based on the new Form 1099-K reporting threshold, the IRS has estimated that it will raise approximately how much over 10 years?

a. $2.4 billion

b. $4.8 billion

c. $8.4 billion

d. $13.7 billion

17. A bipartisan bill (the Red Tape Reduction Act) would raise the reporting threshold for 1099-Ks from $600 to what amount?

a. $1,000

b. $5,000

c. $10,000

d. $25,000

18. Electronic filing is required of all 1099 and W-2 forms when the total number of forms exceed how many?

a. 4

b. 6

c. 8

d. 10

19. The Social Security surplus is expected to disappear by what year?

a. 2026

b. 2028

c. 2030

d. 2034

20. Unless you need the money sooner, you should wait to take Social Security until what age?

a. 67

b. 70

c. 75

d. 84

21. Which of the following IRS news releases includes information about how to avoid Offer in Compromise (OIC) mills?

a. IR-2022-113

b. IR-2022-117

c. IR-2022-119

d. IR-2022-121

22. Which of the following is the #1 arrangement to likely attract additional agency compliance efforts?

a. Charitable remainder annuity trusts
b. Maltese individual retirement arrangements
c. Foreign captive insurance
d. Monetized installment sales

23. Which of the following identifies the local law limit on contribution to a Maltese pension?

a. $5,000
b. $10,000
c. $25,000
d. There is no limit.

24. Which of the following identifies a way in which the IRS may contact you?

a. Phone
b. Text
c. Mail
d. Social media

25. Each of the following is a characteristic of ghost preparers, ***except?***

a. Can provide for a better deal with the IRS
b. Promise bigger refunds
c. Improperly fabricate income, deductions, and/or credits
d. Require payment in cash

26. For email phishing scams, you should send an email as an attachment to which of the following?

a. scams@IRS.gov
b. ghostpreparers@IRS.gov
c. fraud@IRS.gov
d. phishing@IRS.gov

27. Which of the following is something that the IRS would likely do?

a. Contact you by U.S. postal mail.
b. Leave pre-recorded messages.
c. Threaten license revocation.
d. Advise that a warrant has been issued.

28. If failure to file is deemed fraudulent, the maximum penalty increases to what amount?

a. 25 percent
b. 50 percent
c. 75 percent
d. 100 percent

29. When recognizing illegal tax avoidance schemes, which of the following is ***not*** one of the three things to remember?

- **a.** Taxpayers are responsible and liable for the content of their tax return.
- **b.** Anyone who promises a bigger refund without knowing the tax situation could be misleading the taxpayer.
- **c.** Taxpayers should never sign a tax return without looking it over to make sure it is honest and correct.
- **d.** Taxpayers are required to report any suspicious activity to fraud@IRS.gov.

30. Which of the following IRS publications provides a guide with respect to identity theft?

- **a.** Publication 4557
- **b.** Publication 5199
- **c.** Publication 5291
- **d.** Publication 7135

31. Which of the following statements regarding blockchain technology is incorrect?

- **a.** Data is stored on computer nodes.
- **b.** Public blockchains are "open source" and can be used by anyone.
- **c.** Private blockchains are maintained on closed or private networks.
- **d.** Blockchains cannot be hacked or compromised.

32. The first Bitcoin ATM was located in which city?

- **a.** San Diego, CA
- **b.** New York, NY
- **c.** Tokyo, Japan
- **d.** London, England

33. Which of the following is considered to be a fiat stable coin?

- **a.** Bitcoin
- **b.** USD Coin
- **c.** Golem
- **d.** Dogecoin

34. When the FBI shut down Silk Road in October of 2013, it seized ________ in Bitcoins.

- **a.** $2.6 million
- **b.** $3 million
- **c.** $3.6 million
- **d.** $4 million

35. A University of Texas study released in June of 2018 claims the 2017 price increases for Bitcoin were driven by which of the following?

- **a.** Consumer acceptance
- **b.** Investors
- **c.** Government acceptance
- **d.** Price manipulation

36. Which of the following federal agencies wants to regulate initial coin offerings (ICOs)?

a. IRS

b. SEC

c. FBI

d. CIA

37. Which type of virtual currency wallet is the safest from online hacking?

a. Paper

b. Desktop

c. Mobile

d. Web

38. The IRS requires virtual currencies be reported at which of the following?

a. Market value

b. Fair value

c. Exchange value

d. Fair market value

39. Taxpayers who receive virtual currencies for "mining" must report the fair market value of the coins received as which of the following?

a. Passive income

b. Gross income

c. Capital gains

d. No reporting is required.

40. When using virtual currencies to pay wages, employers must also pay ________ tax to the IRS.

a. FICA

b. Worker's compensation

c. Self-employment

d. Excise tax

41. To assist in the transformational opportunities for future tax administration, the Inflation Reduction Act allocates how much to the IRS over the next decade?

a. $45 billion

b. $64 billion

c. $80 billion

d. $134 billion

42. Which of the following will serve as a "guide" for decision-making by IRS leadership and project managers with respect to IRA funding?

a. Investment Operating Plan

b. Strategic Investment Horizon

c. Operations Mandate

d. Strategic Operating Plan

43. The transformational opportunities for future tax administration and how the IRS will deploy the investment involves how many objectives?

a. 2

b. 3

c. 4

d. 5

44. Which of the following is ***not*** one of the five objectives for how the IRS will deploy the IRA investment?

a. Dramatically improve services to help taxpayers meet their obligations.

b. Quickly resolve taxpayer issues when they arise.

c. Focus expanded enforcement on taxpayers with routine tax filings.

d. Deliver cutting-edge technology, data, and analytics.

45. With respect to identifying the resources to seamlessly help taxpayers and paid preparers, one of the objectives of the IRS is to improve the availability and accessibility of which of the following?

a. The IRS Tax Court

b. Customer service

c. Tax forms

d. Data analytics

46. Which of the following identifies one of the initiatives related to quickly resolving taxpayer issues when they arise?

a. Identify issues during filing.

b. Expand enforcement for large corporations.

c. Accelerate technology delivery.

d. Maximize data utility.

47. Developing taxpayer-centric notices is one of the initiatives related to which of the following objectives?

a. Dramatically improve services to help taxpayers meet their obligations.

b. Focus expanded enforcement on taxpayers with complex tax filings.

c. Quickly resolve taxpayer issues when they arise.

d. Attract, retain, and empower a highly skilled, diverse workforce.

48. Employing centralized, analytics-driven, risk-based methods to aid in the selection of compliance cases is one of the key initiatives in meeting which of the following objectives?

a. Focus expanded enforcement on taxpayers with complex tax filings and high-dollar noncompliance to address the tax gap.

b. Dramatically improve services to help taxpayers meet their obligations and receive the tax incentives for which they are eligible.

c. Deliver cutting-edge technology, data, and analytics to operate.

d. Attract, retain, and empower a highly skilled, diverse workforce and develop a culture that is better equipped to deliver results for taxpayers.

49. Which of the following identifies one of the initiatives to meet the IRS objective of delivering cutting-edge technology, data, and analytics to operate more effectively?

a. Attract a talented and diverse workforce.

b. Elevate workforce planning strategy.

c. Apply enhanced analytics capabilities to improve tax administration.

d. Build a culture of service and continuous improvement.

50. Which of the following objectives has the least amount of funds allocated to it?

a. Focus expanded enforcement on taxpayers with complex tax filings.

b. Dramatically improve services to help taxpayers meet their obligations.

c. Quickly resolve taxpayer issues when they arise.

d. Attract, retain, and empower a highly skilled, diverse workforce.

¶ 10,400 Answer Sheets

¶ 10,401 Top Federal Tax Issues for 2024 CPE Course: MODULE 1

Go to **cchcpelink.com/printcpe** to complete your Final Exam online for instant results.

A $192.00 processing fee will be charged for each user submitting Module 1 to **cchcpelink.com/printcpe** for online grading.

Module 1: Answer Sheet

Please answer the questions by indicating the appropriate letter next to the corresponding number.

1. ____	11. ____	21. ____	31. ____
2. ____	12. ____	22. ____	32. ____
3. ____	13. ____	23. ____	33. ____
4. ____	14. ____	24. ____	34. ____
5. ____	15. ____	25. ____	35. ____
6. ____	16. ____	26. ____	36. ____
7. ____	17. ____	27. ____	37. ____
8. ____	18. ____	28. ____	38. ____
9. ____	19. ____	29. ____	39. ____
10. ____	20. ____	30. ____	40. ____

Please complete the Evaluation Form (located after the Module 2 Answer Sheet). Thank you.

¶ 10,402 Top Federal Tax Issues for 2024 CPE Course: MODULE 2

Go to **cchcpelink.com/printcpe** to complete your Final Exam online for instant results.

A $240.00 processing fee will be charged for each user submitting Module 2 to **cchcpelink.com/printcpe** for online grading.

Module 2: Answer Sheet

Please answer the questions by indicating the appropriate letter next to the corresponding number.

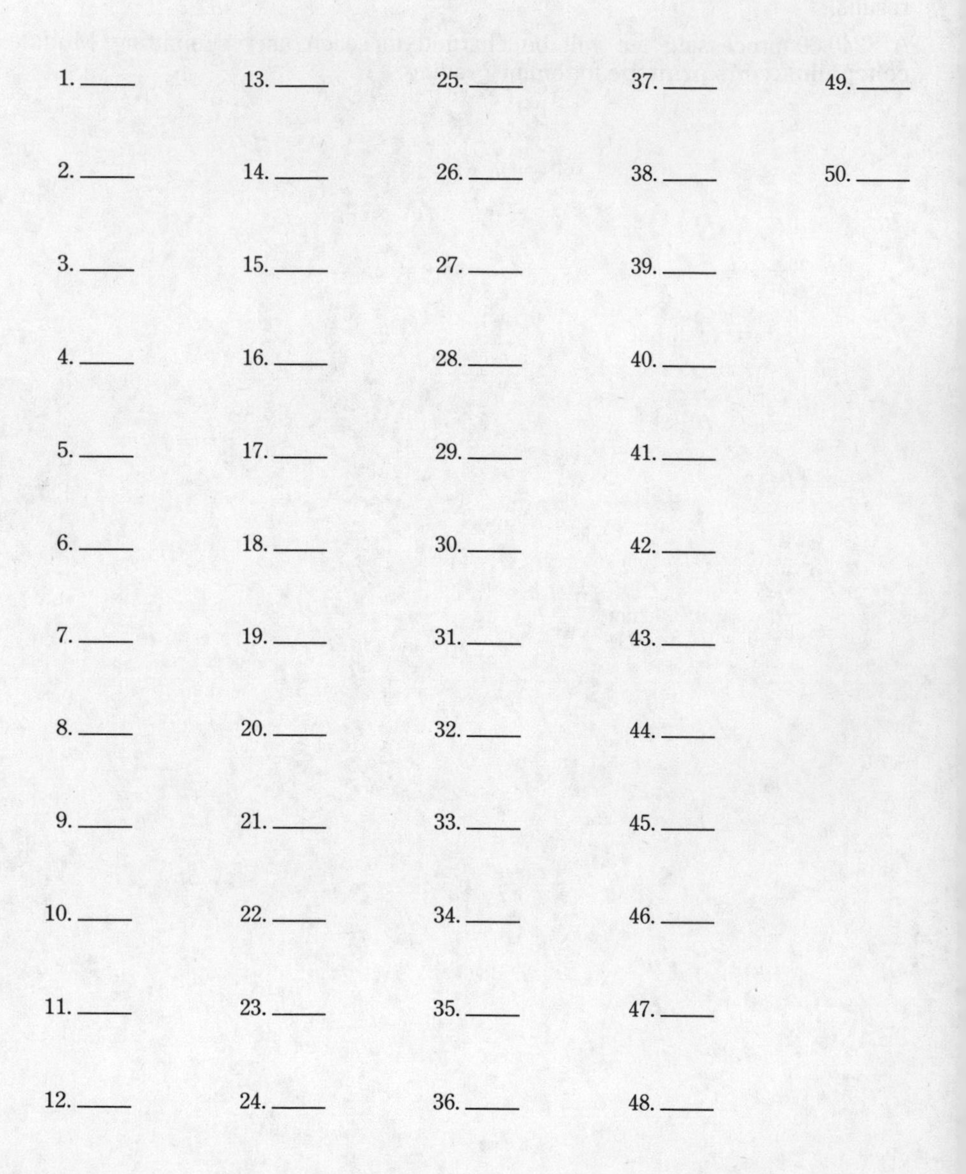

1. ____	13. ____	25. ____	37. ____	49. ____
2. ____	14. ____	26. ____	38. ____	50. ____
3. ____	15. ____	27. ____	39. ____	
4. ____	16. ____	28. ____	40. ____	
5. ____	17. ____	29. ____	41. ____	
6. ____	18. ____	30. ____	42. ____	
7. ____	19. ____	31. ____	43. ____	
8. ____	20. ____	32. ____	44. ____	
9. ____	21. ____	33. ____	45. ____	
10. ____	22. ____	34. ____	46. ____	
11. ____	23. ____	35. ____	47. ____	
12. ____	24. ____	36. ____	48. ____	

Please complete the Evaluation Form (located after the Module 2 Answer Sheet). Thank you.

¶ 10,500 Top Federal Tax Issues for 2024 CPE Course: Evaluation Form

(10024491-0011)

Please take a few moments to fill out and submit this evaluation to Wolters Kluwer so that we can better provide you with the type of self-study programs you want and need. Thank you.

About This Program

1. Please circle the number that best reflects the extent of your agreement with the following statements:

		Strongly Agree				**Strongly Disagree**
a.	The Course objectives were met.	5	4	3	2	1
b.	This Course was comprehensive and organized.	5	4	3	2	1
c.	The content was current and technically accurate.	5	4	3	2	1
d.	This Course content was relevant and contributed to achievement of the learning objectives.	5	4	3	2	1
e.	The prerequisite requirements were appropriate.	5	4	3	2	1
f.	This Course was a valuable learning experience.	5	4	3	2	1
g.	The Course completion time was appropriate.	5	4	3	2	1

2. What do you consider to be the strong points of this Course?

3. What improvements can we make to this Course?

THANK YOU FOR TAKING THE TIME TO COMPLETE THIS SURVEY!